✤ GLOUCESTER CATHEDRAL ✤

VISITOR'S HANDBOOK

GLOUCESTER CATHEDRAL

THAT GREAT ORNAMENT OF THE CITY
-John Dorney 1656

by

DAVID WELANDER

For

Joy and Rachel   Christopher and Timothy
Charlotte and Hugo   Katherine and James

Published in Great Britain, 2001 by David Welander, Sherston, Malmesbury,
Wilts SN16 0NN
© The Reverend Canon David Welander
British Library cataloguing in Publication Data
Welander, David
Gloucester Cathedral : visitor's handbook : that great ornament of the City - John Dorney 1656
1. Gloucester Cathedral
I. Title
914.2'414'0486

ISBN 0951059211

Typeset in Berkeley Old Style
Origination and design by CommunicIT Ltd, Malmesbury, Wilts SN16 0NX
Printed and bound by Bookcraft, Midsomer Norton, Bath

CONTENTS

Preface

ACKNOWLEDGEMENTS

I am grateful to the following for the use of illustrative material: The Society of Antiquaries, Gloucester City Museum and Art Gallery, Dr. C. Wilson, the Dean and Chapter of Gloucester [Waller archives], J. P. Mackechnie-Jarvis {43} and to the National Monuments Record. I am also grateful to those listed in the *Bibliography*. Quotations from their published works enrich these pages.

I am indebted to those who read this *Handbook* in type-script, for their helpful comments and suggestions: Professor M. Thurlby of York University, Toronto, Canada; Father Aelred of Prinknash Benedictine Abbey; Dr.N. Herbert, County Editor of the *Victoria History of Gloucestershire*; Alan Brooks, currently revising the second volume on Gloucestershire in Pevsner's *The Buildings of England* series; Basil Comely, the Architect to the Dean and Chapter, 1983-98; and Sarah Brown for her valuable comments on chapter 8, on the Great East Window. In substance this chapter is the Annual *Margot Eates Memorial Lecture* for 1997 on *The Making and Meaning of a Great Medieval Window*.

PREFACE

The cathedrals of England attract more than fifteen million visitors every year from all over the world. Among the most-visited are Canterbury Cathedral and York Minister, and in London, St. Paul's Cathedral and Westminster Abbey. But among England's other cathedrals Gloucester has a special place because of its historical associations, its importance in the development of English medieval architecture, its medieval stained glass, its extensive monastic buildings and its ancient tombs and monuments.

Those who know the cathedral find it hard not to wax lyrical about it. For example, in 1912, the distinguished architectural historian, Francis Bond, wrote: 'Space fails to speak of the artistic charm of this great church. Internally it abounds above all others in ever-changing vistas and perspectives, and dramatic contrasts of light and shadow. Externally it is magnificently impressive by sunlight and by moonlight, seen near at hand or far away. It is one of the greatest glories of England'.

Paul Johnson, distinguished historian, journalist and author, has been among more recent visitors. In his book *Cathedrals of England, Scotland and Wales* (1993) he reflects on his visit, and on the extraordinary impact the building had on him - its power to enthral and fascinate. He wonders at the skill and daring of the medieval builders, at the 'splendour' and many 'surprises' of its varied architecture. Of the Great East Window he writes 'At the time the window was by far the biggest ever set up in England, and certainly had no rival in Europe. Even today its effect is dazzling, even on those who have visited the church time and again, and know what to expect. What, then, must have been its impact on fourteenth-century men who had never seen, and could not conceive of, anything remotely like it, and who had to take in not only its size and splendour but its vain-glorious heraldic codes which were to them an open book? No wonder the noble lines of its tracery became the matrix of a thousand other windows, and set the stamp of Perpendicular indelibly on English church-building'.

After his visit, he recalled the lines of John Milton, in *Il Penseroso*:

> But let my due feet never fail
>   To walk the studious Cloysters pale,
> And love the high embowed Roof,
>   With antick Pillars massy-proof,
> And storied Windows richly dight,
>   Casting a dim religious light.

Having spent many years walking 'the studious Cloysters pale' and gazing on the 'storied Windows richly dight' I hope this *Handbook* will encourage others to explore this 'ancient pile' and so experience its power to inspire a sense of wonder and mystery. Space is given to sketching in the monastic past of the Cathedral for without some awareness of its origins the building, as it is today, cannot be understood or fully appreciated.

Preface

The sequence of chapters indicates the best route to take, starting at the south porch and moving into the nave. The main headings in each chapter draw attention to features of special architectural and historical interest, and the notes explain their significance and provide background information.

Though the approach has to be analytical, the cathedral is far more than 'the sum of its parts', and far more than stone and glass, wood and metal - however skillfully and beautifully crafted. It was built to serve the needs of a religious community, and through the centuries it has been preserved, with costly devotion, as a place of quiet contemplation, prayer and worship. This is still its *raison d'être*.

Easter 2001   David Welander

Meaning of technical terms   These are often explained, so the general reader should not have too much difficulty. Of course, visitors using this *Handbook* to guide them round the building will be able to relate what they read to what they see. However, a *Glossary of Architectural Terms* is included in the *Appendices*.

Numbering of Windows   The system followed is based on that recommended by the *International Corpus Vitrearum*. The building is divided into north and south sections by drawing a line from the great east window to the great west window. All windows north of the line are prefixed with the letter n. (or in the upper case, N. for those windows which extend to the main vault), and similarly those on the south side of the line by s. and S. The windows are numbered from east to west. The small west window in the choir is numbered W.I and the west window of the nave W.II. see [Pl. 5]. The lady chapel is treated as a separate building, and the great cloister is numbered along each walk from left to right.

References to illustrations   The illustrations in the text of the book are referred to by numbers within square brackets e.g. [5]. For colour illustrations more ornate brackets are used e.g. {5}. References to the Plans in the *Appendices* are prefixed e.g. [Pl.5].

Chapter One

THE HISTORY OF THE BUILDING

(1) The Abbey Church

'The Norman Conquest brought great changes to the English Church, characterized by a building campaign of enormous intensity and vigour. Cathedrals, abbeys and parish churches were destroyed and rebuilt throughout the land on a scale hitherto unknown either in England or indeed in Normandy. Between 1070 and 1100 work on thirty cathedrals and major monastic churches began in England, and many of these were completed by the first decade of the twelfth century. The Norman builders were so thorough in their reconstruction that there is virtually no pre-Conquest architecture surviving in any English cathedral or abbey. The Conquest provided the opportunity to start afresh with a virtually new architectural style - Norman Romanesque - and produced one of the most important periods in English building history' (Rowley, T. 1997).

The foundation stone of the church of the Benedictine abbey of St Peter, Gloucester was laid on 29 June 1089. The Chronicle of the Abbey (*Historia*) records that 'in 1089 on the day of the festival of the Apostles Peter and Paul, the foundations of the church of Gloucester were laid, the venerable and distinguished Robert, Bishop of Hereford, laying the first stone, Serlo, the abbot, being in charge of the work'.

Site of the Abbey Church   The church was built on the site of an Anglo-Saxon convent founded c.679 within the walls of the old Roman town of *Glevum*, by Osric, a sub-regulus of King Ethelred of Mercia. Prince Osric ruled the Hwicce people of the Severn Vale.

* With King Ethelred's assent and a landed endowment which included among its earliest holdings a portion of what would become the Saxon *burh* of Gloucester, Osric founded a community 'intended as a refuge for royal and noble widows and as a facility for educating their children. Resident priests were to provide for the house's spiritual needs' (Patterson, R. 1998).

* The first abbess of the double-foundation was Kyneburga, sister of Osric. She died in 710 and Osric in 729. They were both buried in front of the altar of St Petronilla on the north side of the Saxon church. With the death of Eva, the third abbess, in 769 the convent came to an end.

* The monastery, its buildings and endowments, was then taken over by a college of secular priests. They were not affected by the monastic reforms of the 10th century even though they were in the diocese of one of the leading reformers, Oswald, Bishop of Worcester. They continued to occupy the old convent until c.1022, when they were expelled by Cnut 'for ill lyvynge'.

* Wulfstan, Bishop of Worcester, turned the old convent into a Benedictine house, and in 1058 his successor, Ealdred, built the monks a new church (*de novo* and *a fundamentis*) and installed Wilstan (Wulstan), a Worcester monk, as abbot.

Prince Osric's monastery was built *within* the north-west corner of the former Roman colonia, but when Abbot Serlo began building, the abbey grounds extended further to the north and west, beyond the line of the Roman walls [Pl.4]. Serlo therefore laid out the foundations of his church *across* the north-west corner of the ruined walls, with the crypt positioned *within* the line of the old walls. The precise location of the two earlier churches, that of Prince Osric (c.679) and of Bishop Aeldred (1058) is not certain, but clearly 'when the foundations of the cathedral, the Norman abbey church, were laid, the crypt was planned to receive the existing superstructure and no other' (Willis, R. 1856).

Building the Abbey Church   Serlo, a monk of Mont S. Michel in Normandy and a canon of Avranches, was appointed abbot in 1072 'with the agreement of King William'.   According to the *Historia* he found only two monks and eight boys occupying the old buildings. Assisted by Odo, whom he appointed cellarer in 1077, Serlo built up the community in wealth and numbers, so that when he died in 1104 the abbey was said to be home to about a hundred monks.   The considerable increase in the abbey's income and estates was largely the result of attracting royal and baronial patronage. After a fire in 1088, which destroyed part of the old buildings, Serlo was in a position to mark out the foundations of his new church and to start work on the crypt.

> *Abbot Serlo's church remains the core of the present building [2].*
> In order to build up an impression of the Romanesque church see Clapham, A.W. (1934) plan, Waller, F. S. (1855) isometric drawing of what remains of the church, and Wilson, C. (1985) axonometric reconstruction. Wilson's outline shows the exterior c. 1150 - the apsidal east end and the radiating chapels, the transepts with their corner turrets, the central tower and two western towers, all with conical roofs. These two drawings are invaluable in understanding the architectural development of the building (1100-1540).

'In the year of our Lord 1100 on Sunday 15 July the church of Gloucester which Abbot Serlo of revered memory had built from its foundations was consecrated, with great ceremony, by Bishops Sampson of Worcester, Gundulph of Rochester and Herveas of Bangor' (Florence of Worcester). Though consecrated in 1100, the nave and tower were not completed until some years after Serlo's death, in a second phase of building (c.1100-40).

There are marked contrasts between the eastern arm, the first phase of building, and the second phase, particularly in elevation and decoration.

*   **Elevation**.   The Romanesque choir consisted of an ambulatory arcade, and above it a tribune arcade of similar height. Above the tribune there may have been a clerestory of similar height to the ambulatory and tribune (Wilson, C.); or alternatively a barrel vault springing from above the gallery arches (Thurlby, M.), or even a triforium and then a barrel vault (McAleer, J.P.). In contrast, the nave has immensely tall cylindrical columns, practically the height of the choir ambulatory and tribune combined. Above the main arcade there is a diminutive triforium, and above the triforium there was a tall

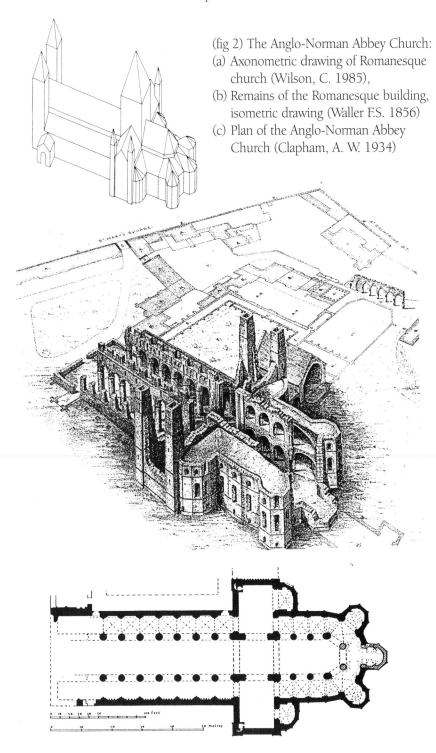

(fig 2) The Anglo-Norman Abbey Church:
(a) Axonometric drawing of Romanesque church (Wilson, C. 1985),
(b) Remains of the Romanesque building, isometric drawing (Waller F.S. 1856)
(c) Plan of the Anglo-Norman Abbey Church (Clapham, A. W. 1934)

clerestory, part of which survives.. The choir aisles are groin-vaulted, whereas the nave aisles had quatrepartite rib vaults. The central area (or, main vessel) of the nave was probably spanned by a high-pitched wooden roof.

* **Decoration** The eastern arm has very little decoration. Where chevron occurs it is on reused material. The capitals throughout are either plain cushion, single or multiple, or volute (with carving on only three in the crypt). The responds and occasional blind-arches relieve the plain ashlar walls, otherwise the pre-1100 work is plain and austere, typical of early English Romanesque.

  However, in the nave the arcade arches are enriched with chevron and bands of decoration including rope and billet, and the aisle windows with chevron. At the west end of the north aisle the capitals of the Anglo-Norman responds are elaborately carved.

The second phase of building was impeded by fire in 1102 (which seriously damaged the chapter house) and by an even more disastrous fire in 1122. According to the *Saxon Chronicles* the fire in 1122 started in the steeple while the monks were singing mass, and burnt much of the monastery including the nave. There is evidence of the fire on the arcade piers; the calcination of the lower courses is thought to have been caused by fallen rafters burning themselves out on the nave floor. Analysis of the fire-damaged stone (1983) has confirmed that the heat of the fire was intense. In 1190 there was another fire which destroyed the greater part of the city and almost all the buildings of the Abbey's outer court.

The **central tower**, completed c.1140, would have been a heavy, square structure, rising no more than its width above the nave and transept roofs. There are examples of such towers at Tewkesbury, St Albans, Norwich, Oxford and Winchester. The main feature of the 12th-century **west front** was probably a central *triumphal arch*, as at Tewkesbury, probably flanked by *towers*. It is recorded that in 1242 Walter de St John, the prior (later abbot for a few weeks) began the building of a new tower on the south side which was completed by c.1246. The west end was demolished by John Morwent (abbot 1420-37) and rebuilt in its present form.

Thirteenth Century Building Works

Following the death of King John at Newark Castle in October 1216 and his burial at Worcester, his eldest son, Henry, was hurriedly crowned at Gloucester (s.ix). The event marked a return of confidence and renewed building work throughout the country. By the end of the 12th century the thick-wall construction, the small round-headed windows, the massive piers and broad arches of Norman Romanesque had given way to a new style. In the Early English (Gothic) style walls were strengthened with buttresses which extended further from the walls, piers became more slender, the semi-circular arches evolved into pointed ones, and graceful, delicately moulded, rib-vaults were to be seen everywhere. Anglo-Norman windows were replaced by lancets, and later by wider windows with simple tracery. In general, the horizontal emphasis of Romanesque was replaced by a new emphasis on the vertical. Towers became taller, many topped with elegant, slender spires.

Early Gothic was marked by simplicity but later decorative elements were added, in particular stiff-leaf carving on capitals, carved roof bosses, and the contrasting colour and texture of Purbeck.

> In England the move away from Romanesque and the development of Gothic came later than on the Continent. There was a transitional period (1140-80) represented, for example, by the nave of Malmesbury in Wiltshire (c.1165) and Abbey Dore in Herefordshire (1170s). The great impetus for change came when Christ Church, Canterbury was destroyed by fire in 1174 and a Frenchman, William of Sens, raised the Gothic choir on the Norman foundations (1184). Gervase of Canterbury, in his year-by-year account of the building work, stresses the use of Purbeck which became characteristic of Early English Gothic. 'Because of the great prestige of Canterbury and the contemporary English love of linear patterning, this festive treatment of interiors was widely imitated in a way that has no precedent whatever on the Continent' (Watkin, D. 1979). The nave at Gloucester was given this 'festive treatment' with the introduction of Purbeck springing for the new vault in 1242.

The 13th-century rebuilding programme at Gloucester was far more extensive than would appear from the modest amount of Early English work which has survived. In addition to work in the church, there was considerable rebuilding around the great cloister and in the precincts. In 1239 the church was rededicated 'in honour of the Apostle Peter, chief of the apostles, by Walter de Cantelupe, Bishop of Worcester, on 18 September 1239, accompanied by the venerable fathers the abbots of Evesham, Tewkesbury, Pershore and Cirencester, and other noble gentlemen with a huge crowd of the common people' (*Historia*).

* *Early English work which has not survived includes:*

The **central tower - the addition of a spire** (c.1222) 'The great eastern tower of Gloucester Church was built with the help of Helias the sacrist' (*Historia*). As sacrist, Helias would have had financial control of the project, but 'with the help of...' suggests he was involved in other ways. His tower is shown in a drawing in the margin of a 13th-century copy of Geoffrey of Monmouth's *Historia Regum Britannie* (Royal MS 13A III f.41v).

> The drawing, made in the mid-14th century, shows the skyline of the town from the west, from the water-meadows, and includes an outline of St Peter's Abbey. The central tower has quite substantial corner turrets and a tall spire. The nave roof is steeply pitched and the west front has a corresponding high gable. The west window appears to be filled with reticulated tracery. The south-west turret, rebuilt in 1246, is shown with a small broach spire, but this may be the west turret of the south transept since it appears to be connected to the central tower by a roof.

The first permanent **choir stalls** (c.1230) Helias also 'constructed the old stalls for the monks' (*Historia*), that is, the choir stalls which were taken out when the present back stalls were built in the mid-14th century. A fragment of one of the stalls was identified by F. S. Waller and preserved behind the canopy of the vice-dean's stall.

The **de Wylington lady chapel** (1227) In 1224 Ralph de Wylington and his wife Olympia provided funds for a lady chapel. 'The chapel of Blessed Mary in the cemetery was completed at the expense of Ralph de Wylington, who gave rents with which to maintain in perpetuity two priests there to say masses for the dead' (*Historia*). The rectangular lady chapel took the place of the eastern-most (axial) chapel off the choir ambulatory.

*   *Early English work which has survived includes:*

The **nave vault** (1242)   At the time of the rededication (1239) work on the new vault may have been in progress.   Proceeding bay by bay beneath the roof 'the new vault over the nave of the church was finished, not with the help of the workmen as at the start, but indeed by the eager efforts of the monks themselves' (*Historia*).

> The quatrepartite vault, which has a ridge rib with finely carved bosses, springs from Purbeck abaci, resting on foliate limestone capitals above a cluster of Purbeck shafts.   In the bays nearest the tower a number of modifications were made, possibly indicating the point at which the monks took over.   The construction of the vault also involved work at the west end, where the tower on the south side was rebuilt (1246).

The **reliquary** (c.1250)   The Early English screen in the north transept is thought to have been a reliquary.

*   *Early English work in the precincts included:*

Improvements to the **water supply** (c.1225)   Helias 'constructed a channel for running water' (*Historia*), that is, a system of conduits for fresh water.   The reservoir or drain (now filled in) outside the *lavatorium* in the north-west corner of the cloister may have been part of Helias' improvements to the abbey's water supply.   Probably built as a reservoir, it became a drain when the cloister was rebuilt in the late 14th century.

A new **refectory** (1246).   The monks' refectory on the north side of the great cloister was demolished, and a new and slightly larger refectory was built on the site.   The doorways at either end of the north walk are part of this rebuilding.

The development of the **infirmary** (c.1240)   There is no reference in the *Historia* to the building of the new infirmary hall but judging by what remains of the south arcade it was built c.1260.   The aisled hall was of at least six bays, and included at its east end a chapel dedicated to St Bridget.

A new **mill**, probably situated in the inner court, was 'built from its foundations' (*Historia*) by Abbot John de Felda (1243-63).

In addition to these projects there were other improvements carried out in the 13th century in the church and around the precincts;   doorways were reconstructed, windows enlarged, and chapels refurbished with floor tiles and piscinae (a fine example of which is in the north-west tribune chapel).

Fourteenth-Century Reconstruction

Fire again ravaged the abbey and its precincts in 1300. 'On the day of the Epiphany, towards the time of the high mass, a fire started in a building above the timber store in the great courtyard of the abbey.   From this fire many buildings were set on fire all through the abbey, including the small bell-tower and the great chamber and cloister.   But after folk ran together from all sides and many prayed, the entire fire was soon brought under control, so that this may be ascribed more to a miracle than to the great efforts of the people' (*Historia*).   Though not mentioned in the Chronicle, the monks' dorter may also have been affected for it was pulled down three years later and a new dormitory built (1303-13).   The first dormitory extended north from the chapter house to the east end of the refectory; the new dorter was aligned east-west along the north side of the chapter house.   It was demolished at the Dissolution (1540).

South Aisle of the Nave (1318-26)   The *Historia* notes that 'in the year of the Lord 1318 the Festival of Corpus Christi began to be generally observed in the whole English Church. At the same time the south aisle of the nave of the church was built with very great expenditure on many items'.

The aisle wall was leaning out so dangerously that the wall and the vault were in danger of collapse. The wall was buttressed along its entire length to secure the Anglo-Norman responds; the window-openings were then enlarged, and three-light windows, festooned with ballflower, inserted. The tracery displays various designs and motifs of the Decorated period (Coldstream, N. 1994). The 'very great expenditure on many items' (*Historia*) refers to the elaborate tracery and labour-intensive ballflower, the stained glass, the impressive buttressing and the array of statuary.

Burial of King Edward II (1327)   On 20 September 1327, King Edward II was murdered at Berkeley Castle, to the south of Gloucester. John Trevisa, who served Lord Thomas Berkeley as chaplain, in his English translation of Higden's *Polychronicon* states that Edward was killed 'with a hoote broche putte thro the secret place posterialle.' The body had to be shown, so it had to look as if he had died of natural causes. He was buried three months later in Gloucester's abbey church. John Thoky (abbot 1307-29) 'brought the king's body with honour from Berkeley Castle in his own carriage painted with the arms of his church, and it was taken to the monastery at Gloucester. The body was received with honour by the abbot with the whole community in solemn vestments, attended by a procession of the entire citizenry, and borne to its burial in the northern part near the great altar'.

> The *Historia* adds that after the king's death 'certain neighbouring monasteries, namely St Augustine's of Bristol, St Mary's of Kingswood and St Aldhelm's of Malmesbury were afraid to accept his venerable body for fear of Roger de Mortimer and Queen Isabella'. Abbot Thoky, in agreeing to receive the body, has been commended for his courage, and credited with foreseeing the financial benefits pilgrims to the king's shrine would bring to the abbey. But he was probably ordered by the Court to do so, and to prepare for the burial. The funeral was delayed until 20 December so that at least some of the royal funeral trappings could be brought from London.   Queen Isabella and her son the young King Edward III were present, together with members of the Court.

Within a year or two a magnificent tomb had been erected on the site of the interment [3]. The burial of Edward II at St Peter's Abbey marked a turning point in the history of the building, and in the development of English church architecture.

Remodelling of the South Transept (1331-36) In the autumn of 1330 the young King, Edward III, assumed full powers. In the following year work began in the south transept (St Andrew's Aisle) which was to mark the beginning of the complete transformation of the eastern arm of the church (1331-74).

Abbot Wygmore (1329-37) was responsible for the first phase of the work. The *Historia* records that 'he did much good for the monastery and, as much whilst in the office of prior as in his prelacy. Whilst he was prior he built the Abbot's Chamber beside the infirmary garden. He adorned the retable (*retrotabulum*) at the prior's altar with polished and gilded figures at his own expense... He greatly delighted in various arts, so that he himself was very often involved in them and he excelled in many different undertakings concerned with the arts, as much in mechanical devises as in weaving'.

Funding the Project The *Historia* states that the gifts of visitors and pilgrims to the king's tomb during the abbacy of John Wygmore were sufficient to fund the work in the south transept. 'The offerings of the faithful and the devotion which the people showed for King Edward who had been buried in the church were such that within a few years there was such a crowd of the common people that the city of Gloucester scarcely held the multitude flowing together from various cities, towns, villages and hamlets.

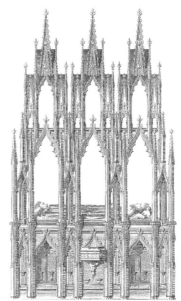

(fig 3) Shrine of King Edward II (Carter, J. 18707)

As a result out of the offerings made there in six years of his prelacy St Andrew's Aisle was completed to the last detail, as may now be seen'.

With the transept completed (1336), the remodelling of the choir began. 'The obvious source of money must have been the new king, whose gifts *in piam memoriam* to Gloucester Abbey were the inspiration and provided most of the wherewithal for the rebuilding' (Pevsner, N. & Metcalf, P. 1985). The king's involvement would certainly have encouraged others to contribute. The display of arms in the great east window may be seen as the Abbey's acknowledgement of the generosity not only of the king and members of his family, but of the king's closest advisers and comrades-in-arms over the whole period of the choir's transformation (1337-55).

Architects involved. There is no record of the names of the architects responsible for the work. But assuming the involvement of the Crown, the king's master-masons must have been consulted and were probably in charge. For some time they had been involved in work at the royal chapel of St Stephen's, Westminster and at Old St Paul's, developing a new and distinctive style of architecture. Because the style was evidently favoured by King Edward II it is sometimes called (at this stage) the *Court style*, but it has the hallmarks of *Perpendicular*. Though unknown outside London, from 1331 features of the style, including the repetitive use of rectilinear panelling over the wall surfaces, appeared in the south transept at Gloucester.

Thomas of Canterbury (d.1336), the second architect in charge of the work at St Stephen's, Westminster, is thought to have been appointed by the Crown to oversee the work in the transept between 1331 and 1335. Another master must have then taken over, directing the work in the choir from 1337. He was familiar with West Country developments of the mid-14th century. This is confirmed by differences in architectural detail between the transept and the choir, for example in the profile of the vaulting shafts [4, Pl.8].

(fig 4) *Method of remodelling the choir (Waller, F.S.)*

Profiles of vaulting shafts -
(a) south transept (b) prebytery

Transformation of the Choir (1337-55)
It was decided to retain the old ambulatory and gallery of the Romanesque choir and to create a Perpendicular choir *within* it. In order to do this, parts of the old choir had to be dismantled including the apsidal east end, the clerestory and the vault (F. S. Waller's isometric drawing [2] shows the extent of the demolition).

In the crypt the apsidal east end was retained and its outer wall used as the foundation of a huge window constructed across the east end of the choir. A tall clerestory was erected on the wall above the tribune arcades, with shafts soaring upwards to a massive lierne vault. In order to construct the vault from west of the choir crossing to the great east window, the crossing piers and base of the central tower had to be radically reconstructed. This, together with the reconstruction of the east end, is an astonishing achievement, displaying the extraordinary daring and skill of the medieval architects and builders. Work on the choir continued throughout the abbacy of Adam de Staunton (1337-51). The *Historia* records that in his time 'the great vault of the choir was built at vast expense, with the stalls there on the prior's side'. His successor, Thomas Horton (1351-77) completed the work. Horton 'began and completed the great altar, with the presbytery there, and the stalls on the abbot's side'. The stalls replaced those erected by Helias, the sacrist, in c.1226. The Black Death in 1349, in which one-third of the population of the country died, may account for an apparent break in the construction of the stalls; those on the north side being put in by Staunton before 1351, and those on the south side by Horton somewhat later (Tracy, C. 1990).

Building the Great Cloister - the first phase (c.1360) The *Historia* states that Walter Froucester (abbot 1381-1412) 'built the monastery cloisters in fine style at great expense. It was begun in the time of ... (the name is erased), and taken as far as the door of the chapter house, and left unfinished at that point for many years'. Almost certainly the name erased was Horton (abbot 1351-77), so that if the work was 'left unfinished for many years...' the first phase probably began *after* the completion of the choir (c.1355) but *before* the remodelling of the north transept (1368-74). This makes the fan vaulting in the first bays of the east walk the earliest, on any scale, to have survived.

Fan vaulting is a peculiarly English form of vaulting, and seems to have originated in the area around Hereford, Gloucester and Tewkesbury. At Hereford a new decagonal chapter house, with a fan vault, was built between 1364-70 by Thomas de Cantebrugge, a master mason and citizen of Hereford; but only the foundations, part of the wall and a few fragments of worked-stone, survive. However, a drawing of the chapter house by the antiquarian Dr. William Stukeley in 1721 shows the fan vaulting as remarkably similar to that in the cloister at Gloucester - assuming Stukeley's drawing accurately represents the vault at Hereford. If so, it seems likely that Thomas of Cambridge (a small hamlet on the Gloucester-Bristol road) was in charge at Gloucester before 1364 and built the first bays of the east walk.

Remodelling the North Transept (1368-74)   Like the south transept, the north transept was given a 'Perpendicular veneer', but after the completion of the choir. This is reflected in the lierne vault which is far more accomplished - the longitudinal ridge rib has parallel ribs either side as in the choir, and the intersections of the ribs are covered by bosses. The design of the clerestory windows also resembles those in the choir. The *Historia* states that the remodelling of the transept was carried out by Abbot Horton and dates it very precisely - it was begun in 1368 and completed in 1374. 'The cost of the work...was £718 1s. 2d. of which the said abbot paid £444 1s. 2d. as is made clear in the records of the work'. Robert Lesyngham may have been in charge before taking up an important commission at Exeter (1376-94). With the completion of the north transept the entire eastern arm of the church had been transformed (1331-74).

Completion of the Great Cloister (c.1385-1400)   Leland credits Walter Froucester (abbot 1381-1412) with having built the great cloister, but the *Historia* makes it clear that the work was begun considerably earlier. After the rebuilding of the bays between the east cloister door and the chapter house, the cloister was 'left unfinished for many years'. When work resumed in c.1390 there was still most of the cloister to build. Anxious to complete the work the Abbot must have instructed his architect to simplified the design of the remaining walks. There are subtle differences in the vault, and some fairly obvious differences in the window tracery, of the later walks.

Fifteenth Century Building Works

The abbey chronicle (*Historia*) ends with a brief reference to Walter Froucester as the 'twentieth abbot of the monastery of St Peter of Gloucester after the Conquest'. In the years from the death of Abbot Froucester (1412) to the dissolution of the monastery (1540) documentary evidence for the building-history of the abbey is fragmentary; but combining this with stylistic considerations it is possible to date the three major works of the 15th century with some accuracy.

West End and South Porch (c.1430)   The west end of the nave was completely rebuilt during the abbacy of John Morwent (1421-37). According to Leland it was

Morwent's intention to remodel the entire nave to make it 'like unto the choir'. He rebuilt the first two bays, but he died before he could carry out the rest of his ambitious scheme. He is also credited with building the south porch.

Central Tower (1450-60)   During the abbacy of Thomas Seabroke (1450-57) the central tower, as modified by Helias in c.1222, was taken down to almost roof-level, and the present tower built on what remained of the 12th-century tower, which was strengthened and buttressed to receive it.   The Anglo-Norman tower and the crossing piers had already stood for more than three hundred years, but they were able to bear the weight (estimated at more than 5000 tons) of the new Perpendicular masterpiece.   The abbot died before the tower was completed, but one of the monks, Robert Tully, who had been responsible for the project, carried on until he left to become bishop of St David's in 1460.

> Anglo-Norman stonework around the base of the 15th c. tower includes parts of circular corner turrets,. 'The north-east one was used as a base for one of the 15th-century tower buttresses, which would appear to indicate the period when these turrets were taken down' (Heighway, C. 1991). Just below this turret, at the north-east corner of the tower, there is a short section of blind arcading which may have continued round the choir and transepts below the eves. Assuming there was a clerestory in the Romanesque choir, the arcading would have been pierced at intervals forming small windows.
>
> Recent research (Heyman, J. 1990) has shown that a considerable amount of 12th-century stonework remains in the base of the present tower. Outside it is faced with fine ashlar, but inside part of the tower's original stonework survives *in situ*, together with rough arches built into the walls to support the tower when the choir vault was being constructed.

Lady Chapel (c.1465-83) was the last major building work of the abbey period. It was begun by Abbot Seabroke's successor, Richard Hanley (abbot 1458-72), and completed by William Farley (abbot 1472-98). The badges of Edward IV, the *Sun-in-Splendour* and the *Rose en soleil*, which still fill spandrels of the windows, suggest the chapel was completed during King Edward's reign (1461-83); the Yorkist badge would hardly have been placed in the windows in such profusion after the accession of Henry VII (1485).

The lady chapel was built on, as was customary, as an extension at the east end of the church but because of the great east window it had to be semi-detached. This was skilfully achieved by making the axial chapel (the 13th. century lady chapel) into a vestibule, and what remained of the axial chapel at tribune level into a west gallery. Access to the gallery-chapel was from an enclosed passage linking the north and south sides of the tribune. The four main bays of the chapel were modelled on the adjoining presbytery, the east end being one large expanse of glass, and the side walls consisting of four large windows separated only by vaulting shafts. Above is a richly decorated vault with a ridge rib and parallel ribs, as in the choir, and bosses at the junctions of the complex mesh of liernes. Chantry chapels extend from the second bay from the east, rather like mini-transepts.

Dissolution of the Monastery (1540)

The last abbot, William Parker (*alias* Malvern, 1514-39) made improvements to the abbot's lodging, including the building of oriel windows in the great gallery. He erected a canopied tomb for the remains of Prince Osric on the east side of King Edward II's shrine, and an imposing chantry for himself on the other side. He also restored the main gateway (King Edward's Gate) on the south side of the precincts. The monastery was surrendered to King Henry VIII's commissioner on 3 January 1540, by Gabriel Morton, the prior, Abbot Parker having died the previous June [5].

(fig 5) The Catherdral from the south-east

(2) The Cathedral Church

The abbey church became the cathedral of the new diocese of Gloucester on 3 September 1541. The Act of Parliament which created the new See states that 'considering the site of the late monastery in which many famous monuments of our renowned ancestors, Kings of England, are erected a very fit and proper place...we have decreed that the said monastery be an episcopal see'. No doubt the decision to create the new diocese saved Gloucester's monastic church from almost certain destruction.

Cathedral Establishment   The first bishop was John Wakeman, the last abbot of Tewkesbury. He occupied the former abbot's lodging on the north side of the precincts. The first dean was William Jennings, the last prior of the nearby Augustinian priory of St Oswald, who occupied the prior's lodging beside the west front of the cathedral. The six prebendaries were given accommodation in the precincts in former monastic buildings, adapted for domestic use, and those who were married were encouraged to set up their own households. The dean and six prebendaries (canons residentiary) formed the cathedral Chapter, the collegiate body whose duties and responsibilities were set out in the *Statutes and Orders for the better Rule and Government of the Cathedral Church* (1544). Others, including minor canons, the organist, the school master, singing men (lay clerks) and choristers were also members of *The College*, some living communally and sharing a 'common table'. A cook, under-cook and other College servants were appointed. The monks' dormitory was pulled down and the infirmary hall partly demolished. What remained of the hall was adapted to provide living quarters for poorer members of the community.

Effect of Reforms on Fabric and Furnishings   Soon after the Dissolution the great rood and the screen across the east end of the nave were removed, though remnants such as the aisle chapels remained [Pl. 7] The medieval choir screen, without its statuary, survived into the 18th century which meant the enclosed monastic choir also survived. But many items which offended the reformers were defaced or removed. Further damage was done in the 17th century at the time of the Commonwealth (see below).

In 1549 the first English Prayer Book was authorized; the process of reshaping the liturgy of the English Church and reordering its worship had began. *The Injunctions of Edward VI* in 1547 initiated various reforms which affected not only the furnishings but the very fabric of churches, for example, stained glass. There were to be only two lights on the altar and no ringing of bells at the words of consecration. Chantries were suppressed; private masses and prayers for the dead, crosses and vestments were all prohibited. All images were to be removed and wall paintings erased. Parish authorities were ordered to 'take away, utterly extinct and destroy all shrines, coverings of shrines, all tables, candlesticks, trindles or rolls of wax, pictures, paintings and all other monuments of feigned miracles, pilgrimages, idolatry and superstition; so that there remain no memory of the same in walls, glass windows or elsewhere within their church or houses'.

In 1551 Archbishop Cranmer, the major architect of the reforms (MacCulloch, D.

1996), consecrated one of the leading Reformers, John Hooper, Bishop of Gloucester. Hooper worked tirelessly to establish reformed doctrine and practice in the diocese. He drew up fifty-two *Articles of Religion* which he required his clergy to accept, and later issued thirty-one *Injunctions*. But on 9 February 1555, during the Marian persecutions, he was burnt at the stake outside St Mary's Gate.

When Queen Elizabeth I (1558-1603) succeeded to the throne the majority of the people were still professing 'the old religion', but gradually the *via media* of the Elizabethian Settlement was accepted and established in law and liturgy. But during Elizabeth's reign the clergy became increasingly lax, and absenteeism and pluralism resulted in the neglect of pastoral care and church buildings. In the Gloucester diocese Dr. John Bullingham (bishop 1581-98) and Dr. Godfrey Goldsborough (bishop 1598-1604) tried to rectify the worst abuses, holding frequent *Visitations*, presided over by William Blackleech, the Vicar-General, with John Jones, the Registrar, in attendance. But as far as the cathedral was concerned, the dean frequently defied summons to attend, as did some of the prebendaries.

Years of Neglect (1540-1620) As early as 1576 'the fabric of the cathedral seems to have been in want of considerable repair' (Masse, H. J. 1899). In 1616 King James I (r.1603-25) appointed Dr. William Laud dean of Gloucester, telling him that 'there is scarcely a church in England so much in decay'. Under Laud, the cathedral Chapter agreed to set aside £ 60 per annum for the repair of the building, and in 1618 an appeal was launched to raise funds for a new organ, the old one being 'very mean and very far decayed'.

Laud also restored discipline, raised the standard of singing and inculcated reverence in worship. He ordered the Chapter to keep a record of its decisions (or *Acts*) in a *Chapter Act Book*. One of the first Acts concerned the 'Communion table' which was 'to be set altar-wise...at the east end of the choir'. It had been 'in the midst of the choir'. A wooden rail (now in the lady chapel) was placed across the sanctuary in front of the altar. Laud's reforms did not go unchallenged. The Puritan-minded bishop at the time, Dr. Miles Smith (bishop 1612-24), was so incensed that he declared he would not set foot again in the cathedral so long as Laud remained dean.

In the 1630s a number of improvements were made, especially in the choir. The Blackleech family gave generously towards new furnishings, and an organ loft was built beneath the south crossing arch in what is now St John the Baptist Chapel.

Commonwealth Period (1642-60) Preaching became popular, as a result of Puritan influence, with large crowds filling the nave for the Sunday sermon or lecture. The Mayor and Corporation occupied seats in the medieval chapel at the east end of the north aisle, which became known as the *Mayor's Chapel*. It already contained a memorial to Alderman Thomas Machen (three times mayor of Gloucester) and the tomb of Abraham and Gertrude Blackleech which stood where the medieval altar had been (the tomb was later removed to the south transept). The choir screen erected by Abbot Wygmore was still in place but without its statuary [6]. A pen-and-ink drawing of the nave, dated 1644, shows the screen and the octagonal bases of the piers before the Georgian pavement raised the floor level and obscured them.

(fig 6) Nave in 1644 (attrib. W. Hollar)

During the Commonwealth the cathedral suffered far less at the hands of the Puritans than might have been expected. But some damage was done, particularly to stained glass in the cloisters where, for a short time, horses were stabled. 'The Scotch soldiers did much mischiefe to ye windows in ye Church and Cloysters during ye late wars' (Prebendary Abraham Gregory d.1690). The wooden effigy of Robert, Duke of Normandy, was smashed at sometime after 1654 (John Evelyn, the diarist, visited the city that year and saw the effigy in its place in the presbytery). At one stage it was proposed to demolish the entire building, a number of leading citizens 'agreeing among themselves for their several portions of the plunder expected out of it'. It was said they began to demolish the lady chapel and the infirmary cloister, and even brought up tackle to take the tower down. But they were thwarted in 1656 when the church was made over to the mayor and burgesses at their own request. John Dorney, the town clerk, appealed for support to 'hold up the stately fabric of the College church, the great ornament of the city'. Thomas Pury jnr. spent a considerable sum fitting out the chapter house as a 'publique librarie', painting his arms on shields at the east end.

Restoration of the Cathedral (1660-65) Dr. William Brough was reinstated as dean in 1660, and before the end of the year six prebendaries had been appointed. On 6 January in the following year, Dr. Nicholson was consecrated bishop. Parliament proceeded to pass the *Act of Uniformity* (1662) which forced the Puritans either to conform or leave the Church. New plate for Holy Communion, silver guilt candlesticks, cushions and hangings were all provided for the choir, together with copies of the *Book of Common Prayer* (1662). John Campion, a gifted local artist and decorator, carried out ornamental painting behind the high altar.

Extensive Reglazing The most urgent need was to make the building wind and weather-proof. Bundles of glaziers' estimates and accounts have survived which reveal that between September 1660 and the end of 1662 most of the windows in the cathedral were repaired or reglazed with clear glass. A certain amount of medieval glass had already been lost through neglect, and during the Commonwealth through vandalism. Some old glass was preserved in the patched windows, and some was removed and stored.

Effigy of Robert, Duke of Normandy Sir Humphrey Tracy of Stanway House, Gloucestershire, who had taken possession of the smashed effigy of Duke Robert had it repaired and returned to the cathedral (1660). John Campion was paid £ 9. 5s. 'for gildinge and painting of Duke Robert, his tombe and about the Quire'.

New Organ In 1663 the Dean and Chapter appealed for funds for a new organ, and Thomas Harris was commissioned to design and build it. The organ case was made by local craftsmen and decorated by John Campion with coats-of-arms of donors, including the royal arms and monogram. He polychromed the pipes with floral patterns and figures. The chaire organ, with its richly carved case (probably the Dallam organ of c.1630) was incorporated into the new organ which was mounted on a loft between the south crossing piers, facing into the choir.

Pedestal font, spherical in shape with a marble bowl was also decorated by Campion and placed between the arcade piers near the south porch. It was later moved to the north transept chapel.

It is surprising that any medieval glass survived considering the depth of religious feeling. Some years after the Restoration one of the Cathedral prebendaries, filled with Puritan indignation, smashed the west window high above the quire (liturgical choir).

> On 23 June 1679 the Chapter, in the absence of the dean, agreed 'by a majority that a certain scandalous picture of ye holy Trinity being in ye west window of ye quire of the church, should be removed, and other glasse put in to ye place'. Dr. Edward Fowler, a prebendary of strong Puritan sympathies, was the prime mover. He later described the glass as depicting 'the old Popish Picture of the Trinity: God the Father represented by an Old man with a very long Grey Beard, and a huge beam of Light above his head; God the Son, by a Crucifix between his knees; and God the Holy Ghost, by a Dove with spread wings, under his beard'. Before workmen could be instructed to remove it, Fowler himself went up onto the nave roof and with a long pole smashed out the offending glass. Dr. Abraham Gregory, another of the prebendaries, of High Church convictions, did not support the Chapter's decision. His objections, however, were deleted from the record in the *Chapter Act Book*. Gregory was so infuriated by Fowler's high-handed action that he put the record straight in a note in his *Register of Leases*.

Eighteenth Century Cathedral

In the early years of the 18th century, when Dr. Knightly Chetwood was dean (1707-20), some notable work was carried out but little of it has survived.

Refurbishing the Choir (1701-20) From 1701 the choir was cleaned and repaired, the floor relaid and much was done 'to beautify and adorn the place' [7, Pl.7].

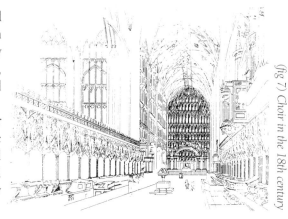

(fig 7) Choir in the 18th century

* It was 'enriched with paintwork and sumptuously provided with embroidered hangings, cushions and new service books'. John Loveday of Caversham wrote in his diary (1736) that the choir 'at great expense has been lately beautified'.
* The organ was moved from beneath the south crossing arch to the west end of the choir.

Later, extra seating was constructed on the platform where the organ had been.

* A handsome reredos of classical design, the work of Michael Bysaak, was set up in 1717. Views of the choir interior by Bonnor (1795) and F S Waller's copy of a lost painting of the choir (*c*.1725) show it in some detail [7]. The reredos remained in place until 1807 when it was sold to Cheltenham Parish Church, only to be returned to the cathedral seventy years later. Parts of it were stored in the south-east chapel of the tribune, and later displayed in the Gallery Exhibition (1981).

* Michael Bysaak also made new stalls, of excellent design and craftsmanship. They were removed during G. Gilbert Scott's refurnishing of the choir (1868-73). Sections of them were later adapted to form choir stalls in the nave. The pulpit and bishop's throne were also transferred to the nave. 'The taste of Bishop Benson's period is now very much admired again, and we can appreciate his choir stalls and other furnishings in the nave today' (Pevsner N & Metcalf P 1985).

  These and other details of the early 18th c. furnishings are shown on Browne Willis' plan of the cathedral in his *Survey of Cathedrals* (1728).

Dr. Martin Benson (bishop of Gloucester 1734-1752) spent vast sums from his personal fortune on various 'improvements'. He must have discussed his proposals with his cousin, Browne Willis (1682-1760).

The Bishop employed the fashionable architect, William Kent, to erect a new **choir screen** (1741), similar in design to the monumental screen Kent had designed in 1739 to enclose the Courts of Chancery and the King's Bench at the south end of Westminster Hall, London.

  The new screen, with its neo-Classical form and Gothic features, was meant to 'lighten' the 'oppressiveness' of the Romanesque nave. Thin shafts carried three wide ogee arches covered with wavy crockets. The parapet above was adorned across the front with decorative panels, probably painted, and crowned by a bizarre cresting of pineapples and pinnacles (Bonnor's etching 1796).

The **Radiance** of white stucco work set into the central compartment of the mutilated medieval reredos in the lady chapel (Bonnor's etching 1796) is also thought to have been Kent's work. Ornate **pinnacles** were added to the exterior of the lady chapel. The Bishop began the **repaving** of the nave and other areas of the cathedral. In the nave this involved raising the floor level by between 0.2m. and 0.3 m. thus covering up the bases of the Norman piers. From 1740 the Dean and Chapter devoted the forfeits (money deducted from prebendaries' stipends for non-residence) to the repaving programme. It was said that Kent wanted to flute the Norman columns but discovering their core was composed of rubble and mortar he gave up the idea. Work on the bishop's palace included the addition of an impressive **portico** in the Palladian style. The portico was on the south side of the palace facing the courtyard. At the time the approach to the palace was through St Mary's Gateway, or King Edward's Gate, and the arched entrance to Miller's Green. There was a rear entrance in Pitt Street. The Bishop also requested that the books and book-cases be removed from the **library** (the chapter house) 'to the isle on the south side of the choir'. The dampness of the room was considered 'prejudicial to the health of persons using and studying in the said library, and having likewise unbound and otherwise impaired many of the books'. The books did not remain there very long for in 1764 they were back in the old chapter house.

Few of the bishop's improvements have survived. The screen was replaced in 1819; the

Radiance removed in 1819 (to Minsterworth church and there lost); the lady chapel pinnacles were removed in the 1890s; and the bishop's palace, with its mid-18th c. improvements, demolished in 1861. The huge memorial erected to the bishop in the south transept was dismantled in 1864.

Precincts (1750-1800)

(fig 8) West end and precincts in late 18th c.

Dr. Josiah Tucker (dean 1758-99) carried through much-needed reforms in the management of Dean and Chapter estates and properties, and in the exercise of its patronage. He also carried out improvements in College Green [8]. The precincts were 'measured, planned and mapped', and the central grassed area of the Lower Green was lined with trees. In 1764 the Chapter required an addition to leases stating that no property 'shall be converted or used as or for an Inn, Tavern, Alehouse or Coffee house, or for a slaughter house or butchers shop, bakehouse or for making soap or candles therein'. Apparently obnoxious smells had been causing a problem! Burials on the south side of the cathedral were discontinued (1771). A proposal in 1794 to widen 'the lower College Lane' (College Street) which was described as 'extremely narrow and inconvenient' was supported by the Dean and Chapter, but nothing was done until the 1890s.

In the 1790s a quantity of painted glass was stolen from windows in the cathedral, culminating in 1798 in the removal of 'painted heads' from the great east window. A reward of fifty guineas was offered for information leading to the conviction of the felons. The old doorway at the end of the west walk of the Great Cloister, which had been bricked up for many years, was partially reopened (1793) and window tracery installed, which Prebendary Small then had glazed with medieval fragments. The work evoked 'much admiration' and probably led to the east window of the lady chapel being repaired using more medieval fragments from windows around the cathedral.

Dean Tucker died in 1799 and was buried in a brick-lined vault in the south transept. A memorial tablet to the distinguished economist and ecclesiastic was erected nearby. A year of two before he died Thomas Bonnor published his *Ten Perspective View'* (1796) showing 'the Beauties of Gloucester Cathedral', and inscribed them to 'the Venerable and Reverend Josiah Tucker D.D., Dean of Gloucester [9].

(fig 9) Cathedral interior in 1796, showing nave, choir, cloister and lady chapel.

Cathedral in the Nineteenth Century

Furnishings (1800-50) Michael Bysaak's 'altar piece' (reredos) was dismantled in 1807, and in its place Dr. John Luxmore (dean 1800-07) erected a very plain screen consisting of stone panelling attached to the outer wall of the feretory. An oak table served as an altar, with chairs for the clergy behind it. Bysaak's stalls, the bishop's throne and mayor's stall of the early 18th c. remained in place. The medieval stalls were described as 'very much mutilated and defaced'. Beneath the north and south crossing arches there were wooden galleries, providing additional seating. The pedestal pulpit, now in the nave, stood centrally at the presbytery steps. Dean Chetwood (1707-19) had moved the effigy of Duke Robert, and the mortuary chest on which it rested, to the north-east ambulatory chapel where it remained until 1905 [10].

(fig 10) Choir in 1827

Kent's choir screen (1740) was taken down in 1819, and the present screen erected (1823). It was designed by Sir Robert Smirke (1780-1867), and donated by Dr. Griffiths, one of the prebendaries. The old Consistory Court at the west end of the south aisle was boarded up in 1833, and part of the wooden railings around the inner enclosure was later placed in front of the tomb of King Edward II. The Court furniture was finally removed in 1847. Memorial tablets, mainly of the 18th century, attached to the piers of the nave arcade were removed, but the remains of medieval niches were left. In 1825 a monument to Dr. Edward Jenner (1749-1823), by Sievier, was placed at the west end.

Restoration (1800-1867) F. S. Waller's Report (1855) to the Dean and Chapter on the condition of the fabric marked a turning point in the restoration of the cathedral in the 19th century. Some of the work he detailed had already been carried out or was in progress.

Crypt Bonnor described the crypt at this time as a 'hypogeum converted into a bone-house'. A drawing shows the central chamber piled high with debris and skeletal remains. But in 1850 the bones were removed to the south-west chapel and later interred in the garden at the east end of the cathedral. The floor of the crypt was drained and concreted. A quantity of soil which had accumulated around the outside of the crypt and lady chapel was thrown back to form beds for shrubbery (see below).

Cloister The great cloister was cleaned and much of the paving relaid. Some of the windows, which had been bricked up since the 17th century, were opened and glazed. The first to be glazed, by Messrs Hardman of Birmingham, were small two-light windows at the west end of the south walk (1856).

West Front Most of the stone-work of the great west window was replaced (1846-48), and the whole west front restored. The porch was also extensively restored, with its west side having to be 'practically rebuilt'.

In his *Report*, Waller not only described 'the present state of the cathedral' but added proposals for its restoration. Some of his recommendations were immediately accepted, including the removal of all limewash. This had already revealed interesting medieval paintwork, particularly in the lady chapel. In the south transept the eastern chapel was opened up and the buttress across its entrance refaced. But priority was given to reglazing, with donors being asked to pay for the repair of the stonework as well as for the stained glass.

> **Dr. Francis Jeune**, Master of Pembroke College, Oxford, and Canon of the Cathedral from 1843-64, took a particular interest in the College School (King's School), and as Treasurer raised funds for the restoration of the cathedral. In particular he designed the lay-out of the grounds around the east end, creating lawns and beds for shrubbery, and footpaths and a 'carriage drive' (1855). The area remains much as he designed it. He also proposed a theme for the reglazing of the cloister in which the windows, from the south east corner along the east walk and around the other walks, would depict the *Life and Work, the Death and Resurrection of Christ.*

In the nave, the reglazing of the great west window (W.II) in 1859, in memory of Dr. J.H. Monk (bishop 1830-56), encouraged others to donate glass for the aisle windows [15]. It seems that donors were allowed to decide the design of the glass and to commission the firm of their choice.

In 1860 the great east window (E.I) was restored by Ward and Hughes under the direction of Charles Winston.

Restoration of the Choir (1867-73) In 1867 the Dean and Chapter asked George Gilbert Scott to undertake the restoration of the choir. A decade earlier he had been asked to comment on Waller's proposals and had expressed certain reservations, particularly with regard to the choir. He agreed that the early 18th c. stalls should be removed and the floor repaved. But he was opposed to moving the organ to the tribune, and to removing the choir screen and return-stalls, which would have opened up the choir to the nave. He laid his own proposals before the Chapter in April 1867. They were accepted almost in their entirety and work began in the autumn.

The **choir was repaved** with encaustic tiles, their designs being copied from medieval tiles in the choir and elsewhere. Larger than the medieval tiles, they were made by the well-established firm of William and Henry Godwin of Lugwardine, Hereford. A series of **sgraffiti**, made at the Minton works and probably designed by Scott himself, was laid down in the presbytery. They depict scenes from the Old Testament. In the centre of the presbytery, Scott laid a small rectangular area of brown tiles, bordered with strips of black marble, to mark the traditional burial place of Robert, Duke of Normandy (d.1134). The **medieval pavement** (*Seabroke pavement*) in the sanctuary was repaired, and an extra step made to the high altar. The old tiles on the original altar level were removed and relaid in the south-east chapel of the tribune. The reredos, designed by Scott himself (1871), replaced the panelling against the feretory wall. Before the **reredos** was erected the area was excavated revealing the bases of the two ovoid piers of the inner apse. The medieval **feretory** was recovered, with its chambers for relics. Messrs Farmer and Brindley made the reredos, J. F. Redfern (1838-76) providing the sculpted groups and figures for the niches and canopy. However, the **sedilia** on the south side of the sanctuary had to be reconstructed since much of the old canopy had been removed. The angels with musical instruments on the canopy survived from medieval times. Redfern carved twelve more figures to enrich it. A credence table and communion rail completed the sanctuary. In the quire the **medieval stalls** were restored. The 17th c. paint-work was removed from the canopies, and the seats were extensively repaired. Twelve new misericords, copied from other medieval series (principally at Chester and Worcester) were carved. The **sub-stalls**, designed by Scott, were made by Messrs Farmer and Brindley who also supplied the bishop's throne and stall for the mayor. The **clerestory windows** on the south side had been reglazed by Hardman in 1865, and the north clerestory by Clayton and Bell in 1869. The great east window had been restored in 1860 by Ward & Hughes, under the direction of the stained glass historian Charles Winston (1814-64). Clayton and Bell polychromed the vault in 1888.

But by the end of 1873 the restoration of the choir was all-but completed. In five years it had been transformed from a shabby relic of early Georgian times to the choir we see today. It is rightly judged one of Scott's most successful restorations.

Restoration of the Lady Chapel (1892-1905) In 1892 J. L. Pearson, the London architect who had recently designed Truro's new cathedral, was asked to advise on the restoration of the lady chapel which, as he noted, has been 'almost ruinous for twenty years'. The old furniture was cleared out, the vault and walls cleaned, stonework repaired and the floor relaid. In his first Report (1891) Pearson stated that 'the windows on the south side are in an almost ruinous condition from the decay of masonry, and the mullions are in a most unsafe state'. Following repair of the stonework, one of the windows (S.IV) was restored by C. H. Dancy who preserved medieval fragments in the cusping and tracery lights. In his second report (1895) Pearson urged the reglazing of the entire chapel. Meanwhile, having carried out the basic repairs, the chapel was reopened for services on the Feast of St Michael and All Angels, 29 September 1897.

> *The Builder* supported the proposal to reglaze the windows provided 'the stained glass is really modern art work and not mere ecclesiastical shop production' (October 1897). Advised by William St John Hope, Secretary of the Society of Antiquaries of London, Christopher Whall of the Arts and Crafts Movement was commissioned 'to reglaze the windows...excluding the windows in the sanctuary'. A few months earlier, the Dean had allowed the family of the late Sir Joseph Lee of Ross to glaze the south sanctuary window (S.II), and as a result Whall's iconographical scheme was never completed.

When the repair and reglazing of the lady chapel was completed, preparations began for a major restoration of the central tower (under the direction of F.W. Waller 1846-1933). Work began on the south face in 1907 and continued around the tower for several years. The external flying buttress at the south east corner of the tower was taken down and rebuilt.

Electricity was introduced into the building in 1910, and the gas lighting which had caused considerable damage to the stonework was removed.

Cathedral in Two World Wars Some repair work was carried out during the First World War (1914-18), notable in the choir where the great east window was scaffolded and many rusty iron bars and cracked mullions replaced.

During the inter-war years (1918-39) F.W. Waller reported regularly to the Dean and Chapter but because of a lack of funds he often had 'Nothing of importance to report...' But from the 1930s Colonel N.H. Waller (the third of the Gloucester dynasty of architects) took over from his father, and Dr. H. Costley-White succeeded Dr. Gee as dean in 1938. Concern began to be expressed about the state of the cathedral roofs, in particular the roof of the central tower. In spite of the outbreak of war in 1939, repairs to the tower roof were completed. The stained glass of the great east window was taken out, each panel being carefully packed and labelled. Roughly half the glass was taken to Miserden Park, about eight miles outside the city, and the rest was stored in the crypt. Certain monuments, including that of King Edward II, were protected by sandbags.

> The effigy of Robert, Duke of Normandy, was packed in a wooden crate and put in the crypt. On 2 September, on the eve of the declaration of war, a mysterious wooden crate was received from Westminster Abbey in London. Both crates were bricked up in the crypt for the duration of the war. It was a closely guarded secret, but the case from the Abbey contained the Coronation Chair. Later, one of the masons, Harry Pearce, recalled how he put Robert on top of the case from the Abbey, which prompted Bernard Ashwell (Architect to the Dean and Chapter 1960-85) to remark that 'Duke Robert got nearer to the throne of England in the twentieth century than he ever did during his life time!'.

Restoration of the Cathedral (1945-2000) In May 1945 Messrs. Whall and Whall were consulted about restoring the medieval glass to **the great east window**, but it was decided that Wallace Beck of Cheltenham should undertake the work 'as he could collect the glass in his car, otherwise it would have to be sent to London'. When the crates were opened it was found that many of the labels had become detached from the panels. But with the aid of photographs by Sydney Pitcher taken before the war, Beck completed the work by September 1946. Working on the window in 1998-9, the Canterbury Conservators concluded that 'the window has not been substantially releaded since 1860, so that what we see today is pretty much as Winston & Hughes left it' (Brown, S. 2000).

Through the 1950s and 1960s **the roofs** of the cathedral, including the great cloister, were renewed or repaired. Some medieval roofs had survived, but they had been repeatedly patched up and were in a precarious state.

The *nave roof* was reconstructed in 1953-1954 using steel trusses resting on a continuous reinforced concrete beam on the north and south walls. New concreted guttering was constructed, and the lead on the roof recast and relaid. In 1955 the nave wall above the south walk of the cloister was refaced with Tetbury and Painswick stone. The roof of the *south walk* of the cloister was reconstructed with pre-stressed concrete beams and purlins with planking laid over the top (1955-57). The old lead was recast and laid. The other *cloister roofs* were rebuilt using light-weight concrete (1964-66). In 1956-1958 the *choir roof* was rebuilt using the same method of construction as on the nave roof, except that the medieval gutter behind the parapet walls was not disturbed as it still 'bound together the whole of the top of the wall' (B. Ashwell). The *north transept roof* was rebuilt in 1961-62. Though steel trusses were used, oak was used for the purlins and rafters. Grey-blue slates on the south transept roof were replaced with lead in 1966. The *slate roofs* of the library, the chapter house and infirmary slype were renewed in 1967-68, and the north aisle roof in 1975-76 (using the same slates). The roof of the infirmary slype was relaid in 1996 and the north aisle roof in 1998.

The **washing of the exterior** of the building began with the porch (1963) and lavatorium (1964). Ten years later it resumed, first on the south aisle, then on the south transept, crypt and choir ambulatory. It continued, on and off, for the next twenty years.

> The exterior of the lady chapel was cleaned 1986-89, the north side of the choir, north transept and adjoining buildings from 1990, and the cloister interior from 1990-94. The cleaning of the cloister walks revealed traces of medieval paint. The grime of centuries had hidden and hastened the decay of the stone. Washing revealed unmatching pointing and other ugly aspects of earlier restoration work. A certain amount of stone had to be replaced but with the increasing difficulty of obtaining good quality local limestone Lepine stone from Chauvigny, east of Poitiers, France was used from the early 1970s.

Extensive work was carried out in **the tower** in the late 1970s under the enthusiastic direction of Gilbert Thurlow (dean of Gloucester, 1973-83), an authority on bells and bellringing. A new bell frame of Iroko wood was constructed, a number of the bells were recast and two new bells added to form a peel of twelve. *Great Peter*, England's only remaining medieval Bourdon, or 'great bell', was rehung to swing.

In 1976-77 the eastern slype, which was said to be 'dark, dirty and desolate' was made into a **Treasury** for church plate. Two sections of blind arcading on the south side of the slype were dismantled (and the stones taken into store) in order to make a way through from the north transept.

With the growth of tourism in the 1970s the number of visitors to English cathedrals dramatically increased. A restaurant was opened in the undercroft of Church House (1980), with toilet facilities and a shop. In 1981 an Exhibition was mounted in the tribune as part of the cathedral's celebrations marking Prince Osric's founding of the Saxon monastery.

> As in earlier centuries, the restoration of the cathedral in the 20th century was financed, in the main, by the Dean and Chapter making periodic public appeals for funds for specific work. But in the late 1980s Government funding became available for agreed programmes of conservation and restoration. Thus in the last decade of the century a major programme of work was carried through by an enlarged workshop of experienced craftsmen, stone-masons and carpenters. Basil Comely, the Architect to the Dean and Chapter, worked closely with the newly formed Cathedral Fabric Committee, which in

turn referred proposals to the Cathedrals Fabric Commission and to English Heritage for approval and funding.

This **major restoration** of the cathedral began in 1989. The tower, found to be structurally sound, needed extensive stone replacement (1990-94). The south-east ambulatory chapel was refurbished to mark the 900th anniversary of the founding of the Norman abbey church and rededicated in 1993. The altar and fixed furniture was made in the cathedral workshop by Carol Feasey and the stained glass, designed by Tom Denny, was made under his supervision in Bristol. At the same time the lady chapel west screen was glazed and the great cloister cleaned, bay by bay (1989-92). In 1992-3 the south porch was restored and imposing gates, designed by Basil Comely, were erected in College Street. The repair of the parapets and clerestory windows of the choir (1993-2000), together with the north parapets of the lady chapel and nave, was followed by extensive repairs at the west end. In the choir twenty eight of the misericords were restored by Carol Feasey. Following a Report (1998) by Dr. S. Strobl on the condition of the great east window, stonework and tie-bars were renewed, and a conservative restoration of the glass was put in hand.

In recent years work on the fabric has been going on almost without a break under the direction of the Architects to the Dean and Chapter, B.J. Ashwell (1960-85) and C.B. Comely (1985-2000), working with the Clerk of Works, first T. Dorrington (1981-1992) and then A. Norton (1992-2001) and a team of highly-skilled craftsmen and women. As a result the cathedral is now in a far better state of preservation than it has ever been.

Chapter Two

THE NAVE

'Walking down Westgate, and turning into College Green, we are face to face with the Cathedral {1}. It is without question one of the great cathedrals of England. Outwardly it appears all Perpendicular, with its sumptuous central tower, its rows of Perpendicular windows in the nave, a large Perpendicular window in the south transept, and above all the grand Perpendicular features of the choir and the lady chapel. But there are a few clues to its Norman origin; the unmistakably Norman turrets and pinnacles of the south transept, and the rounded chapels and ambulatory at the east end, where many windows are clearly Norman but filled with later tracery' (Thorold, H. 1986)

The **porch** was built during the abbacy of John Morwent (1421-37) and replaced a smaller porch dating from the 12th century [11]. The front of the porch is buttressed at the angles and enriched with canopied niches either side and above

(fig 11) South porch in 1829

the doorway. In the spandrels of the doorway there are shields for coats of arms. Above the niches and around the sides there is an open parapet and pinnacles, and in the front a graceful ogee arch rises to a finial. The parapet and perforated corner-turrets were later to be echoed in the *corona* of the central tower {1}.

There is a **room over the porch**, but it was never finished or furnished. There is no staircase leading up to it from either the porch or the nave as, for example, at Malmesbury Abbey, Wiltshire. The only access is by way of the newel stair at the west end of the south aisle which leads up to the aisle roof where it is possible to cross, behind the parapet, to a door at the

back of the room. Because of its inaccessibility and unfinished state the room was probably never used, except possibly for storage. A section of the early-14th c. decorative frieze which ran the full length of the south aisle wall beneath the eaves is preserved in the room in almost pristine condition, having been protected from the weather.

The **sculpted figures** which originally filled the niches were removed either soon after the Dissolution (1540), or during the Civil War (1642-51). Drawings of the porch from the late 17th century show the niches empty, but for a while in the late 18th c. the two central niches contained a sundial with words from Martial: *Peruent* *et imputantur* (trans: 'The hours pass away and are set down to our account'). In 1868-70 the niches were restored, and filled with figures sculpted by J. Frank Redfern (1838-76).

Over the doorway, in the centre, stand St. Peter and St Paul to whom the abbey was jointly dedicated. On either side of them are the Gospel-writers in biblical order from the left. In the niches either side of the entrance are Prince Osric (as king of Northumbria), founder of the Anglo-Saxon monastery, and Serlo, the first Norman abbot. The figure of Serlo was pulled from its plinth and damaged in 1999. The four figures in the niches in the corner buttresses represent St Jerome, St Ambrose, St Augustine and St Gregory. Early 19th-century prints and Carter in his *Plans* (1807) show the arms of England and France on the left, and the arms of the Abbey on the right in the spandrels [12]

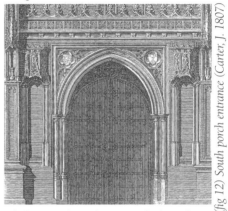

(fig 12) *South porch entrance (Carter, J. 1807)*

Inside the porch there are stone benches on either side, and the walls are enriched with **stone panelling**. The panelling is pierced on the east and west sides to form windows. As a result the windows on the inside seem rather odd, the uprights of the panelling forming mullions, but outside the windows appear perfectly normal. The porch has a **lierne vault**. The central boss depicts a half-length figure of Christ, with pierced hands outstretched, surrounded by attendant angels.

The **great wooden doors**, being round-headed, must have been made for a large Anglo-Norman doorway, probably the central doorway of the original west front. If so, when the west end was rebuilt in the 15th century the great doors were adapted to fit the archway of the new porch (with its ogee outer arch, pointed inner arch and segmental tympanum). In the mid-20th c. a wicket was made in the right leaf.

The doors should be examined on both sides for their timber construction and fine medieval ironwork [12b].

The 'iron of Gloucester' was well known at the time. In Domesday Book it is recorded that Gloucester had to supply the king with 36 'dicres' (units of ten, probably horseshoes) and 100 rods of iron for making nails for the king's ships. Gloucester's control of the land routes out of the Forest of Dean made the town the natural centre for working the iron produced in the Forest. Ironworking remained one of the town's most important industries throughout the Middle Ages (Herbert,N.1988). The type of ore found in the Forest of Dean is limonite, a hydrated iron oxide, used in the production of a wide variety of ironware including nails, hinges, grilles, straps etc. for the building industry. Such items could be obtained nearby in Ironmongers' Row (College Court).

The doors have sickle hinge-work of the thirteenth century (before1280), and lobed bars and adossed Cs of the mid-fourteenth century, trimmed when the doors were moved to their present position (c. 1430). The sickle hinges are like those at Foy in Herefordshire, which belonged to Gloucester Abbey 1100-1280.

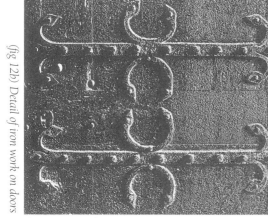

'The doors originally hung from three pairs of strap hinges, but only the two upper pairs survive. These are decorated with a chiselled surface pattern of a single groove outline and double-line zig-zag or cross-hatch. The hinge straps end in a pair of sickle shapes with raised lips, and a central lobe on a stalk. Between and above the hinge straps are six horizontal bars on each leaf of the door. These are made of thinner iron than the hinges. They are decorated with three cut-out discs or lobes at each end and have a pair of back-to-back Cs. in the middle. The original Cs are welded to the decorative bars. Similar Cs. and short scrolls are also placed along the hinge straps but are not welded on. Some of the lobed bars have circular punched surface patterns, some have a double-line zig-zag. The two lobed bars at the top have been cut to fit the present curvature of the door (Geddes, J. 1999).

The **stained glass** on the west side is by Messrs Powell (1854), and that on the east side by Heaton, Butler and Bayne (1869, restored 1994). Appropriately, the windows depict angels ringing bells calling people to worship.

The Nave is dominated by the massive cylindrical columns of the north and south arcades {2}. These reduce the triforium to little more than a narrow decorative band, and later alterations have reduced the clerestory to comparative insignificance. The lowest order, the arcade, is more than equal in height to the other two combined [13]. Similar columns were used in the naves of other Benedictine churches of the Severn Vale, notably Tewkesbury, Pershore and Evesham. These contrast markedly with the great Norman naves of eastern England, such as Norwich, Ely and Peterborough, where the nave arcade and the triforium are very nearly equal in height and width, whilst the clerestory is of little less importance.

Where did the idea of these great columns come from? There is nothing of the sort in Normandy. Even elsewhere in France it is difficult to find a parallel, except in the case of the lofty cylinders of the nave of Eglise S. Philibert, Tournus, Soane-et-Loire (c.1040). Prof. J. Bony (1939) found a possible connection with Tournus through the now-demolished upper episcopal chapel at Hereford (from a drawing by Dr W. Stukeley). When the chapel was built the Bishop of Hereford was Robert of Lorraine (bishop 1079-95), a monk of the great abbey of Cluny, which is not far from Tournus. Furthermore, it was Bishop Robert who laid the foundation stone of Gloucester Abbey in 1089 - not the diocesan bishop, Wulfstan of Worcester.

Because of the rebuilding of the west end of the nave in the 15th c. only seven bays of the Anglo-Norman nave survive [14]. The **columns**, so close together (about

(fig 13) Nave in 1829

3.8 m) that they nearly hide the aisles, are 9.3 m. high and 6.4 m. in circumference. However, because their original plinths are concealed beneath the Georgian pavement they are effectively shortened by up to 0.3m. Since the bare columns would have looked decidedly odd rising from the paved floor, plinths were attached to the columns to make them appear more normal (and to cover any rough work in the paving where it abuts the piers). At medieval floor level there are the remains of a tiled pavement. The convex capitals of the great columns, which are similar

(fig 14) Nave, north elevation in section (Carter, J. 1807)

to those at Tewkesbury, are surmounted by semi-circular **arches** of three contrasting orders, namely a pair of strong soffit rolls, a straight edge, and chevron set at right-angles to the wall. The cable moulding above the arches passes around some of the western vaulting shafts but is cut away from those at the east end. At the apex of the arch of the most westerly bay, on the north side, is a 12th century grotesque. Above the arches, and dwarfed by them, is the diminutive **triforium** which has no wall-passage, and is set back on the wall behind a string-course. The string course serves to emphasise the division in the elevation. Each bay of the triforium is made up of twin openings with short columnar piers and responds, scallop capitals and chevron set at right-angles to the wall. Behind each bay an over-arch supports the clerestory, but these arches, which are only visible from the aisle roof-space, were later filled in. The aisle roof-space is no longer open to the nave. The Anglo-Norman **clerestory** was practically demolished when the main span of the nave was vaulted in the 13th. century. The jambs, or what remains of them, can be seen in most bays. In some bays the chevron curves over at the top indicating that it once formed a small arch. Evidently the clerestory consisted of a pair of small round-headed arches resting on colonnette, and between them a round-headed window deeply splayed and set high in the wall. The windows were later enlarged and Perpendicular tracery inserted. Because so much of the clerestory was demolished, it is difficult to determine whether the **main vessel** (central area of the nave) was originally stone vaulted or not. 'The evidence points in favour of quadripartite rib vaults over single bays' (Thurlby, M. 1981). This is possible, but the calcination around the lower part of the piers has long convinced most scholars that the central area had an open timber roof, until it was replaced by the existing vault. The roof, which may have been ceiled but probably not, was severely damaged by fire at least once in the 12th century.

The **vault**, constructed during the abbacy of Henry Foliot (1228-43), was completed in 1242. The stone-masons began work at the west end and, working beneath the roof, proceeded bay by bay towards the tower. They used a certain amount of tufa, a light porous stone, in the construction of the web. The bosses along the ridge-rib were richly coloured, as were the capitals and corbels of the vaulting shafts. The shafts terminate in a series of heads; *on the north side*, a nun, two women, a man with long hair and a tonsured monk and *on the south side*, a monk, a youth, a head with a cadaverous expression, a nun and two anchorites.

The first five bays of the 13th c. vault spring from Purbeck abaci set on a cluster of three short Purbeck shafts with capitals of leafage. These rest on brackets supported by shafts which descend between the arches of the piers. But, partly due to an error which developed in the course of the work, the vault is stilted slightly from its lower position at the west end, the apex of the vault rising from west to east by 0.4 m. Furthermore, the vault and its springing was altered in the eastern bays. Here, instead of springing from an abacus resting on a cluster of Purbeck shafts, the springing is from the level of the triforium floor, with single, tall shafts rising either side. It is noticeable that the window arches on the tower side have a curious kink. The explanation of these changes may lie in the statement in the *Historia* that 'the new vault was completed... not with the help of craftsmen as at first but by the ardent devotion (animosa virtute) of the monks'. For some reason, perhaps lack of funds, the monks had to complete the work themselves, leaving 'a bit of a botched job' (Ashwell, B). But, in their defence, as work progressed towards the tower crossing something had to be done to correct earlier miscalculations in the spacing of the vault.

West End The two western bays are the work of Abbot Morwent (1420-37). He pulled down the Anglo-Norman bays intending (according to Leland's informant) to reconstruct the entire nave in the Perpendicular style, to make it similar to the choir. 'It is a matter of rejoicing that he was not spared to carry out his intention' (Masse, H. J. 1899). The original west end may have been similar to that at Tewkesbury but with the addition of two large western towers. According to Giraldus Cambrensis one of the 'large and high' towers collapsed in *c*.1164. But whether, as Verey suggests, the entire west end was in danger of collapsing 'due to faulty foundation' is open to question. Nor is it entirely clear whether Morwent built on the Anglo-Norman foundations or having demolished the earlier work shortened the nave by a bay [Pl. 1].

At the west end the columns of the arcade are fluted, with flat sides and single shafts facing into the nave. The end bay is wider than the adjoining bay, probably because the foundation wall of the western towers projected from the west wall along the line of the arcade. Morwent decided to dispense with a triforium, being content with a small clerestory. A lierne vault was constructed with a longitudinal ridge-rib and parallel subsidiaries in the style of the choir vault. But, unlike the choir vault, a similar arrangement runs north-south between the clerestory windows. The vault is studded with bosses, the central boss depicting the *Coronation of the Virgin* (possibly another echo from the choir). The vault in the side aisles is particularly well-constructed, needing no plaster to cover up roughly-cut stone.

East End The **choir screen** (1823) was designed by Robert Smirke (1780-1867), later Sir Robert, the leading Greek Revival architect who had recently (1816) designed Shire Hall in Westgate Street. The screen, which replaced William Kent's screen, was given by Dr. Griffiths, one of the prebendaries, to whose memory a tablet was placed on the north-east crossing pier. The **bishop's throne and stalls** were made by Michael Bysaak for the choir (c.1716). They were moved into the nave after Scott's restoration of the choir (1868-73). The hexagonal **pedestal pulpit**, a fine example of late-17th or early 18th century craftsmanship, was removed from the choir in 1840 when the present stone pulpit was built. A new staircase and sounding board, designed by Stephen Dykes Bower, were added in 1946. With the installation of an electronic sound-reinforcement system the sounding board was considered unnecessary and so was 'taken into store' (1985). Dykes Bower also designed the nave altar and a floral frontal. The **wooden lectern** (c.1655) may have been made for the public library which was set up in the chapter house during the Commonwealth. In the 18th c. the lectern was removed to the choir where it stood between the stalls, facing east, until 1866. When the present choir lectern was given to the cathedral the old wooden lectern was available for use elsewhere, eventually finding its way to the nave.

The **Great Organ** is a Restoration instrument (completed in 1666) by Thomas Harris, the father of the celebrated Renatus Harris {48}. The cost (£400) was raised by public subscription. The main case, which was made by local craftsmen, contrasts with the case of the Chaire organ attached to the Great organ on the east side. The smaller organ dates from c.1630 and is probably the work of Harris's father-in-law, Thomas Dallam. It is similar to that provided by Dallam in 1609 for St George's, Windsor.

> The finely carved and decorated organ **case** was designed with two fronts, the present west front was originally the back when the organ stood on a loft between the south crossing piers, and consequently faced into the south transept. The organ was moved to its present position in 1718. In 1741 William Kent added gothic pinnacles to the towers, probably to match the pinnacle over the bishop's throne, but they were removed in the late-19th century restoration. They may be seen in drawings by Bonnor, T. (1796) and Bartlett, W. H. (1829).

> The **pipes**, with their heraldic designs, and the case were painted by John Campion, a local artist and craftsman, who also restored the paint-work on the tomb-chest and effigy of Robert, duke of Normandy. Campion's decoration is said to be 'of a type fairly common on pre-Commonwealth organs, but already something of a decorative anachronism by the time the Gloucester organ was built' (Gillingham, M. 1971). The arms include members of the royal family, Charles II and James, Duke of York and other benefactors, including members of the Cathedral Chapter. The cipher of King Charles II

was painted on the principal pipes below the tower caps on the west front of the organ. In 1970 Ralph Downes and John Sanders undertook to re-design the organ and 'to bring it into line with musical thought about the function and capacity of organs at the present day' (Seiriol Evans, dean of Gloucester 1953-73). The tonal scheme adopted was much more classical, one which was 'forward looking and one of the best examples of the 1970s' (David

Briggs). In 1999 Nicholson and Co. of Malvern, Worcestershire, carried out further extensive work, detailed in the brochure issued on the occasion of the re-opening of the organ in January 2000.

North Aisle Apart from the two western bays, the north aisle retains its Anglo-Norman rib-vault {3}. The **responds** (half-shafts attached to the outside wall), which rise to the same height as the nave arcade, are divided into five orders [16].

> On the left, a nook-shaft rises to a capital from which springs a wall arch, circling the top of the adjoining window. From the capital of the next shaft, springs a rib of the quadripartite vault. The central capital supports the transverse arch which crosses over the aisle to the pier of the nave arcade. And so around to the right-hand side of the respond and the next bay.

(fig 16) Nave, north aisle and capital

The **capitals** of the responds in the three western Anglo-Norman bays are carved with designs derived from contemporary metal work, and with motifs from Anglo-Saxon and Viking art [16]. The capitals are examples of the revival of pre-Conquest art in the early decades of the 12th century (Zarnecki, G. 1989). The carving is remarkably similar to that on the south doorway and chancel arch of Kilpeck Church, Herefordshire, which was given to St Peter's Abbey in 1134. It is possible that the same mason who carved these capitals also worked at Kilpeck. The **vault** (*c*.1110), with ribs of two rolls and a spur between, is an example of an Anglo-Norman quatrepartite vault.

'Rib vaults appear in English architecture at the end of the eleventh century and by the early part of the next had spread throughout most parts of the country and across the Channel into Normandy. Rib construction was pioneered by the builders of great churches, first apparently at Durham, and was then developed and elaborated at sites such as Winchester, Gloucester, Peterborough, Lessay, Saint-Etienne in Caen, and many others' (Hoey,L.R. in *The Antiquaries Journal (1997)*.

On the underside of the transverse arches near the west cloister door there are remains of medieval decoration in the form of stars. In the south-west corner of the same bay, springing from the capital of the arcade pier, there is the beginning of a vaulting rib which appears to be the continuation of the adjoining 15th century vaulting. This is taken as evidence that Abbot Morwent intended to continue eastwards with his reconstruction of the nave. The **windows** are set high in the north wall in order to clear the lean-to roof of the adjoining cloister walk. Though they have been enlarged and filled with Perpendicular tracery their zig-zag mouldings and side shafts have survived. The stone bench at the foot of the wall is also Perpendicular work. The **doorways**, one at each ends of the aisle, lead into the great cloister. They were designed to fit Anglo-Norman openings in the thickness of the wall, dating from the early 12th century. Like the great west door of the nave both doorways are half-groined in the recesses into which the doors open. The *west cloister* door which led into the monks' living quarters (that at the east end of the aisle being beyond the nave screen) was once even more impressive than it is today. A crocketed canopy rises above the entrance, with panelling in which there were painted-figures of the apostles; their outline is still visible. On each side of the door are niches for sculptured figures {14}. Though Haines (1867) identified a *green man*, the *rebus* of Thomas Braunche (abbot 1500-10) on the inside of the doorway, the wooden doors are thought to be much earlier, probably *c.*1390 (Hewett, C. 1985).

> In monastic times, the monks returned through this doorway at the conclusion of processions around the east end and claustral buildings. They processed down the centre of the nave and, after a station in front of the main altar (the Jesus' altar), returned through the doors on either side of the altar to their places in the quire. For bystanders the doorway with its carved stonework and painted figures would have added to the impressiveness of the monks' entry.

The *east cloister* door is also Perpendicular work but not so richly decorated. The arms of the See, the Bishop and Dean, and the Canons, as well as the Darell and Nightingall families were emblazoned above the door at the end of the 19th century. With the nave floor gradually rising towards the east, steps down to the cloister walk were required at the east door.

South Aisle The aisle was rebuilt, in the Decorated style, during the abbacy of John Thoky (1307-29). Originally the **vault** was similar to that in the north aisle, but by the early years of the 14th century the aisle wall was leaning outwards (in places by nearly 30cms. from vertical) threatening, or actually causing, the collapse of the vault. Thoky tried to save the vault by buttressing the wall, but in the end he had to take the vault down and build a new one. In 1318 he appealed to the bishop of Worcester to appropriate the church of South Cerney to the abbey for reasons that included 'the fabric is threatened by ruin'. Something had to be done, urgently. At the west end of the aisle the wall is practically vertical, being supported by the earlier porch. The vault there was eventually replaced by Abbot Morwent (*c.*1430). The vaulting in the bays to the east is similar to the nave vault, on a smaller scale; but then in the remaining bays, up to the end of the aisle, the ribs are of a different profile and enriched with ballflower, and the web is more clearly defined. In spite of the variations, the vaulting to the east of Morwent's bays is part of the same programme of reconstruction (*c.*1318-28). The ballflower, a labour-intensive form of decoration, may have been dropped because of cost or because of time. The work may have been overtaken by the murder and interment of Edward II and hurriedly completed. By buttressing the south wall, Thoky saved the Anglo-Norman **responds**, but this meant the ribs of the new quatrepartite vault had to spring, rather awkwardly, from the capitals of the old responds.

The marks left by the stonemasons' tools are very evident in this aisle, with the tooling usually vertical on rounded surfaces, and diagonal on flat surfaces. Towards the east end of the aisle, at or slightly above eye-level, there is a number of **masons' marks** on the arcade piers. At least three of the marks which occur on the Anglo-Norman work at Gloucester are also found at Tewkesbury.

At Tewkesbury masons' marks occur which are also identical to ones seen in France. The stonecutters had clearly crossed the Channel from one building site to the other. These marks are personal signatures just as initials are today. The stonecutters were renumerated on piecework, the marks allowing the quality of their work to be checked. The eventual disappearance of masons' marks was linked to the adoption of other forms of payment (by the day or by the volume of work done at a bench) when the need for such detailed attention to the work of individual masons was no longer necessary.

There are several Roman bricks incorporated in the most-easterly pier of the arcade, making up for ill-fitting ashlar. Other building material lying about from the Roman period was used elsewhere, including an inscribed centurial stone, set into the wall behind the triforium at the west end of the aisle. Massive stones from the broken-down Roman city wall may well have been used in the foundations, or cut up and used in building work.

Thoky removed the arches of the Anglo-Norman windows (some springers remain *in situ*), enlarged the openings and inserted a series of three-light **windows** with unusual 'butterfly' tracery [Pl. 10]. The tracery displays several motifs of the late Decorated period and like the rest of the window is smothered in ballflower. A horizontal line drawn just below the springing of the arch cuts through no less than thirty-two ballflowers. There are more than 1,400 ballflowers in each window. The master who introduced ballflower was active in Herefordshire, Gloucestershire and the West Country for it also occurs in profusion at Ledbury and on the tower of Hereford Cathedral, at Leominster and at Badgeworth, Gloucestershire.

The window at the east end of the aisle was probably altered when the recessed tomb below it was constructed early in the 15th century. The new window was also studded with ballflower to match the others in the series, even though this particular form of decoration had long since gone out of fashion.

In the wall of the third bay, from the east end of the aisle, there is a small recess, possibly a *piscina*. In monastic times, in line with the respond beside this recess, there was a screen extending across the nave to the far wall, with an altar in front of the screen in each aisle. The *piscina* was associated with the south aisle altar.

At the side of the altar there was a door in the screen, leading through to the south transept and choir ambulatories. In the centre of the nave, backing onto the screen, was the main nave altar, commonly known as the *Jesus' Altar*, with the *Holy Rood* high above it. There were doors either side of the central altar leading through to the choir. It is possible to identify the place, high in the columns of the arcade, where the rood beam was secured [Pl. 7].

Stained Glass [Pl. 5]   There is medieval glass incorporated into two of the north aisle windows (n.viii & n.x), and fragments in the clerestory windows (in the ornamental borders, and medallions and script).   One of the clerestory windows, the third from the west end on the north side, was restored to its original design by Hardman in 1856.   The rest of the glass in the nave is Victorian, with examples of the work of eight firms.

The glass is of very uneven quality, and there is no overall iconographical scheme. 'There was no systematic controlling spirit at work to suggest, to guide, or to check. Just imagine the difference in the south aisle if there had been a scheme carefully planned beforehand instead of the haphazard process of a window offered, a window accepted, a window put up, and no questions asked as to designer or artist. Imagine what the effect might have been had the windows, as a set, been designed by Burne-Jones and executed by William Morris' (Masse, H.J. 1899).

The **great west window** (W.II), on the *Nativity of Christ and the Doctrine of Baptism*, is by Wailes of Newcastle (1859). It was erected at the expense of the Revd. Thomas Murray-Browne, Hon. Canon of Gloucester Cathedral, to Dr. J. H. Monk, Bishop of Gloucester (1830-56) 'in grateful remembrance of many years of sincere friendship'[15].

In the tracery lights are six crowns and below these fourteen angels, eight playing musical instruments

(i)   Above the upper transom are three instances of Christian baptism from the Acts of the Apostles, each scene occupying three lights: the baptism of Paul, of Cornelius and of the jailor of Philippi.

(ii) Above the lower transom, in the central three lights is the Nativity, and on the left the Angels appearing to the Shepherds, and on the right the Magi worshipping the infant Christ.   No transom divides these scenes from the scenes above.

(iii) These scenes are, from left to right: the Presentation in the Temple, the Baptism of Jesus, and John the Baptist preaching by the river Jordan.

(iv) Below the lower transom are 'types' of baptism from the Old Testament: Noah after the Flood leaving the ark; the Israelites after passing through the Red Sea; and Naaman washing in the River Jordan.

The tracery heads and cusps, as seen from inside the building are not repeated on the outside - a plain transom crosses the lights. This unusual feature was copied from the great east window.

The **north aisle**, from the east end:

The first (n.v): The Risen Christ, with St John the Evangelist and the Virgin Mary, by Frederick Preedy (1820-98) from his London period (1865), to the Darell family (see inscription at base of the window).

The second (n.vi): The Miracles and Resurrection of Christ, by Clayton & Bell (1861) to Thomas Turner (1783-1859), a Gloucester banker, and treasurer of the Gloucester Infirmary.
The third (n.vii): The Martyrdom of John Hooper, Bishop of Gloucester from 1550, deprived 1554, and burnt at the stake outside St Mary's Gateway 1555. From the Clayton & Bell

(fig 15). Nave, the great west window (Wailes, W. 1859)

studio (1865). This is the earliest recorded work of C.E. Kempe, who was serving his apprenticeship with the firm at the time. Donated by Kempe's aunt, Mrs. Claxson. It was a mistake to depict so Protestant a bishop in Catholic vestments at his burning, and to call him Richard Hooper in the inscription.

The fourth (n.viii): Three Saints (St Dorothy, St George, and St Thomas as bishop) by Hardman (1865). The faces of the angels with censers have faded, probably due to inadequate firing. This window contains some medieval glass, mainly in the upper half. 'The most successful restoration of 15th c. glass I have ever met with' (G. Gilbert Scott in 1867).

The fifth (n.ix): The Nativity, by Clayton & Bell (1866), to Dr. G. H. Hall, Master of Pembroke College, Oxford and Canon of Gloucester (d.1843), and his wife, Sarah (d.1859), and their daughter Charlotte (d.1839).

The sixth (n.x): Three Saints (St Patrick as bishop, St Oswald as king and St James the Great) restored by Hardman (1865). The saints in the tracery lights are St John the Baptist and St Margaret of Antioch. There is some late-medieval glass in the upper part of the window, but much of the lower half is 19th century.

The seventh (n xi): Faith with cross and chalice, Charity with children around her, and Hope with an anchor, by Ward & Hughes (1865), to Frances, widow of William Price of Tibberton Court (d.1860). Ward & Hughes had just completed the major restoration of the great east window (1859-1861) under the direction of Charles Winston, glass historian and restorer.

The eighth (n.xii), of two lights only: The Burial and Resurrection of Christ, by Clayton & Bell (1876) to Thomas Churchus of Clevedon (d.1870).

The window (n.xiii) at the west end of the aisle: The Lucius Legend, by Hardman (1862), to William Viner Ellis of Minsterworth. The four men in armour in the tracery lights represent, Robert of Normandy d.1134, and three dukes of Gloucester, Thomas d.1397, Humphrey d.1447, and William d.1534. According to tradition, Lucius was baptised and died in Gloucester, and was buried in the nearby church of St Mary de Lode.

The south aisle, from the east end.

The first (s.v), over the recessed tomb: The Four Evangelists, by Rogers of Worcester (1864), to Lt.Col. Sir Harry Frances Colville Darell Bt. (d.1853).

The second (s.vi): The Crucifixion, with the Virgin Mary and St.John, to J. N. Balme d.1857. The window is signed: 'William Warrington, London 1859.' Another window in this series (s.x) is by the same firm, but probably the work of Warrington's son, James.

The third (s.vii): The Burial of Edward II, by Clayton & Bell (1859), to Elizabeth, wife of William Viner Ellis of Minsterworth (1777-1865), a yeoman farmer who prospered and eventually occupied Minsterworth Court, near Gloucester. The next-but-one window, also by Clayton and Bell, depicts another historical event associated with St Peter's Abbey.

The fourth (s.viii): The True Vine, with scenes illustrative of the life and teaching of Christ, by Bell of Bristol (1860), to Mary Caroline Evans of Hygrove House, Minsterworth (d.1837). Her daughter, Maria (d.1848) is commemorated in another Bell window in the series (s.xi).

The fifth (s.ix): The Coronation of Henry III (which took place hurriedly at St Peter's Abbey in 1216) by Clayton & Bell (1860), donated by Sir William Guise (1816-87) of Elmore Court, the fourth baronet. He claimed descent from one of the barons present at Henry's first coronation in the abbey church, Hubert de Burgh, from whom the family derived the Manor of Elmore.

The sixth (s.x): The Passion of Christ, by Warrington (1861), to General Sir W. G. Davey KCB (d.1856). He is buried in the cloister. See note on s.vi.

The seventh (s.xi): Acts of Mercy, by Bell of Bristol (1861), to Maria Evans (see note on s.viii). *The eighth* (s.xii), west of main entrance: Justice, by Hardman (1865), to John Elliott, a Gloucester solicitor (1864). The theme is developed in scenes from biblical and apocryphal stories to do with the administration of justice. A window of excellent design and execution. The west window (s.xiii) in the south aisle: Christ's Healing Miracles, by Clayton & Bell (1865), to Dr. Edward Jenner (1749-1823), discoverer of vaccination, who was born and brought up at Berkeley in Gloucestershire, where he practiced medicine from 1773 until his death. Also to Dr. John Baron, his friend and biographer. Paid for by public subscription. Nearby, at the back of the nave, is a large statue of Jenner, by R. W. Sievier of London 1825.

Memorials in the nave include examples of the work of nationally important sculptors and provincial monumental masons, mainly of the 18th and 19th centuries. Classical columns and Grecian urns abound. There is much of the history of the county and diocese in the memorials, as well the life and work of a number of Gloucester's distinguished (and not so distinguished) citizens.

The **north aisle**, from the east end:

The painted monument to Alderman Machen, his wife, Christian, and their family (1615) 'perhaps by *Samuel Baldwin* of Stroud' (Verey,D. 1978). A good example of the style popular at the time among merchants and landed gentry. Machen, wearing his gown as mayor of Gloucester, kneels with his Prayer Book open, opposite his wife, and below are their children, seven boys on the left and six girls on the right, all dutifully kneeling. The canopy is supported on Corinthian columns. Several of the memorials have been repainted at different times (e.g. for the Three Choirs Festival in 1797) but this, to Alderman Machen, retains the original red paint of his mayoral gown.

At the side of the memorial is an Art Nouveau memorial by *Henry Wilson* to Canon E. D. Tinling (d.1897). A bronze figure with marble detail is depicted kneeling. Wilson also designed the face of the clock on the west wall of the north transept, [44] and a memorial in the south transept.

(fig 18) Nave north aisle, Morley memorial

Opposite, on the Norman pier, is a small tablet by *Bryant Fedden* to Ivor Gurney (1890-1937), poet and musician of the Cotswold hills and Severn vale.

Further down the aisle is a large memorial to Mrs. Sarah Morley (d.1784) by *Flaxman*, aptly described by Verey as 'Classical in style, Gothic in feeling'. Mrs. Morley 'impelled by a tender and conscientious Solicitude to discharge her parental Duties in person, embarked..' on a ship bound for India, and died at sea. Three angels receive her and her baby from the waves [18].

Nearby are three memorials in the classical style: to Samuel Hayward of Wallsworth Hall (d.1790), by *Bryan* of Gloucester; to Ralph Bigland (d.1784), Garter Principal King of Arms; and another to Hester Gardner (d.1822), by *James Cooke*.

Further to the west is a monument, Gothic in style, to Col. Edward Webb d.1839 by H. Hooper of London. A tablet near by to the Rudge family is by *Millard*.

On the left of the cloister door are three charming medallions to members of the Rudhall family of Gloucester, master bell makers: Abraham Rudhall (d.1798), Charles (d.1815) and Sarah (d.1805). Elizabeth's of 1699 has a bell at the base.

The massive monument to Charles Brandon Tyre (d.1811), with bust in a medallion held by two angels, is an ungainly memorial filling (with depressing effect) far too much space. But its size, and the inscription, reflect the esteem in which the good doctor was held at the time.

On the west wall, there are memorials to Bishop Warburton (d. 1779), by *T. King of Bath* (the ledger covering his tomb is nearby); and to Bishop Martin Benson (d.1752). Both inscriptions are worth reading: Warburton is described as 'a prelate of the most sublime genius and exquisite learning.' A large memorial was erected to Dr. Benson (bishop of Gloucester 1734-52) in the south transept, but in c.1862 it was dismantled, part of it being preserved in the tribune.

The **south aisle**, from the east end:

The **recessed tomb** contains the recumbent effigies of a medieval knight and his lady, probably Sir John and Lady Bridges of Coberley (d.1407). He wears the SS collar which means the effigy cannot be earlier than the reign of Henry V (the first decade of the 15th century). The Bridges' crest appears on the knight's sword belt. The lady also has an SS collar. The knightly figure is depicted in plate armour, mail gorget, an under-helmet, or *chapelle de fer*, and shoes of mail. His feet rest on a lion, and his head on a helmet, partially covered by a drape. His lady has flowing hair and a striped riband across her breast. Her dress reaches to her feet, and at her feet is a collared dog.

> The canopied tomb has an ogee arch, with foliated crockets and finials. The recess is panelled at the sides and back, and like the south transept has a vaulted roof without bosses. On either side is a canopied niche, with a three-dimensional ogee arch with pinnacle. The cornice has a single rose and double roses and leaves. The window above may have been enlarged as part of the overall design, and glazed accordingly. The present glass is by Rogers of Worcester (1864).

The **chantry chapel**, known in medieval times as the chapel of the *Salutation of the Blessed Virgin Mary*, commemorates Thomas Seabroke, Abbot of Gloucester (1450-57) who was responsible for the building of the central tower. His alabaster effigy rests on a tomb chest, and shows the abbot in full pontificals of a mitred abbot, with his pastoral staff on his right side. The abbot's burial staff was discovered in his coffin in 1741. It is now in the custody of the Antiquarian Society of Newcastle-on-Tyne (a replica by Carole Feasey was displayed in the Gallery Exhibition in 1981). The effigy remained in its original position in the recess on the north side of the chapel until 1741, when Bishop Benson moved it to where the altar had been, against the east wall (Britton, J. 1829). In 1874 King lamented that 'the chantry and effigy have been much mutilated and shattered' (King, R. J. 1874). Within a few years the chapel was restored and the effigy returned to its recess on the north side.

The carved figure of St Peter, the Fisherman (1987) on the left of the tomb is by Carole Feasey. High on the west wall of the chapel is a tablet with twisted columns and emblems of death, to Frances Baber d.1669. Above the chapel there is early 17th c. linen-fold panelling, similar to that in the Laud Room of Church House.

Other memorials in the south aisle include:

Mary Clarke (d.1792) and Richard Clarke (d.1796), both by *W Stephens* of Worcester. Prebendary William Adams (d.1789) by *T. King* of Bath. Jane Webb (d.1811), by *Wood* of Gloucester, and John Webb of Norton Court d.1795 by *Bryan* of Gloucester. The tablet to Mary Singleton (d.1761) by *J. & J. Bryan* incorporates coloured marbles in the Baroque style. Sir John Guise of Highnam (d.1794) by *Millard* of Gloucester incorporates a draped broken column in the Classical style. The monument to Dame Mary Strachan (d.1770), widow of Sir William Strachan, by *Thomas Ricketts* of Gloucester is 'well above the usual provincial level' (Verey, D. 1978). A cherub holds Lady Strachan's portrait in a medallion, and underneath are the baronet's arms with little male supporters. Nearby is another memorial by *Ricketts*, to Dr. Anthony Ellys, Bishop of St David (d.1761).

Further along the aisle are memorials to: Richard Raikes (d.1823), by *Thomas Rickman*; to Eli Dupree (d.1707), with a bust, and a broken pediment; and to Jane Fendall (d.1799) by *King of Bath*. Richard Raikes was the younger brother of Robert Raikes (1735-1811) the prison reformer and pioneer of the Sunday School movement. Other famous sons of Gloucester in the 18th century were George Whitfield (1714-70) the charismatic preacher and associate of John and Charles Wesley. He was educated at the College School, and is said to have preached his first sermon at St Mary de Crypt in Southgate Street. And John Stafford Smith (1750-1836), also educated at the College School, arranged a traditional English tune which, with words by Francis Scott Key (1779-1843), was adopted (in 1931) as the United States national anthem: *The Star-spangled Banner*. There is a plaque to him, and to his father, Martin, Cathedral organist 1740-82, at the east end of the north aisle.

The free-standing marble sarcophagus, with a bust on the top, by *Sievier*, is to Sir George Onesiphorus Paul Bt. (d.1820). The inscription gives details of his life and work, especially as a prison reformer. "Sir George is regarded as a very major figure in the history of prison reform. 'This county has become the example and model....' is probably no exaggeration" (Herbert, N.).

By the south porch entrance there is an impressive tablet to Dr. William Nicholson, bishop of Gloucester (1660-1671). To the right of the west window there is a tablet to Sir Hubert Parry (d.1918), musician and composer. Sir Hubert was the owner of the Highnam Court Estate near Gloucester which he inherited from his father, Thomas Gambier Parry. An impressive statue to Edward Jenner (1749-1823), the discoverer of vaccination, by Sievier, stands nearby at the back of the nave.

Alderman John Jones' memorial: Under the west window is an unusual and interesting memorial to Alderman John Jones (d.1630). A painted half-length upright effigy 'by the Southwark workshops' (Verey, D. 1978). The monument is full of detail, such as quill pens and packets of deeds, with their seals and dates exposed to view, pigeon holed and dated 1581-1630. Jones was registrar to eight bishops of Gloucester, and a member of Parliament at the time of the Gunpowder Plot. The monument was erected in his lifetime, but he died as soon as it was completed. It does not give the date of his death, but the date on the packet of deeds (1630) was meant to indicate that he was still hard at work when, having just approved his memorial, he suddenly died.

Chapter Three
THE SOUTH TRANSEPT

'Abbot Thoky (1307-29) had done a good deal in improving the lighting of the south aisle of the nave, and the aisles and chapels, and the tribune. Abbot Wygmore commenced operations in the south transept. The north transept was in daily use, as the cloister was on the north side of the nave, and the monks passed through the north transept to their daily services in the crossing. The cultus of Edward II was just now at its height, and the surroundings of the shrine were crowded every day and all day with pilgrims. But in the six years before 1337, Wygmore had cased, lighted and vaulted the south transept' (Bond, F. 1912).

In 1331 work began in the south transept which led on to the complete transformation of the eastern arm of the building. The *Historia* connects this work with the interment of the body of King Edward II four years earlier. A fine tomb had been raised over the burial place which immediately became a place of pilgrimage.

'There was such a crowd of the common people that the city of Gloucester could scarcely hold the multitude flowing from the cities, towns, villages and hamlets of England. As a result out of the offerings made there in six years... St Andrew's Aisle (south transept) was completed to the last detail, as may now be seen' (*Historia c.* 1400).

By the end of the year 1336, the Anglo-Norman transept with its high-pitched open roof, its small round-headed windows and plain wall surfaces was transformed.

(fig 19) South transept, east side

Architectural Features The most noticeable feature of the remodelled transept is the **wall panelling**. Rows of tall narrow panels with cusped heads are repeated tier upon tier from the floor to the vault [19]. The way the panelling is attached to the old stonework is best seen from the tribune. On the south side the panels rise from floor level and continue up in front of the wall passage, and up the wall to the sill of the window. They then form window tracery (and each panel a *light* for stained glass) with the mullions rising directly to the main arch. The use of rectilinear panelling in this way, over wall surfaces and arched openings and continuing as tracery through windows, is a defining characteristic of Perpendicular. But on the side walls the mullions do not rise directly to the apex of the windows but end in the graceful flow of Decorated tracery. Integrated with the wall panelling on the east side is an **internal buttress**, considered necessary to strengthen the south-east crossing pier which was leaning to the south. The wall panelling had to be rebated into the pier to ensure that it was truly vertical. The buttress crosses the opening of the gallery and extends down to cross the arched entrance to the eastern chapel. There is also a buttress on the west side but this is less intrusive, part of it being outside the west windows. The **twin doorway**, with its frilly top and angels set in trefoils, leads to the choir ambulatory and into the crypt [22]. It is a beautiful composition, incorporating a number of motifs of the Decorated style. Other decorative elements in the transept are the quatrefoil frieze at gallery level, four-centred arches, ogee shapes and moon-like curves in the cusping of the panelling and window tracery. The **vault** is an

(fig 20) South transept, lierne vault

example of lierne vaulting [20], with short ribs (*liernes*) connecting the main ribs, which first appeared (at some time after 1288) in the choir at Pershore. The design of the south transept vault owes little to the contemporary style of net vaulting at Bristol, but there is a direct relationship to work at St Stephen's, Westminster in the 1320s. The geometric pattern is not nearly as complex as in the choir vault, and there are no bosses 'to cover up the inexact junctions of the ribs' (Verey, D. 1979). Masse, however, noted 'the clever joining of the masonry', and Willis commented 'the ribs join perfectly'. Anyone with a pair of binoculars can judge for themselves. The **vaulting shafts** are not crossed by any of the horizontals or decorative features of the elevation. They rise uninterrupted from floor to vault reinforcing the overall impression of soaring height. In section they are far more complex than the vaulting shafts in the choir [4]. The tall bowtells, with their hexagonal bases, provide each of the main ribs of the vault with its own point of springing. The **windows** on the east and west sides show the transitional character of the reconstruction, drawing as they do on the vocabulary of the Decorated style whilst at the same time foreshadowing elements of Perpendicular (Coldstream, N. 1994). The tracery in all four windows is extremely graceful, with ogee curves and flowing lines, and with cusped heads and quatrefoils. In the larger of the west windows a single transom crosses the tall, narrow lights at the level of the sill of the neighbouring window.

The **great window**. Either side of the strong central mullion, with its Y division, the mullions rise directly from the base of the window, through the transoms, and continue up to the main arch. This is the earliest surviving Perpendicular window in the country. But in this prototype, the bifurcation of the central mullion distracts attention from the as-yet tentative verticality. By contrast, in the great east window of the choir, constructed some years later, the two major mullions defining the

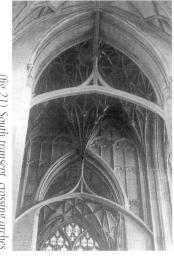

(fig 21) South transept, crossing arches

central bay continue to the head of the window with uncompromising directness. Below the window, behind open panelling, is a **wall-passage**, entered from the staircase in the south-west corner. The passage leads across to the gallery on the east side of the transept where there is a chapel (above the transept chapel) which had only recently been updated with Decorated windows, niches and piscinae.

St Andrew's Chapel The chapel is apsidal though outside the wall is polygonal. The arched opening from the transept was bricked up in 1755 so that a huge memorial to Dr. Martin Benson (bishop of Gloucester 1734-52) might be erected against the wall. The chapel was then used as a lay-clerks' vestry, access being through a narrow passage from the south ambulatory. It was opened again in 1855 and the obtrusive but necessary 14th-century buttress was refaced.

The **interior decoration** (1866-8) in spirit frescos is the work of Thomas Gambier Parry of Highnam Court (who also completed the painting of the vault of Ely Cathedral, left unfinished by the death of L'Estrange). He undertook the work for his friend Thomas Marling in memory of Marling's wife who died in 1863 (see the brass in the north-west corner of the chapel). The frescos depict, *inter alia*, scenes from the life of St Andrew. The Perpendicular **stone reredos** was restored, polychromed and gilded in 1977 in memory of Basil Guy, bishop of Gloucester 1963-75 (see tablet on left of steps from the transept). The 19th c. statuary is by Roddis of Birmingham. The central figure of Christ is flanked by St Andrew and St Peter, and the eight smaller figures represent Job, Solomon, Moses, David, Isaiah, Jeremiah, Ezekiel and Daniel. The other figures form an angel choir. The **floor tiles**, with St Andrew's initial, cross, and fishes, were laid down in 1856. Their use for the risers of the steps from the transept is regrettable.

Chapel of St John the Baptist, beneath the crossing arch, is screened off by a wooden parclose screen (*c*.1500). Inside the chapel the panelling on the back of the choir stalls is covered with monograms of S and B alternately, surmounted by crowns. The **entrance** into the chapel used to be on the south side in the centre of the screen where there was a slab with a mutilated cross incised on it, and the remains of an inscription: *Kyrie eleison anime*
                                        Fratris Johis Lyon

Masse states that 'this Johannis Lyon was the monk who made the reredos in this chapel'. There are, in fact, the remains of two medieval reredoses behind the present reredos (1965). Stone used in making the early 12th c. reredos was merely reversed and recut to make the second. The present **reredos and canopy** were designed by Stephen Dykes-Bower and carved by Tom Wellard, Clerk of the Works at Gloucester for more than thirty-five years after the Second World War. It was part of the restoration and embellishment of the chapel in 1964-5 in memory of Dr. C. S. Woodward (bishop of Gloucester 1946-54). At the same time a cartouche was mounted on the panelling to the right of the altar in memory of Dr. H. Costley-White (dean of Gloucester 1938-53).

Four Doorways In addition to the twin-doorway [22], there is a doorway in the south west corner of the transept leading to the choir gallery, roof-spaces and tower, and two doors in the south wall. The **south-east doorway**, behind a late-Elizabethan memorial, has a double-bodied monster on the lintel.

> In the reconstruction of the transept (1331-36) the present wall-passage was built below the great window, with a series of steps up to the gallery at its east end. This meant that any stair in the south east turret was cut off. Originally, the upper part of the staircase provided access to an Anglo-Norman clerestory passage which ran along the east side of the transept and possibly around the choir. But since the 14th-century the only access to the upper part has been from the transept roof-space by way of a narrow gallery behind the balustrade over the south window.

The other door in the south wall is probably an old **sacristry door**, though it was known for many years as the *Pilgrims' Door* on the mistaken assumption that it was used by pilgrims visiting the shrine of King Edward II. There is no decoration on the outside of the doorway but elaborate decoration on the inside which suggests the door led, not into the transept from outside, but from the transept into a room or building of some importance. A sacristry was commonly found in this position, providing the sacrist or his assistant with ready access to the altars in the eastern arm of the building. Carter in his plan of the Cathedral (1807) shows a sacristry adjoining the transept on the south side, though no trace of foundations has been recorded. However, a small recess in the outside wall adds credence to the suggestion.

> It is not known when the doorway was blocked up, presumably when the sacristry was demolished. Early drawings of the exterior of the south transept do not show the door which suggests it was closed at least from the 17th century [59]. In 1880 it was still blocked up, but in 1899 Masse noted 'it has now been opened'.

Resting, almost casually, on the projecting arms of the doorway, are two standing figures. The pose and the carving of the garments show them to be the work of a master craftsman. It is not known when the heads were removed, mainly because some writers have commented on their 'fair countenance' without ever having seen the faces. Beckindale (1948) noted that 'the Pilgrim's Door is guarded by angels with faces of great beauty'. He could not have seen the doorway, and was probably relying on the first edition of Masse (1899) who noted 'the sculpture is extremely graceful and pleasing, the expression of the faces particularly charming, and the drapery is arranged in a masterly manner'. Both writers were probably mislead by the frontispiece of Carter's *Plans and Elevations* (1807), which is a drawing of the doorway in which the angels are depicted with seraphic expressions. Carter, however, says nothing about their countenances, only that 'their attitudes are well conceived and pleasingly varied'. Haines (1865) noted that the heads 'have long since gone'. The condition of the stone where the heads were severed indicates that the damage was done centuries ago, possibly at the time of the Commonwealth or even earlier. Not only have the heads been removed, but also the figures have been badly hacked about.

The **south-west turret door** opens to a newel stair which provides access to the wall passage beneath the terminal window, and to the roof space above the transept vault and so to the roof-space over the crossing and choir. From the transept roof-space there is access to a stair at the south-east corner of the tower, which leads up to the ringing chamber and the bell chamber. This stair continues to the roof of the tower from which on a clear day there are spectacular views of the Severn Vale and the Malvern Hills, the Forest of Dean and the Cotswolds, and in the distance the Border country and the Welsh mountains.

Stained Glass The **east windows** (S.VII & S.VIII), over the gallery, contain some of the best and earliest medieval glass in the cathedral. The glass was restored by Hardman in 1863-4 'on the original pattern and re-using all the old glass belonging to them'; that is, incorporating the fragments of 14th c. glass which had survived from the original glazing of the remodelled transept. In the head of the window there is white scroll-work of vine leaves on a fine ruby ground and, below, plain quarries with simple borders. The window nearest the crossing contains a number of line-edged quarries decorated with star-like designs similar to those used extensively in the great east window. The **chapel of St Andrew** contains glass designed by John Powell and executed at the Hardman works in Birmingham (1868). It was inserted at the time of the restoration of the chapel by Thomas Marling of Norton Court.

The **great window** (S IX) was given by Thomas Marling when he was Mayor of Gloucester, and made by Hardman (1871); it depicts, in biblical sequence, incidents from the life of St Peter. It is well above the average quality of Victorian so-called trade glass and repays careful study (with binoculars). The larger of the **west windows** (S.X & S.XI), by Clayton and Bell (1889), is a memorial to Thomas Gambier Parry (1816-88) of Highnam Court. Its design reflects his artistic gifts and antiquarian interests. He invented the spirit fresco process and was responsible for the fresco painting in St Andrew's Chapel, opposite.

He was an able linguist and musician, a great traveller and an enthusiastic archaeologist. The main lights depict: Thomas Seabroke, Abbot of St Peter's (1450-57), seen designing the central tower; St Barbara, whose prayers were sought for protection against thunderstorms and fire, which were constant hazards in building work; St Luke, the Gospel writer, physician and companion of St Paul on his travels, and according to tradition, a sculptor and painter; Fra Angelico (1387-1455), the painter of the Florentine school.

Memorials A number of the **ledgers** have been moved from their original position. In the floor, at the angle of the west wall and the nave aisle there is a copy (1981) of a small tablet (the original was placed in the Gallery Exhibition in 1981) with the inscription: 'Here lyeth under this marbell ston Robert Leichfi (Lichfield), organist and Maister of the Choristers of this cathedral church, 20 years. He dyed the 6 of January 1582' (or, 1589). He was the first recorded organist of the cathedral, and appears to have been in post from 1562. In 1593 his two daughters, Bridget and Elizabeth, died of the plague and were buried in St Nicholas Church in Westgate Street.

The **monuments** set against the south wall are (i) An Elizabethan monument to Richard Pate (d.1588), founder of the Grammar School at Cheltenham and builder of Matson House, Gloucester. He was Recorder of the City of Gloucester and an MP for the city. The figures are missing; only the painted canopy remains. And (ii) a large black marble tomb with recumbent effigies of Abraham Blackleach who died in 1639, and his wife, Gertrude. 'It was not for her beauty that Dame Gertrude was thus commemorated' (Haines, H. 1867). Blackleech was not an alderman: 'This seems to be a time-honoured cathedral mistake. He was the son of a former chancellor of the diocese, and a prominent resident of the close' (Herbert, N.M.). The monument was moved here from the chapel at the east end of the north aisle when the chapel there was finally dismantled (Browne Willis' plan 1728).

> Blackleech is in cavalier costume, and his feet rest on an eagle, whilst his wife's costume is exquisitely detailed and her feet rest on a mailed fist holding a dagger. The effigies are carved in alabaster with great skill and attention to detail; note the boots, rosettes, sword belt and sword handle, and lace-work. 'According to Mrs. Esdaile they are either by Epiphanius Evesham or Edward Marshall, with faces like those by Evesham and hands like Marshall's. But whomsoever they are by, they are good examples of the Nicholas Stone period' (Verey, D. 1979).

The **wall tablets** on the west wall include one by Henry Wilson to Dr. Evan Evans, Master of Pembroke College, Oxford, and Canon of the Cathedral (d.1891). The memorial consists of a bronze tablet, bordered by a frame of marble and inlaid with other marbles. The bronze at the top is inlaid with shell of an iridescent colour. It should be compared with Wilson's memorial to Canon Tinling (d.1897), by the east cloister door. Another tablet worthy of note is a marble bust of T. B. Lloyd-Baker (d.1886) by W. S. Frith. The bust in relief is set in a medallion above a relief of Justice. The memorial to Dr. Charles Ellicott, bishop of Gloucester (d.1905) in the south ambulatory is another example of Frith's work. There are also tablets to Benjamin Baylis (d.1777), by Bryan of Gloucester; and to Mary, wife of Thynne Gwynne (d.1808), by Reeves of Bath.

On the east wall there is a tablet, with a lengthy inscription, to Dr. Josiah Tucker (dean of Gloucester 1759-99). He was interred in a brick-lined vault beneath a ledger nearby.

The **mason's memorial**, to the right of the crypt doorway, is a wall-bracket in the L shape of a mason's square. On the under side a master-mason is seated with the tools of his trade on his lap. Depicted above the mason is a section of the transept vault, in miniature, and a young man spread-eagled over it. This has given rise to the quite plausible suggestion that the bracket was erected as a memorial to a stone mason, or an apprentice, who fell to his death while working on the construction of the vault. Dowel holes in the upper surface of the bracket may indicate that it once supported a lamp (for lighting the approach to the crypt stairs) or more probably a figure of St Barbara who was invoked, particularly by builders, for protection against lightning, fire and sudden death.

(fig 22) Crypt entrance (1828)

THE CRYPT

The idea of a crypt goes back to the early Christians' use (for burials) of subterranean quarries or excavations among the hills around Rome. The catacombs, as they were called, became hiding places during periods of persecution, and later Christians visited them believing that prayers offered at the tombs of the saints and martyrs buried there were particularly efficacious. In c.600 Pope Gregory the Great added a crypt to old St Peter's at Rome. Later larger crypts were built in Carolingian and Ottonian churches, e.g. Speyer in Germany.

> 'The ultimate source of spacious crypts was Italy, but there were also common in the Rhineland in the eleventh century. Cushion capitals were also familiar there and, if crypts and cushion capitals come together, the Rhineland would be the obvious centre from which they reached England' (Kidson, P. 1979).

In medieval times, apart from forming the foundations of the building, crypts were furnished with altars and used for worship, and for burials, particularly of local saints and martyrs.

Gloucester's crypt is entered from the south transept [22], and is one of six in the country founded before 1090, the others being St Augustine's Abbey at Canterbury, Canterbury Cathedral, Winchester, Worcester and Rochester. The crypt extends beneath the whole of the presbytery (that part of the choir to the east of the tower crossing) including its ambulatory and radiating chapels, and beneath the chapels on the east side of the transepts.

It was in the crypt that work on the abbey church began in 1089. 'In that year the foundations of the church were marked out...and the first stone laid by Robert, Bishop of Hereford, Serlo being the abbot' (*Historia*). The eastern end the church was planned as a three-storey building, the basic plan of the crypt being repeated above at each level.

Crypt Plan Because of the demolition of the east end of the choir in the 14th century, it is only in the crypt that the late-11th century plan is preserved in its entirety [23]. Indeed, for this reason the periapsidal plan can be studied better at Gloucester than anywhere else. Its great merit, as Francis Bond pointed out, was that it provided a processional path (*via processionum*) around the sanctuary which did not exist in a plan such as that at

(fig 23) *Crypt, south aisle facing west*

Durham, with its three parallel eastern apses after the fashion of the abbeys of Normandy. Moreover, it provided for three eastern chapels instead of two, and readier access to each of the chapels.

> It is probable that Westminster Abbey (in that part of the Norman church begun by Edward the Confessor in 1050 and dedicated in 1066) had a similar arrangement. Documentary evidence points to the existence there of a sanctuary with a processional path, of upper as well as lower chapels, and of an upper as well as lower aisle encircling the sanctuary. This upper aisle may have had a *demi-berceau* or half-barrel vault as at Gloucester. A *demi-berceau* in this same position can be seen in St Stephen's, Caen, and the springing of one at Cerisy-la-Foret in Normandy.

In one respect Gloucester surpasses in planning all the Romanesque churches of Normandy and England, in that, having a crypt, the three radiating apses are each of three stories high, thus providing nine eastern chapels. And if to these are added the transept chapels with those below and above, in crypt and tribune, there is a total of fifteen around the eastern arm of the church, an extraordinary number for such an early date.

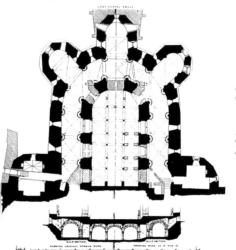

(fig 24) Crypt plan and cross section

The processional path was also important. Gloucester did not have was a Saint's chapel at the back of the high altar. But as Gloucester never had a local saint it never required such a chapel. The mother church of Worcester had in St Wulfstan and St Oswald two local saints. Later its eastern limb had to be reconstructed in order to provide them with adequate 'habitation'. Gloucester, in contrast, remained unaltered in plan, except that in order to provide room for a full monastic choir at the services of the Blessed Virgin, the easternmost (or, axial) chapel was twice rebuilt on a larger scale.

Date of the Crypt A detailed examination of the crypt has led some to conclude that there are remains of an earlier, pre-Conquest, church incorporated in its structure.

F.S.Waller pointed out that the bases and capitals of the piers in the central chamber are 'much out of level from east to west, and from north to south, and in design they are strikingly different to the half columns with cushion capitals attached to the outer walls. So different, indeed, are they as to make it questionable whether a larger portion of these columns do not belong to an earlier church'. He also noted that the masons' marks found on Anglo-Norman work elsewhere in the church are only found in the crypt on the later strengthening work (see below) and not on the Early Norman work, a fact which made Dr. Francis Bond wonder whether part of the church which Aldred, Bishop of Worcester, built for the Benedictine community in 1058 may not survive in the central chamber. 'In the crypt there is Norman work of two dates, the earlier part of which may be Aldred's... though the great bulk of the work was undoubtedly done by Abbot Serlo.' (Bond, F. 1912).

The level of the floor in the central chamber, as defined by the bases of the columns, is considerably lower than that of the aisles and radiating chapels, suggesting that it belongs to a separate building programme. This possibility is supported by the appearance of two layers in the arcade walls, with the outer built onto the inner i.e. the wall of the central chamber. 'If one assumes that the outer layer, along with the ambulatory chapels is Serlo's, then the earlier phase could either be a false start in 1089 or a remnant of the church built by Ealdred, Bishop of Worcester, and consecrated according to the *Anglo-Saxon Chronicles* in 1058. The normal attribution of this work to the late eleventh century gives some indication of the thoroughly Norman character of its volute capitals, tooling, vaulting and general layout' (Fernie, E. 1983).

Whether or not there are remains of an earlier building in the central chamber, it is clear that '*when the foundations of the building were laid, the crypt was planned to receive the existing superstructure and no other*' (Willis, R. 1860).

Central Chamber The central chamber is divided into three by two rows of small columns from whose capitals spring arches and a groin vault [25]. The volute capitals and groin vaults are typical of late-11th century work, as are the twin-scalloped capitals of the wall-shafts. The **piers** are further apart north-south than they are east-west. As a result, whilst the arches aligned east-west are more-or-less semi-circular, those aligned north-south are three, if not four, centred. But though

(fig 25) *Crypt, central chamber*

these arches are comparatively 'flat' the **vault** has proved strong enough to support the floor of the presbytery for more than nine centuries. 'Faced with a severe limit on height, less unpredictable designers might have been content to copy Worcester's subdivision of the central space into four aisles covered by vaults of small span and elevation. However the Gloucester master opted for three broad aisles and covered them with vaults of a daringly shallow profile' (Wilson, C. 1985). The **floor** level in the central chamber is about 0.8m. below the level of the ambulatory, and the ambulatory on average is 2m. below the level of the ground outside. As a result the central chamber has long been subject to flooding. Water to a depth of 25cms. can often be seen around the bases of the eastern piers. The danger of flooding meant the central chamber was seldom, if ever, used for worship. There is no evidence in the fabric of liturgical use, even though the apsidal chapels remained in use for much of the medieval period.

During restoration work in the crypt in the 1850s a mass of debris was cleared out and the central chamber drained. A quantity of rubble was brought in to raise the level of the floor, and concrete was spread over it from wall to wall. In the 1960s the four most eastern piers were in danger of collapse, possibly due to the weight of the choir reredos above them, so the piers were dismantled and reassembled around steel rods driven well into the substrata. At the same time the concrete and rubble around the piers was removed and the ground excavated to expose their bases. More recently the pits have been lined.

The **capitals** of the central arcade are an interesting mixture of volute and cushion, with twin-scalloped capitals on the wall responds. Two of the volute capitals of the north arcade are carved with acanthus leaf decoration, and a neighbouring capital has a face, or *mask*, on its north face [26].

(fig 26) Crypt, 'mask' carving on capital

The **mask** has almond-shaped eyes and prominent eyebrows, a 'handlebar' moustache and goaty beard. It is similar to a mask, dated to 1063, found during excavation in 1945-55 on a damaged capital at Rouen Cathedral. 'Such capitals with crudely carved masks and prominent volutes in the upper register are very common in Romanesque Normandy especially between 1050-1080. The nearest parallels to the Rouen capital are found in the crypt of Bayeux Cathedral (*c*.1050), in Thaon old church (*c*.1060), in the nave of the Trinity abbey church in Caen (*c*.1070) and in S. Etienne, Caen. Although this type did not spread as widely in England, it may be found, with some differences, in Gloucester Cathedral crypt (*c*.1089), in Blyth Priory Church (*c*.1080) and elsewhere' (Bayle, M. 1984).

At the west end of the central chamber there is a fenced area containing mainly masonry fragments, some of considerable archaeological interest.

Crypt Ambulatory A broad ambulatory surrounds the central chamber. The outer wall, no less than 2.5m. thick, is an impressive example of Norman 'thick wall' construction. Set into the wall are small round-headed windows, deeply splayed.

But *the crypt is not entirely as originally built.*

(1) The *responds*, or wall-shafts between the windows, were comparatively narrow. They have been encased to strengthen them. In several bays the corners of the original capitals protrude.

(2) The *piers* of the main arcade were compound and quite substantial, with attached shafts facing into the ambulatory and into the arched openings. It was hoped the piers would prove strong enough to support the weight of the choir and tribune arcades.

(3) The *vault* in the ambulatory was originally *groined*. But when the ambulatory was strengthened, by encasing the arcade piers and half-shafts against the outer walls, supporting-arches were constructed *under* the original transverse arches. At the same time a system of quatrepartite ribs was constructed in each bay. In some of the irregular bays around the eastern section of the ambulatory the apex of the groin vault is exposed.

(4) The *ribs* which were put in to support the groin vault have no key stone at their intersection (for example, in the first bay at the foot of the entry steps). Instead, whilst one rib crosses the vault diagonally the other, consisting of two quarter-ribs, simply abuts it at the apex. The way some of the ribs rest on the pier capitals, suggests the strengthening work was done in a hurry, or at least without regard to its finished state.

(5) The inserted ribs varying in profile; some are of plain rectangular section, others of one broad half-roll with two smaller quarter-hollows, and others have chevron decoration.

When was the strengthening work carried out? * Some have argued it was carried out soon after the crypt was completed. The way the original transverse arches on the south side of the crypt appear to be out of shape and in danger of giving away is taken as evidence that, early on, it was realised that the crypt was not strong enough to support the superstructure. Victorian antiquarians even suggested that the damage to the transverse arches was caused by an earthquake which occurred, according to the *Historia*, in the same year that work on the crypt began (August 1089). * Alternatively, the work may have been carried out in the early years of the 12th century when a high vault is thought to have been constructed over the choir. The lateral pressure of the vault and the additional weight on the foundations made it imperative to strengthen the crypt, which was already showing signs of weakness through settlement. * Some of the strengthening work was put in when the choir was reconstructed in the 14th century. The massive lierne vault would have greatly increased the weight bearing down on the aging crypt, and made its strengthening imperative. The use of discarded chevron, possibly from the reconstruction of the south aisle (*c*.1320) or the south transept (1331-36), is taken as evidence of a later date for at least some of the work.

Thus, the strengthening work was not carried out at any one particular time but at different times as weaknesses in the structure became evident, or its stability was threatened by new pressures. The arcade around the central chamber, originally open, has been filled in with solid masonry in some bays, and in others with discarded window tracery. At the east end, against the inner apse, blocks of masonry (*c*.1340) provide firm foundations for the two additional vaulting shafts at the east end of the choir. These foundations blocks were made up of ashlar from the demolished east end (note, the nook-shafts at the outer corners, and masons' marks, which are noticeably absent from the original work in the crypt).

Crypt Chapels The **first chapel** (*closed to the public*), at the foot of the entry steps houses the junction and distribution of the cathedral's electricity supply. The chapel has a double piscina with a shelf, the remains of two sets of hinge posts, and holes for the moveable bar with which the door was once secured. Over the door there is an inscription in Latin explaining why the crypt was known for many years as the *Bone House*.

> A large quantity of bones had been brought in from around the east end of the cathedral, an area which had been a burial ground for centuries. When the crypt was restored by F.S.Waller in the early 1850s the remains were stored in this chapel before being taken out and reinterred in a large grave on the north side of the choir. The drawing (1828) by W.H.Bartlett shows the central chamber piled high with rubble and human remains. Opposite the entrance to the chapel a strengthening wall creates a rather inaccessible chamber.

The **second chapel**, the south-east chapel, contains a wall arcade of five plain arches with ornament above and the remains of a stone bench (*sedilia*) below. A large stone slab from the floor of the south porch has been placed here to serve as an altar. The window in the apse was enlarged in the 13th century, but the side windows are little altered. The chapel retains its original groin vault, with transverse arches springing from attached columns with twin-scallop capitals and abaci. On either side of the entrance are the remains of a stone screen. As with the other chapels off the eastern section of the ambulatory there is a step into the chapel (the floor level rising gradually towards the east). The axis of the two lateral chapels is not aligned due east; consequently their altars did not face east, as was customary. There are relaid medieval tiles along the step into the **third chapel**, the axial chapel. The chapel retains its apse, but outside the side walls have been extended eastwards making it necessary to form a 'tunnel' through to the windows. These alterations and the blocking up of the east window are cited as evidence that the chapel was extended in the 13th century so that a lady chapel, of Early English design, could be built above.

> The **font** which stands in the chapel was designed by G. Gilbert Scott (1875) and stood originally at the west end of the south aisle of the nave. It was given in memory of William Gibbs of Tyntesfield by his widow, and made by Messrs Farmer and Brindley of London in Inverness granite. There are three carved panels in low relief on each side of the font, surrounded by foliage. The font was little used and the granite was considered out of place in the nave (built predominantly of limestone) so it was banished to the crypt.

The **fourth chapel**, the north-east chapel, is whitewashed and contains nothing of note apart from the remains of an external stair and a blocked doorway. This was opened in the 18th century to provide access to and from *The Grove* (the garden around the east end of the cathedral).

> *In the ambulatory outside the chapel note:* * The foundation-block, made up of reused Anglo-Norman masonry, corresponding with that on the south side. * The chevron of the under-arch, made up of separate stones each with a single chevron. * To the west of the chevron arch the exposed apex of the groin vault * Further along the ambulatory, the

window tracery fitted into the arcade arch. * The next bay to the west is entirely filled in, except for a small doorway which leads through to the central chamber. Originally the door opened into a small cupboard, or recess, in the thickness of the wall (Carter, J. 1807). The entrance is made up of stones from an old doorway, already rebated to receive a wooden door. Note the hinge-holes and the latch. Incorporated into the left jamb is an arched stone which once formed the lintel of a small door or cupboard.

Opposite the entrance to the **fifth chapel** is a cresset, a small recess in the wall for a burning wick, to light the foot of the steps from the transept (long-since removed) and the passage through to the chapel. Further evidence of the blocked doorway and stair has recently (1998) been discovered. In the eastern recess of the chapel, where the altar stood, there are the remains of a 13th *c.* rib vault. The ribs, the stiff-leaf decoration and the bosses are all much decayed, as is the *piscina*. On the north side there is a recess, probably an *aumbry* (cupboard) which would have been used to store the sacred vessels. The steps lead up to the eastern slype (presently the Cathedral Treasury) which was a *locutorium* in monastic times, and served as a passage from the cloister walk to the monks' cemetery.

Chapter Five
THE CHOIR AMBULATORY

The ambulatory with its radiating chapels reminds us that behind and beneath all the glorious Perpendicular work of the choir the Norman east end survives. A semi-circular or polygonal aisle around the east end of the choir was a feature of many monastic churches. It was designed for processions, which were an important feature especially of Benedictine life and liturgy. It was also used by pilgrims visiting a shrine behind the high altar, or elsewhere at the east end of a church. At Gloucester it formed part of the pilgrims' route to the shrine of King Edward II.

Leaving the south transept by the steps to the choir ambulatory a vista opens up that has remained almost unaltered since the late 11th century. The windows have been enlarged and filled with Perpendicular tracery and 19th-century glass; there is a Perpendicular screen in front of the south-east chapel, and the piers, vault and walls have been stripped of medieval colour. But the main structure is early Anglo-Norman work, dating to *c*.1090.

South Ambulatory

Architectural Features In the transept the double-doorway backs onto the late-11th-century **arched entrance** to the ambulatory. A broad semi-circular arch spans the entrance, with twin responds at the sides, cushion capitals and shared abaci. Before the reconstruction of the crossing (1337-55) the twin responds against the tower piers would have risen to a similar arrangement. Between the enlarged windows the 11th c. **responds** remain intact, with single scallop capitals supporting transverse arches and a groin vault. The **transverse arches** are distorted, but not as badly as those in the crypt below. Willis described them as 'broken backed' (Willis, R. 1860). The **massive piers** of the choir arcade, with their small convex capital bands (as later in the nave) and broad arches of plain square section, stand firm on their foundations in the strengthened crypt. On the choir side the piers were cut back to the width of the outer order of the arches so that the vaulting shafts could be attached (this is best observed from the ambulatory); but there is evidence that, in places, the rounded surface of the piers was shaped to the same profile to form part of the vaulting shafts [4].

Memorials On the right of the steps to the ambulatory is a memorial and brass *in mem.* the Revd. John Kempthorne (d.1838). Close by is a brass, by Messrs Heaton, Butler & Bayne, *in mem.* the Revd. H. Haines (d.1872), for twenty-three years second master of the King's School. A cast of *The Nativity* by Josephena de Vasconcellos (from the original sculpture made for St Martin's-in-the-Field, London) is usually kept here. Opposite the south-east chapel is a memorial-tomb to Dr. Charles J. Ellicott, a distinguished Victorian divine and Bishop of Gloucester and Bristol 1863-97, and of Gloucester 1897-1905. The memorial, which is

1. Cathedral from the south west

2. Nave, looking east

3. Nave, north aisle looking west

4.

5.

6.

4. Lady Chapel, interior, looking west

5. Lady Chapel, Margery Clent (*nee* Smith) memorial

6. Lady Chapel, north chantry, Godfrey Goldsborough, Bishop of
   Gloucester (1598-1604)

7. Lady Chapel, Sir John Powell (d. 1713)

8. Lady Chapel, monument to Elizabeth Williams, detail

7.

8.

10a Female saint

10b Monks in possession

9 & 10 Lady Chapel, east window and details of five lights

King
m choir clerestory series)

10d Madonna and Child

10c Bishops or abbots in possessio

11 & 12. Lady Chapel,
Christopher Whall window
S IV. and details, St. Louis
from the Chapter House

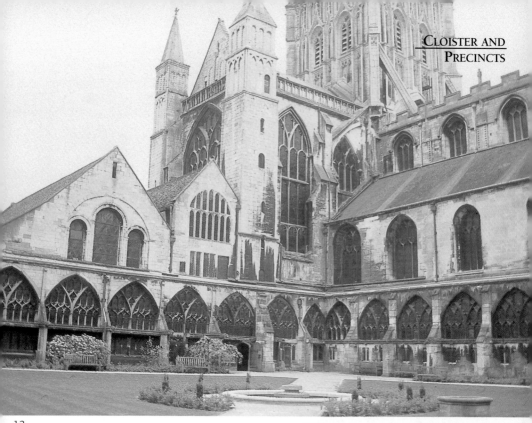

13

13. Great Cloister, garth, looking south east
14. Great Cloister, nave west entrance
15. Great Cloister, south walk looking east

15

14

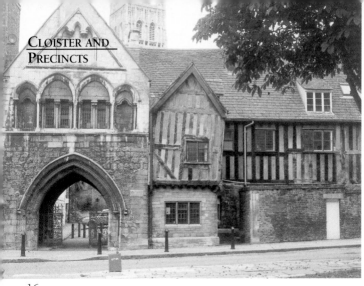

16

17

18

16. Precincts, St. Mary's Gate

17. Precincts, outer parlour
(west slype)

18. Precincts, Great Hall
(Parliament Room)

19. Junction of Great East
Window and Lady Chapel

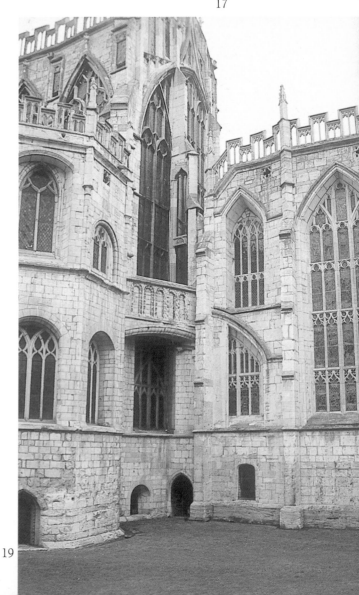

19

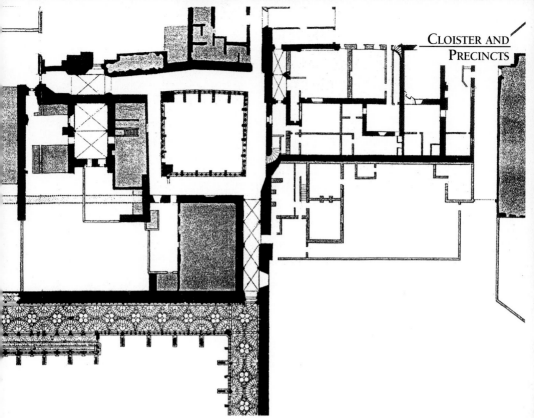

20. Plan of Infirmary area in 1807 (Carter, J.)

21. View, Infirmary area from the tower

22. Cathedral from the south east

23. Cathedral from the south west, aerial view showing Cloisters and Precincts

signed, is by W. S. Frith, the Gloucester monumental sculptor.

> Dr. Ellicott was an eminent biblical scholar, working with a group of others on the translation of the New Testament for the Revised Version (1880) of the Bible. His episcopate of forty-two years was the longest in the history of the diocese. He was buried at Birchington-on-Sea, near Margate.

Cope Chests Opposite the effigy of Duke Robert are two rare 14th-century cope chests, designed as quarter-circles so that copes, which were semi-circular when laid flat, could be conveniently stored [27]. The chests have four legs and straight sides with early examples of fielded panels. The boards have skewed and

(fig 27) South ambulatory, cope chests

square edge butt-joints, edge-to-edge. The ironwork is undecorated and difficult to date, but the chests may be associated with Robert Lesyngham's work in the north transept and cloister from c.1368 (Hewett, C. A. 1985). The chests were kept for many years in what-is-now the choir vestry (Carter, J. 1807).

Monument to Robert, Duke of Normandy Robert, the eldest son of William the Conqueror was given Normandy when his father died, whilst his younger brother, William, nicknamed Rufus, was given the English throne {44}.

> Duke Robert participated in the First Crusade, fighting gallantly, but on his return to Normandy his still-younger brother, Henry, was crowned King of England. Duke Robert became a focus of discontent until King Henry captured him in 1106 and confined him to Cardiff Castle for the rest of his life. On his death in 1134 his body was 'carried to Gloucester and buried *cum magno honore* in the pavement that is before the altar of the church' (Florence of Worcester).
>
> His connection with Gloucester Abbey went back to his father's support for the first Norman abbot, Serlo, who was one of the Conqueror's chaplains, and to the King's visits to the town for his Christmas Court (or, Witan). It was at Christmas in 1085 that King William ordered the survey of the country and the compilation of *Domesday* Book. Duke Robert is commemorated, along with other early benefactors, on the walls of the Chapter House: *Hic jacet Robertus Curtus.*

Judging by the style of the armour, the **effigy** of Duke Robert [28] dates from the reign of King Henry III (1216-72), probably c.1240. The hauberk of chain-mail and the long surcote ceased to be worn after the 13th century. Some believe it was carved within sixty years of Robert's death. 'From the coat of mail and long surcote it would seem to be twelfth-century' (Bond, F. 1912). A wooden effigy of this date is a rare survival. A shield was attached to the black strap on the left side, as on a similar effigy of roughly the same date at Dorchester, Oxon. The two effigies, one in wood and the other in stone, may have been made in the same workshop (Hurtig. J, 1979). The 15th-century **mortuary-chest** was probably made for the abbey, specifically for displaying the effigy. The earliest drawing (Robert Cooke, 1569) of 'the tombe...in the middle of the quyer' shows the effigy and chest as one, as does Nicholas Charles in 1610. Earlier, Leland (1541) wrote: 'Rob'tus Curthoise, sonne to William the Conqueroir, lyeth in the middle of the Presbitery' - presumably on the chest. There is a frieze of leafage around the chest which may have been carved by Simon Werman who worked in the West Country, around Taunton, at the end of the century (Poyntz-Wright, P. 1991). A series of ten shields with coats of arms adorns the sides of the chest, nine of which were originally intended to commemorate the nine worthies of the world.

> They are, *on the right side*, Hector, Julius Caesar, King David of Israel, and King Arthur, *and on the left*, Edward the Confessor, Alexander the Great, Judas Maccabaeus and Charlemange. At the ends are Godfrey of Bouillon and the arms of England and France quarterly. The inclusion of the royal arms in this form means the chest must be later than the time of King Henry IV (1399-1413).

The effigy was badly damaged by soldiers in the Civil War (1642-51) but the pieces were preserved by Sir Humphrey Tracy of Stanway, Gloucestershire. At the Restoration (1660) it was repaired, repainted (together with the chest), and placed in its traditional place in the presbytery. The tomb of King John (d.1216) occupies a similar position at Worcester, as did that of Edward the Confessor at Westminster

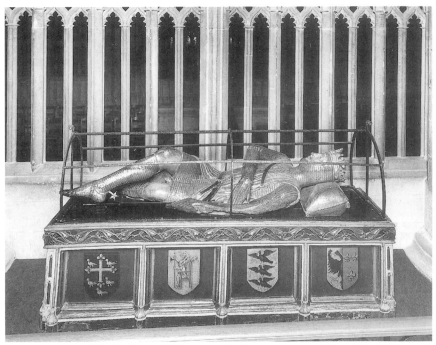

(fig 28) Choir ambulatory, south side, monument to Robert, duke of Normandy

up to 1245. The monument remained in this position until it was removed by Dr. Knightly Chetwood (dean, 1707-20) to the north-east ambulatory chapel. It was returned to the presbytery in 1905 but moved to the south ambulatory in 1988. During the 19th-century restoration of the choir Gilbert Scott marked the traditional place of the Duke's burial in the tiled pavement.

Stained Glass The stained glass in all six ambulatory windows is by C. E. Kempe (1837-1907). Only one of the windows is 'signed' with his wheat-sheaf trademark, but there is no mistaking his style which, at the time, was becoming extremely fashionable, attracting even Royal patronage. The richness and ebullience of his windows caught the mood of high Victorian society and reflected the growing influence of the Catholic revival (Stravidi, M. 1988).

From east to west:

(i) *The Lamb of God* (s.ii) 1882 *in mem.* Sir John H. Culme-Seymour (1800-80), Canon of Gloucester for fifty years.

(ii) *God, our Saviour* (s.iii) 1886 *in mem.* Dr. Henry Law, Dean of Gloucester (1862-84), a leader of the Evangelical party in the church (see dedication).

(iii)*Four Saints* (s.iv) 1890, with a highly personal choice of subjects *in mem.* the Revd. R. and Mrs. Harvey. Richard Harvey was a Canon of Gloucester from 1858 until his death in 1889 aged ninety-one, and survived his wife by only 12 hours (see inscription).

Apart from the ambulatory windows, there are three other Kempe windows in the cathedral - in the north aisle of the nave (n.vii) which he designed when he was an apprentice with Clayton & Bell (1865); in the north chantry of the lady chapel (1895), and a large window (N.X) on the west side of the north transept (1894).

South East Chapel Behind its Perpendicular screen, the chapel retains its Romanesque character. The apse is semi-circular, though outside the wall is three-sided. On each side of the chapel there is a narrow stone bench, now hidden by a wooden bench, and above the benches there are slightly pointed wall-arches. At the base of the wall shafts, there is dog-tooth moulding, typical of the late 11th-century. The bases of the two colonettes which supported the stone altar also remain *in situ* beneath the wooden floor, as does a circular stone set into the tile-pavement which may have been the base of a pedestal piscina. The piscina set into the wall on the south side dates from the 14th century. The base of the late-medieval reredos also remained exposed until the chapel was refurbished in 1993-94.

The chapel was refurbished in commemoration of the 900th anniversary of the laying of the foundation stone of the abbey church in 1089. The painting of the vault over the apse (by Burlison and Grylls 1869) was retained. The subject of the painting reflects an earlier dedication of the chapel to St Philip. But the window glass, by Clayton and Bell (1868), *in mem.* of Sir C. W. Codrington Bt. MP (d. 1864) was removed. A large part of it was given to St Saviour's Church, Eastbourne.

C.B.Comely designed the new interior to provide for 'worship in the round'. Much of the furniture was made in the Cathedral Workshop by Carol Feasey. The theme of Thomas Denny's glass (1992) is *Praise*, in celebration of the centuries of worship by monastic community and cathedral choir and congregation. The side lights are based on Psalm 148 in which the whole creation is summoned to offer praise to its Creator, and the central section 'is concerned with a more personal form of praise, St Thomas's moment of realisation in which he worships Christ - 'My Lord and my God' (St John 20.19-29)). The colour, unified and stable in the small space of the chapel, and the movement and rhythm of light and dark are themselves a shout of praise' (Denny).

East Ambulatory

Originally, the ambulatory continued on past the axial chapel to the north side of the choir, with the same comparatively low vault adapted to the apsidal plan. The original vaulting system spanned the ambulatory between the inner three-sided apse and the seven-sided outer wall. But the eastern section was demolished during the remodelling of the choir in the 14th century, including the arches and piers of the inner apse [2]. What remained had to be strengthened with a new system of ribs and arches to ensure the stability of the new structure which consisted, in the main, of a huge wall of glass.

* From outside the south-east chapel the contrast between the strength of the Anglo-Norman arcade and the slightness of the new vaulting-shaft is very apparent, yet it was expected to carry the same weight as the rest without the backing of an 11th. c. drum-pier.
* In this new eastern bay the sides of the choir splay outward to accommodate the great window, which is wider than the choir itself.
* The great shafts on either side of the window rest on a mass of masonry in the crypt (at the junction of the crypt ambulatory and the lateral chapels). The window itself, built on the apsidal outer wall of the crypt, is canted (bowed). The whole concept and construction of the 14th-century east end must rank among the most innovative and daring works of medieval monastic engineering.

Note

(i) The arches of the additional bay are pointed, in contrast to the arches in the bays to the west which follow the line of the Anglo-Norman arches.

(ii) In the outer wall, on either side of the entrance to the lady chapel, there are attached half-shafts (or, responds) with cushion capitals which formed part of the original vaulting system around the eastern ambulatory.

(iii) The wall opposite the entrance to the lady chapel encloses the *feretory*, a shrine for relics behind the high altar.

(iv) The vast expanse of stained glass in the great east window (the size of a tennis court), and in the choir vault *Christ, surrounded by an angel orchestra*.

North Ambulatory

This is similar in construction to the south ambulatory, retaining its essentially Romanesque character. Features of the 14th-century reconstruction noted on the south side are duplicated on the north side.

North East Chapel Now known as the *War Memorial Chapel*, it was earlier known as the *Chapel of St Edmund and St Edward*, or *Boteler's Chapel* after Reginald Boteler, *alias* Butler (abbot 1437-50). The chapel was refurbished in the mid-15th century, and retains a number of late-medieval features; for example, a stone **screen** which may well date from the time of Abbot Boteler, and a **reredos**, of one central and eight small niches, with statuettes which had traces of medieval pigment on the shields of the frieze, providing sufficient indication for their repainting. There are fragments of **medieval glass** in the window tracery. A **piscina** has been adapted as a credence shelf. The floor tiles are badly worn, due partly to the trampling of feet around the effigy of Robert, Duke of Normandy, which stood here for nearly two hundred years (*c.*1715-1905).

Memorials of various wars have been brought together in the chapel and in the ambulatory outside. The *Books of Remembrance* record the names of men and women who served in the Gloucestershire Regiment, the Royal Air Force and British Navy and who gave their lives in the World Wars of 1914-18 and 1939-45 and in more recent conflicts. In the windows there are commemorative panels, two by Edward Payne (1906-91) installed respectively in 1974 and 1978, one to the 8,100 officers and men of the Gloucestershire Regiment who gave their lives in the First World War (1974), and the other to the 723 officers and ratings of HMS Gloucester sunk off Crete in May 1941 (1978). The memorial window by Alan Younger commemorates the Glosters' Korean Campaign (1950-1). The design incorporates a Chinese trumpet and the Regimental bugle. Outside, in the ambulatory, there is a cross made by Lt.Col. J. P. Carne VC. DSO. during his captivity after the battle of the Imjin River (22-25 April 1951), and used at services held in the prisoner of war camp at Pyn-chong-ni, North Korea (1951-53). Standards of the Gloucestershire Regiment were displayed for many years in the north ambulatory.

Stained Glass The windows were glazed by C. E. Kempe. From east to west:
(i) *Four Holy Women* (n.ii) 1878, given by the Dean and Chapter *in mem.* Catherine Maria Tinling d.1876, wife of Canon Edward Tinling. In the scene, bottom left, note the gentleman with the spectacles! Sufficient old glass survived in the tracery of this window to suggest its original design, which Kempe adopted for this and the other windows in the series.
(ii) *Four Patron Saints* (n.iii) with related scenes, *in mem.* Lt.Gen. Sir Joseph Thackwell (1781-1859) with the Thackwell arms. In the Battle of Waterloo (1815) this 'very brave and dashing officer' lost an arm, and had two horses shot from under him.

(iii)*Four Builder Abbots* (n.iv) 1892, was the last of the series to be inserted. Given
     in mem. Alfred George Price of Tibberton Court. The Kempe trade mark of three
     wheat-sheaves is in the tracery.

Tombs and Monuments

Some of the monuments in the choir ambulatory are of more than local interest -
they are of national importance.   There is the memorial to Robert, Duke of
Normandy, in the south ambulatory which is important for its historical association
and as a rare survival of 13th c. memorial wood-carving. In the north ambulatory
there is the shrine of King Edward II which is an outstanding example of 14th-
century canopied-tomb design.

Monument to Prince Osric Erected by William Parker, the last abbot of St Peter's
(1514-39), in honour of the founder of the first monastic house on the site - see
inscription on the pier at the foot of the effigy - *Osricus Rex primus fundator hujus
Monasterii 681*.   Osric is shown holding a model of a church, and wearing a tunic
and a laced mantle with fur hood or collar. He is crowned, and holds a sceptre, and
his feet rest on a lion. The effigy is roughly carved, perhaps deliberately to make it
appear more ancient than it is {45}.

Above the tomb there is a canopy with a panelled soffit, and in the spandrels are
the arms of Abbot Parker and the attributed arms of Northumbria, reflecting the
belief that Prince Osric (d.729) became king of Northumbria. Leland (1541) wrote:
'Osric, founder of Gloucester Abbey, first laye in St Petronell's Chapell, thence
removed into our Lady Chapell, and thence removed of late dayes and layd under
a fayre tomb of stone on the north syde of the high aulter' The tomb, of Tudor date,
was investigated in 1892 but the remains were left undisturbed.

Shrine of King Edward II This magnificent tomb was erected over the burial place
of Edward II by his son, King Edward III (r. 1327-77) and Queen Isabella (Wilson,
C. 1985).   Large ogee-headed niches were cut out of the Anglo-Norman piers at
either end to allow for movement around the tomb {42}.   The capitals were
decorated with the device of Richard II (a white hart, chained and gorged, with a
ducal coronet) to mark the king's visit to Gloucester and to the tomb in 1378.

The chest: A feature of contemporary tomb chests at Westminster was the use of
two kinds of stone, of contrasting colour; for example, the Eltham tomb which is of
Purbeck with alabaster cladding. Edward II's tomb has a chest of oolitic limestone
which is clad with Purbeck. In the Purbeck cladding are ogee-arched recesses,
cinque-foiled, with crocheted heads.

Shallow and deep recesses alternate [29]. Each of the smaller niches contain a
pedestal for a figure, while the larger recesses have two pedestals. Dowel holes and
iron studs (to secure the figures) survive in several of the niches. There are four small
shallow niches on each of the long sides of the chest and two on the short sides,
making twelve niches in all. There were sixteen figures in the larger recessed niches.

152

Honoratissimo et Nobi... ...lissimo, Domino, Dno.
GEORGIO Baroni BERKLEY. ...de BERKLEY in agro
Gloverniensi. Tumuli ...hanc Regis EDWARDI
Secundi, Figuram. H. D. D. D. F. S.

(fig 29). Shrine of King Edward II (Francis Sandford 1683)

In Francis Sandford's *Genealogical History of the Kings of England* (London 1683) there is an etching of the shrine showing shields in the spandrels above the arches framing the niches. This would suggest that the double niches contained secular figures, perhaps members of the Royal house and of the Court (presumably some of those whose arms are also found nearby in the Great East Window), and the twelve smaller niches figures of the Apostles (who also feature in the Great East Window).

As Dr. Anne Morganstern shows in *Gothic Tombs of Kingship* (Pennsylvania 2000) 'this hypothesis gains strength by analogy'. She compares such tombs as that of Robert de Vere,? the fifth Earl of Oxford (d.1296) at Earl's Colne, Essex, and the tomb of Elizabeth de Montfort (d.1354) at Christ Church, Oxford. Earlier genealogical tombs, with shields in the spandrels, include the tombs of Aveline de Forz (d.1274), of Edmund, earl of Lancaster (d. 1296), and of Aymer de Valence (d.1324), all at Westminster Abbey. Sometimes the shields are placed beneath each niches as, for example, on the tomb-chest of Richard Beauchamp, earl of Warwick (d. 1439), at St Mary's, Warwick.

The bracket in the front of the base was for a light, or a receptacle for offerings.

> King Edward III when in danger of shipwreck vowed an offering of a golden ship at his father's tomb. This was duly presented but later redeemed at the request of the Abbot and the community for one hundred pounds. The Black Prince offered a golden crucifix containing a portion of the holy Cross, the Queen of the Scots a necklace with a ruby, and Queen Philippa a heart and ear of gold. Such offerings were no doubt hung about the tomb in the usual way.

The effigy: The effigy of alabaster is London work of c.1330. The head is very fine [30], to be compared with the head of Edward III at Westminster and the head of the Black Prince at Canterbury. There is a striking resemblance, especially in the arrangement of the hair and beard, in all the Plantagenet effigies. At Gloucester 'in this royal head are concentrated the outstanding features of early-14th-century English sculpture, the passion for undulation, the lack of stern masculinity and the hint of

(fig 30) King Edward II, detail of alabaster effigy

decadence, and close attention to detail and finish' (Coldstream, N. 1994). The Gloucester angels are practically identical to those on the tomb of John of Eltham (d.1334), earl of Cornwall and second son of Edward II, in Westminster Abbey.

> Masse, H.J. (1899) suggested that 'judging from the expression of the face, there may have been some attempt at portraiture'. An earlier 19th c. writer wondered whether 'the king's features were possibly chiselled from a waxen mask, taken after his death' (King, R. J. 1874). But in an effigy of this date this is now considered unlikely.

Dr Morganstern sees the king as 'gazing heavenward, as if transfixed by a great light. The impression of a vision is confirmed by the participation of two angels who look upward as they gently support the monarch's head. The translucent glow of the albaster, employed here for the first time in a royal effigy in England, contributes to the effect of a transcendental event'.

The king holds the royal septre, and an orb which until 'this time had been used as a symbol of royal power in England only on the king's seal' (Morganstern). Though, since the 11th century, *Christ* had been depicted holding an orb this appears to be the first use of an orb on an English royal tomb. Thus, in the medieval mind, the orb would have associated the effigy and remains of Edward II with Christ himself. The king is shown in all the sancity of medieval kingship as *Christus Domini*, the Anointed of the Lord. Like the Old Testament kings and like Christ himself [who was compared with Melchizedek(Genesis 14.18-24: Hebrews 6.20 -7.28)] he is *rex et sacerdos*, both king and priest.

He lies in a magnificent shrine, fit for any saint, identfied mystically and symbolically with Christ himself. 'Small wonder this was seen as a place of miracles, a place where the sick found healing and the penitent forgiveness, and where the mass of pilgrims came to gaze in amazement'. But at the same time, the shrine and its effigy made a political statement, following the violent death of King Edward II, about the status and sanctity of kingship.

The canopy: The sumptuously pinnacled two-tiered triple canopy was carved from local limestone. 'The alabaster effigy is set among towering, delicate cages of stone, with ogee arches, pinnacles and cresting. The resemblance to a shrine was deliberate' (Coldstream, N. 1994). There are two stages of ogee-headed arches, with close cusping at the sides of the arches and ogee foils which are surmounted by finials, with buttresses placed diagonally and terminating in pinnacles. In style it is akin to the south transept remodelling (1331-36), and was probably designed by the same architect. 'It is the work of a genius' (Verey, D. 1978). The tomb is, indeed, worthy of a greater king than Edward II.

> **King Edward II** (1284-1327), son of Edward I (r. 1272-1307), married Isabella, daughter of Philip the Fair of France in 1308. In his early years Edward was fond of luxury, gambling, horse-breeding, dog-training, music and swimming and, it was said, of such 'vulgar' pursuits as boating, thatching and ditching. As king he had his favourites, first Gaveston, Earl of Cornwall, and later the Despensers, much to the fury of the barons. Mortimer, one of his baronial opponents, on his escape from custody in the Tower of London, joined Queen Isabella, his lover, in France. On their return to England in 1326 Edward was forced to abdicate. He fled westward, but was captured at Neath and later murdered at Berkeley Castle, Gloucestershire (20 September 1327). He had proved an utterly incompetent ruler.

In the 18th century, finials and other details were restored by Oriel College, Oxford (founded by King Edward II) using plaster rather than cut stone. The dates of the restoration are on a shield on the pier at the head of the tomb: *Hoc fundatoris sui monumentum, situ vetustatis deformatum, instaurari curaverunt Praepos. et Soc. Coll. Oriel, Oxon A D. 1737 - 1789 - 1798.* The tomb was investigated in 1855, and when the leaden coffin was opened the body was found 'in a wonderful state of preservation'.

Chantry of Abbot Parker The tomb is set within a Perpendicular stone screen. The *effigy* shows Parker vested in full pontificals {46}, including a jewelled mitre (the abbots of Gloucester were mitred from c.1381). The effigy lies on a high *tomb*, with three panels on each side, the first and third bearing emblems of the Passion of Christ, and the middle one Parker's arms. In the frieze above the panels are the Tudor rose, the pomegranate, a lion's head, oak leaves, *fleur-de-lys* and the initials WM for William Malvern (*alias* Parker). The Abbot's arms, surmounted by a mitre, are set on the pier at the head of the tomb. The floor of the chantry is paved with contemporary tiles, some well-preserved with the arms of the Abbey and of Parker.

> **William Parker**, as a young monk, distinguished himself at Oxford. On the death of Abbot John Newton (*alias* Browne) in 1514, he was unanimously elected abbot even though he was not yet thirty years old and thirty-fourth in the community (which was said at the time to number no less than sixty-five). St Peter's being a mitred abbey, Parker had a seat in the House of Lords and was summoned from time to time to advise the king, Henry VIII (r.1509-47). His life-style was typical of a late-medieval Prince of the Church in that he was often away from Gloucester on business for his Order or for the Crown; or enjoying leisure, for example, at his hunting lodge at Prinknash, where his brother was woodward (estate manager).

Parker had his tomb and effigy made and the chantry built during his lifetime. But at the time of the dissolution of the monastery it was left to the prior, Gabriel Morton, to surrender the abbey to the King's Commissioner. The reason for the abbot's absence has been the subject of much speculation, but it now appears that Parker had died early in June 1539, six months before the abbey was surrendered. Exactly when and where he died is not known for certain, nor where he was buried. The tradition that he was not buried in the tomb apparently derives from the mistaken belief that at the dissolution of the abbey in 1540 he was still living and was contumacious (V.C.H. Glos. 1907).

The tomb was investigated in 1919 and appeared to contain two coffins, which led Dr. Henry Gee (dean 1917-38) to suggest that the papist bishop of Gloucester, James Brookes (1554-58) and the first Elizabethian bishop, Richard Cheney (1561-79) were buried in the chantry, but this is pure speculation.

At the west end of the ambulatory there is a **stone lectern** which was associated with the monks' attendance in the choir (rather than with pilgrims visiting the shrine of Edward II). Near by, in a case, is an *Art Nouveau* processional cross by Omar Ramsden (1922), and a memorial tablet to Henry Hugh Arthur Fitzroy, 10th Duke of Beaufort (1900-84).

> The memorial recounts his long years of public service including his unfailing support, for more than fifty years, of his parish church at Badminton and cathedral church at Gloucester. He was 'greatly admired, much loved by friends. He heeded not his years nor lost his courage on his horse'. He was Master of the Horse (Beaufort Hunt) 1936-78, hence the oval medallion at the foot of the memorial. The original design included foxes, but these were left out to avoid offending the anti-hunt lobby. The memorial was unveiled by HM. Queen Elizabeth II in the presence of six other members of the Royal Family on 14 April 1986.

THE CHOIR

Around the middle of the 14th century the Perpendicular style began to supplant the Decorated in many parts of the country. It continued until the middle of the 16th century though there are good examples of the style as late as the time of James I, and even Charles I. It is a peculiarly English style of architecture being used during this period for buildings of every kind - churches, houses, castles, barns and cottages.

The name is derived from the arrangement of the tracery, which involves the repeated use of perpendicular lines, with the frequent use of *transoms* crossing the mullions at right angles in large windows. Bands of quatrefoils and other similar ornaments are frequently employed, and often carried across panelling creating a rectilinear arrangement. Panelling is widespread on walls, both internally and externally, indeed some buildings are entirely covered with it, for example, Henry VII's Chapel at Westminster. Fan vaulting is generally characteristic of the style.

The term was given currency by Thomas Rickman (1776-1841) through his published lectures entitled *An Attempt to Discriminate the Styles of Architecture in England* (1817). The south transept at Gloucester is the earliest *extant* example of the style; the choir remains one of the most impressive {25}.

After the death and burial of King Edward II in 1327 an ambitious programme of building works began which transformed the eastern arm of the abbey church. First, the south transept was remodelled (1331-36), and then the choir (1337-55). The project was completed with the remodelling of the north transept (1368-74).

At first sight the choir appears to be a fine example of Perpendicular architecture with stone panelling covering the entire north and south elevations, a huge window at the east end with a Perpendicular grid-pattern, and vaulting shafts soaring upward to an elaborate lierne vault [31, Pl.8]]. But behind the 'lattice' of stone panelling the ambulatory and tribune of the Romanesque choir remain virtually intact. The great east window rests on the apsidal east end of the crypt, and the clerestory rests on the wall above the tribune arcade. However, though much of the Anglo-Norman choir remains, much had to be demolished.

REMODELLING THE CHOIR (1337-1355)

Extent of the Demolition F. S. Waller, in his isometric drawing [2], shows what remains of the Anglo-Norman building, and the extent of the demolition around the choir: * The high-vault, together with its supporting walls, was taken down to just above the tribune arcade. * The great central apse, with its semi-dome, was demolished leaving a great gap between the lateral chapels at the east end. * The broad semi-circular arches spanning the tower crossing on the north and south sides were replaced with pointed arches and extraordinary 'flying spans' [21]. * The arch on the east side of the crossing was taken down, without disturbing the tower,

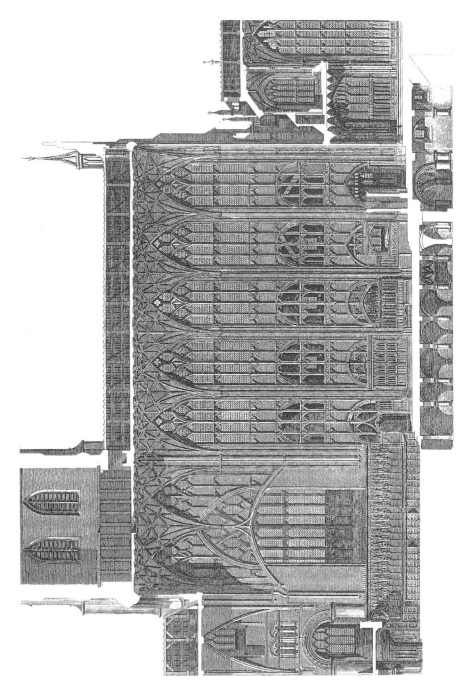

(fig 31). Choir, north elevation (Carter, J. 1807)

so that a new vault could extend unbroken (except for a low ribbed arch) from west of the crossing to the great east window. * The side walls were pared down for the wall-panelling to be applied and the wall above the tribune arcade prepared to receive a lofty clerestory [4]. * Foundations were prepared on the outer apsidal wall of the crypt for the construction of a great wall of glass at the east end.

Purpose of the Reconstruction The intention was * to bring the diverse elements of the Anglo-Norman choir together into a single *rectangular* space. The two compartments of the old choir, the liturgical choir (*quire*) and the presbytery, were unified through the removal of the Anglo-Norman arch on the east side of the crossing, and the construction of a new and magnificent vault over the whole area. * to raise the *height* of the choir by constructing a tall clerestory, and to emphasise the sense of soaring height by allowing no horizontals to cut across the vaulting shafts. * to *unify* the interior by applying stone panelling to the wall surfaces and over the open spaces of the ambulatory and tribune arcades, and continuing the panelling, as tracery, through the clerestory windows. * to *enclose* the liturgical choir with high-backed stalls which have the effect (together with the spans beneath the crossing arches) of isolating the transepts and enhancing the sense of enclosed space. * to flood the choir with *light and colour* through the construction of the high clerestory and huge window at the east end. The interior was filled with light, and with the brilliant colours of extensive areas of stained glass. * to emphasise still further the *visual unity of the choir* by using the same design (of saintly figures-in-niches) in the glazing of the clerestory as in the great east window.

Principal Elements in the Design

Wall Panelling In many English cathedrals a screen, about the height of the altar screen, separates the choir from the side aisles, and often from the transepts as well. But at Gloucester the stone screen is carried up to the vault.

'They appear to have intended to separate the presbytery from its aisles by the usual stone screens - designed to correspond with the tracery of the clerestory windows. This would have left an ugly cavernous arch - that of the eleventh-century tribune - in each bay, between the screen below and the clerestory above. The pattern of the tracery of the clerestory window had been repeated once in the screen below, so what could be more natural than to repeat it a second time in the shape of a screen set in front of the open arch of the tribune? It remained merely to join up the mullions of all three - lower screen, tribune screen, and clerestory window - and the three members were welded together into one composition. Harmony and unity reigned from pavement to vault. Here again we have at Gloucester not only the commencement, but the full development of what became the leading principle in later English Gothic (Perpendicular) - the determination to impose unity on the elevations of their churches by repeats of window tracery. With the vaulting shafts rising sheer in unbroken flow from the pavement to the vault above, the choir became to all intents and purposes a one-story design. Nowhere had anyone dared to conceive the possibility of bring out the organic unity of an interior by reducing it to a single storey. This was done first at Gloucester; and, moreover, at Gloucester only was it ever worked out successfully' (Bond, F. 1912).

The panelling even extends around the pointed arches on the north and south sides of the crossing where it is formed, in part, by cutting back the surface of the stone. Even the wall around the high west window is decorated in the same way, and with niches with brackets for figures. Since the same rectilinear panelling forms the grid-pattern of the great east window the entire choir is 'wrapped around' in the same decorative motif. The balance of the *vertical* and the *horizontal* in the wall panelling is remarkable. The vertical members take the eye ever upward towards the clerestory and the vault. This is reinforced by the uninterrupted vertical thrust of the vaulting shafts. However, though the panelling hides the horizontal lines of the old Romanesque choir, the *horizontal* is there in the new design, and if anything emphasised, creating a sense of perspective and depth. The horizontal members are slighter than the vertical, but they cross the elevation at several levels; within the openings of the ambulatory arcade; through the quatrefoil frieze at the tribune floor; within the tribune arcade openings; along the sill of the clerestory, and by the transoms of the clerestory windows.

Clerestory Windows In the reconstruction, the walls of the choir were taken down to a few courses above the tribune arches. Much of the demolished stonework was reused in the clerestory windows and in strengthening work around the tribune.

> The windows on the north side are filled with glass by Clayton & Bell (1870). They depict named-figures from the New Testament. At the time a certain amount of medieval glass remained in the windows, sufficient to show that the original design consisted of figures in niches in the lower lights, with flowered quarries, and patterns and borders in the upper lights. The Victorian glass is similar in design, with fragments of medieval glass preserved in the tracery lights.
>
> The windows on the south side are by Hardman (1865). He used stamped quarries (by Powell of Whitefriars) with central medallions and coloured borders copied from remains of medieval glass.

West window Because the vault at the tower crossing is higher than the roof of the nave, it was possible to construct a window in the tower west wall. The window contains glass by Hardman (1866). It takes up the theme of *Christ in Majesty* surrounded by an angel choir. The original 14th c. glass was smashed by Prebendary Fowler in 1679, but Hardman incorporated fragments of the old glass 'together with fragments from other windows collected at different times' (Haines, H.1867)

Beneath the window there is a Latin inscription referring to the building of the tower. The writing was restored in the 19th century; it reads: 'This work which you behold constructed and adorned, is the result of the labour of Tully, Abbot Seabroke ordering these things'.

Tower Crossing The great piers of the Anglo-Norman crossing survive, and the inner face of the north and south piers retain their attached half-shafts {26}. But at the top of the piers the capitals and shared abaci have been removed and the half-shafts merged into one. The great semi-circular arches which spanned the openings to the transepts were taken down and replaced by pointed arches [21].

> An inscription on a stone high up on the south face of the north-east crossing pier (best seen with binoculars from the south side of the tribune) records that behind the inscribed stone are the remains of the springing of the demolished presbytery arch.

Beneath the north and south arches are **flying spans**, four-centred arches which apparently support the springing of the ribs of the most westerly bay of the vault. [21] 'On the not-very-pronounced apex of each arch there is a vertical member, supported on either side by counter-curves. The result is an ogee arch in mid-air, from which springs the seven ribs of the vault' (Verey, D. 1978). But these arches are so depressed that they are hardly capable of bearing their own weight let alone supporting the vault which, in fact, rests securely in the wall behind. Their purpose is not so much *structural* as *aesthetic*. Their effect is to isolate the transepts and so increase the sense of *enclosure* within the choir. The spans have been called 'pieces of carpentry in stone', and 'very original stylistic conceits'. As with other aspects of the 14th c. remodelling these spans show the innovative streak of the architect, and the skill and daring of the stone masons.

Tower Reconstruction   It has long been assumed that the lierne vault could not have been constructed over the liturgical choir without taking the tower down. 'As far as the springing of the flying arches the crossing piers are Norman, and so to this point the walls of the tower, choir and presbytery must have been taken down' (Ashwell, B. in memo to author 1982). 'Part of the mid-14th-century reconstruction must have embraced the lower portion of the tower (as far as the adjoining roofs) since there is no break in the vaulting and the work is of the same character throughout' (King, R. J. 1874). More recently, however, evidence has some to light to show that the vault was, in fact, constructed without taking down the Anglo-Norman tower and its 13th-century embellishments.

In the 1980s Professor J. Heyman made a detailed examination of the fabric in the roof space above the crossing, and identified a *relieving* arch above the apex of the choir roof vault on the west side. (For examples of relieving arches see the crossing of Pershore Abbey, Worcestershire). Heyman believed that the stonework above this arch could be 12th century though it includes randomly placed reddened blocks as well. Clearly, the wall had been disturbed and repaired. He also found evidence of a relieving arch above the vault on the east side. This arch is wider than that on the west side, and includes much re-used 12th c. stone, many voussoirs and some reddened blocks.

'Since the choir vault extends through the crossing, it had to be made to pass through the east wall of the Norman tower at a considerable height above the original chancel arch. Before the vault could be completed, therefore, about 10 m. of the east wall of the tower had to be taken down. The way this was done may be seen from the top of the vault in the space below the floor of the ringing chamber. Above the present surface of the vault can be seen a roughly-cut arch, about 600mm. deep, let into the east face of the Norman masonry. The lower surface of this arch is perhaps 300mm. above the top surface of the vault. The roughly-cut arch collects the forces due to the weight of the tower. Once the arch was inserted, the 10m. of masonry below it could be taken down in safety. The vault could then be built, and the 300mm. gap plugged with small pieces of stone cut to fit it'. Heyman added: 'The insertion of the relieving arch is an extraordinary conceptual feat'.

Lierne Vault The lierne vault is the largest and one of the most complex in the country [32]. By tracing the main ribs from one side of the choir to the other it will be seen that the vault is basically a double quatrepartite vault, that is, the ribs make up a geometric design covering two bays {27}. However, the main rib system is complicated by a myriad of short inter-connecting ribs (*liernes*). Their purpose is decorative rather than structural but, with the tiercerons, they make the vault look extremely complex.

(fig 32) Choir, lierne vault

Springing from the vaulting shafts are four ribs either side of the transverse rib:

(i)   The transverse ribs crosses to the vaulting shaft opposite;

(ii) The adjoining rib passes through the main boss at the mid-point of the bay to the next vaulting shaft on the opposite side;

(iii) The next rib crosses through the boss at the intersection of the next transverse rib, and on to the opposite vaulting shaft but one;

(iv) The next does not cross to the opposite side of the choir, but ends very soon within the arched space of the clerestory window;

(v)   The last forms a wall-arch around the head of the adjoining window.

Another feature of the vault is its longitudinal **ridge rib** with parallel ribs either side. This feature was thought to have been invented at Gloucester but the nave vault at Tewkesbury, constructed *c*.1330, also has parallel ribs. The Tewkesbury vault may well have been the precursor of Gloucester's. Nevertheless, it was a feature which the Gloucester masons made their own and used later in the vault of the north transept, at the west end of the nave and in the lady chapel. The vault is studded with **bosses**, some four hundred in all, mostly of realistic foliage. But at the east end, above the high altar, there is a figure of *Christ in Majesty* surrounded by an **angel choir** (see below). In the vault, above the liturgical choir, there is a **bell hole** through which the bells were, and still are from time to time, raised and lowered. The largest of the bells, *Great Peter* (cast in the 15th *c*. and weighing more than three tons) was made a fraction smaller in diameter than the hole so that it would pass through. The vault was painted in 1895 by Clayton & Bell, but 'when the white-wash on the vault was removed, no trace of medieval painting was found' (Masse,H.J. 1899).

Angel Choir Among the bosses above the high altar is a group of angels holding various musical instruments {43}. These are:

On the south side from the east end, a citole with three strings, a very short wind instrument with a large bell, a long trumpet probably a bozine, a recorder or shawn, a psaltery, and cymbals.

On the north side from the east end, a gittern, bagpipes, rybybe with three strings, a pipe and tabor, a portative organ, timbrels with jingles, a symphony showing the crank for turning the wheel, and a harp.

Two of the angels, one on either side, are holding instruments of the Passion, a large tau-cross and three large nails, a spear and a crown of thorns.

In the centre of the group is a figure of *Christ in Majesty*, seated, bare-headed and with no nimbus. His long hair falls over his shoulders. He has a long beard, and is wearing a robe with very full sleeves fastened with a large circular clasp on his chest. He holds an orb, symbolizing his universal sovereignty, and his hand is raised in blessing.

Angel choirs had been a feature of English church decoration since the 13th century. Groups of angels with musical instruments are found;

(i) in stained glass windows, for example, at Malvern Priory and the Beauchamp Chapel at Warwick;

(ii) as stone carvings on west fronts, in the spandrels of choir arcades, on doorways and on sedilia, as here in the sanctuary;

(iii) carved in wood on choir screens and stalls, including misericords. There are three great 14th c. collections of musical angels in the West Country, the others are the Minstrels' Gallery at Exeter c.1360, which is the only medieval English gallery of its type to be adorned with musicians, and the roof-bosses at Tewkesbury Abbey. The idea of having an angel choir at Gloucester was probably taken from the slightly earlier series at Tewkesbury.

Bracket Memorial The effigy on the bracket on the south side of the presbytery is older than the bracket itself [33]. The bracket dates from the mid-14th century, but the effigy dates from the 13th century. The effigy is set beneath a triple canopy, of Early English design, which still has some of its original paint. In the pediments of the canopy there are two angels. The effigy is of an abbot, without a mitre, holding a model of a church with his right hand, and on his left side there is a pastoral staff. At his feet are two monks. It probably represents Abbot Serlo, the first Norman abbot (1072-1104), being a survival from his tomb erected in the time of Abbot Henry Foliot.

During Foliot's abbacy (1228-43) the church was extensively restored and rededicated (1239). Leland, visiting the abbey in 1541 wrote: 'Serlo, Abbot of Gloucester, lyeth under a fayre marble tomb on the south side of the presbytery'. The bracket is hardly a 'fayre marble tomb' but it is on the 'south side of the presbytery'. Abbot Serlo may have been buried in the chapter house, or somewhere in or around the choir. If he was buried, as Leland states, on the south side, near the apse of the Anglo-Norman choir, the tomb would have been dismantled during the 14th c. reconstruction and the ledge formed for the effigy.

(fig 33) Choir, 13th c. effigy (?) Abbot Serlo

Monks' Stalls The liturgical choir (*quire*) has always been within the crossing {26}. On either side of the choir a high screen, formed by the backs and canopies of the   stalls, encloses the choir.   The return stalls face east, and back onto the wall either side of the west entrance to the choir. The stalls on the north side were completed during the abbacy of Adam de Staunton (1337-51) and those on the south side during the abbacy of Thomas Horton (1351-77).   There may have been a break in construction owing to the Black Death (1349), but since Horton had been sacrist for some years before being elected abbot he probably continued supervising their construction. Dr. C. Tracey (1987) points out that 'the shape of the standards is archaic, with the rectangular lower section and the elbow projecting well out from the top of the capping. The unusual treatment of the base of the leading edge of the standard is not paralleled in any surviving stalls in the country'. He notes that for some reason a piece of new wood has been let into every standard at the arm rest. This tends to 'give the impression that the standards have been deepened, but this is not so because otherwise the panel at the bottom with its inset trefoil would be correspondingly narrower. It is admittedly difficult to envisage the problem that necessitated this particular method of repair'. (Tracey, C. 1990).

In drawings of the Georgian choir (e.g. Bonnor, T. 1798, and Ansted, H. 1827) the backs of the Bysaak stalls (c.1718) are set hard against the medieval stalls. It would seem, therefore, that the back row of the Bysaak stalls were secured to planks set into the standards of the medieval stalls. If this was so, the medieval stalls could not have been used for many years, (c.1718-1871). Such indeed was the case, for when the Georgian stalls were removed the medieval stalls were described by G. Gilbert Scott as being in 'a derelict condition'. The extent of Scott's repairs confirms this.

The stalls have three-dimensional ogee-arched canopies.   There are two main designs, alternating regularly on the south side but not on the north. The dean's stall (the abbot's stall) on the south side of the west entrance is wider than the rest and the canopy more impressive. Behind the canopy of the vice-dean's stall (the prior's stall) on the north side there are fragments of one of the early-13th-century stalls put in by Helias, the sacrist. The sub-stalls, together with the bishop's throne and mayor's stall, are part of Scott's refurnishing (1868-73).

Misericord Carvings   The seats in the stalls of a medieval choir were usually secured with hinges so they could be turned up. When this was done the broad up-turned ledge was sufficiently deep to enable aged and infirm monks to squat, taking some of the weight off their feet during the long hours they spent in the quire. It was common for the underside of such seats to be carved. The subjects chosen varied widely, some based on classical myths and legends, others on popular romances and folk tales, and others were scenes from everyday life, domestic and rural. At times the carvers indulged their keen and often ribald sense of humour. In most series religious subjects account for only a small percentage. There are roughly 8,600 medieval misericords in England of which about 5% have specifically religious or biblical subjects. At Gloucester five of the original series which have survived have religious subjects, but seven of the twelve 19th c. replacements have religious subjects - reflecting the preference of Victorian clerics. Unlike other mid-14th-century series, the Gloucester misericords are without supporters, or secondary subjects, instead the carvings are enclosed within a raised border enriched with foliation and cusping {47}.

List of subjects, numbered from the dean's stall and along the south side, then across to the north side and back to the vice-dean's stall.   * indicates a 19th c. replacement.
- \> 1   *Adoration of the Magi
- 2   Two dragons fighting
- 3   Giant with a club being slain by a knight
- 4   Delilah cuts off Samson's hair
- 5   Bear-baiting
- 6   Two bearded men running at each other, one with sword in hand
- 7   *The Coronation of the Virgin (Chester Cathedral)
- 8   The Flight of Alexander (compare 22)
- 9   An Owl pestered by other birds.
- \> 10   Lady, with a dog, in an orchard with birds in trees
- 11   Two monsters
- 12   Knight riding at full speed, possibly St George slaying the dragon
- 13   *The Sacrificing of Isaac (Worcester Cathedral, compare 49)
- 14   Mermaid swimming, holding a fish in each hand
- 15   Three shepherds,with crooks, and dog following sheep. Middle shepherd gazing into the sky. Possibly the shepherds of the Nativity
- 16   The Pelican in her piety.
- 17   *Man being swallowed by a monster (Worcester Cathedral)
- 18   Nude female figure, with one foot on ground, covered with a net, carrying a rabbit and riding a goat (Old Norse tale of Queen Disa)
- 19   Male figure riding a goat, facing backwards, blowing a horn (Worcester Cathedral compare 28)
- \> 20   *Moses reading the Commandments to Israelites (Worcester Cathedral)
- 21   *Hawking (copied from 27)
- 22   *The Flight of Alexander, king seated on throne being raised by griffins (compare 8 & 26)
- 23   *Two angels playing instruments (Chester Cathedral)
- 24   Two dragons, their necks joined in jester's head, with cowl and asses ears
- 25   Crowned figure reclining
- 26   The Flight of Alexander (compare 22)
- 27   Hawking (compare 21)

28 Male figure riding a goat (compare 19)
29 Man lying down, embracing a donkey (Balaam and his ass, or an Aesop's fable)
> 30 (*First on north side of choir next to mayor's stall*) A boar and swine feeding on acorns
31 Two four-footed dragon-like monster
32 Two youths, possibly jugglers, playing with balls or discs
33 Two youths, similarly dressed as 32, playing with a large ball.
34 Lion fighting a dragon, with bat-like wings
35 Elephant, with cart-horse feet, horse's tail, trumpet-shaped trunk and carrying an embattled howdah
36 Eagle, with huge talons, attacking a beast of prey
37 Winged human figure, possibly St. Michael, thrusting his spear through head of dragon
38 Huntsman, riding at speed
39 *Temptation of Adam and Eve (Worcester Cathedral).
> 40 A heavy horse, carrying a four-footed animal with curling tail and semi-human face
41 Lion or wolf attacking a fox
42 Gentleman, finely dressed, reclining
43 Lion attacks a two-legged dragon, biting its neck
44 Huntsman on foot, with his dogs, and with a (broken) long-bow, aiming at animal, possibly a fox, in a tree
45 Lion fighting a dragon
46 *Presentation in the Temple (Worcester Cathedral), or possibly the child Samuel at Shiloh
47 Man reclining on left arm
48 Fox, carrying off a goose
49 The Sacrificing of Isaac (compare 13).
> 50 Large griffin, a four-footed beast with head and feet of an eagle
51 The Vintage (grape harvest)
52 *The Tournament, or combat of knights (Worcester Cathedral)
53 Human figure, reclining on left arm, with stall in right hand (compare 47)
54 Deerstalker discharging an arrow (long-bow broken in left hand); a large stag is brought down
55 Angel, reclining holding a book. Band across his body for the angel's message
56 Two boys (heads missing) felling a tree, animals forage nearby
57 Wrestlers
58 *Beast of prey, possibly a lion, attacking a winged dragon (Worcester Cathedral)

This magnificent choir was the centre of the life of the monastic community. Through the night and through the day the monks gathered here for prayer and worship, recalling the words of the Psalmist: 'Seven times a day will I praise thee...' St. Benedict's working day was basically divided into three more or less equal parts: the *Opus Dei* which had pre-eminence, meditation and study, and manual work. The year was divided into two seasons, winter (from mid-September to Easter) and summer. The day was the natural day from sunrise to sunset and it was divided into twelve equal hours (whose length varied from season to season).

The day began at midnight when the first and longest service (Matins) took place. This was followed, after a brief pause, by Lauds. The monks then returned to their dorter. They were 'summoned by bells' at daybreak and assembled again in the quire for Prime which was immediately followed by the early mass for servants and manual workers. Only the necessary participants attended the service, the rest went to the cloisters where they attended to their toilet. The senior priests then said their private masses, the other monks took their books for study and the novices began their lessons. If it was not a fast day, a light breakfast (*mixtum*) was taken as the bell rang for morning mass (Lady Mass or Chapter Mass). This was followed by their meeting in the Chapter House, and then in the quire for the office of Terce and the solemn High Mass which on Sundays and festivals was preceded by the great procession. Sext followed and the community then returned to the cloister and, after washing, gathered in the refectory for the main meal of the day, taken shortly after noon. The next quire service was None which in the summer was followed by a brief siesta. A short period of recreation was sometimes fitted into the afternoon and any other time was occupied by work until Vespers at about six o'clock. This was longer than any other quire office (apart from Matins) and was followed, except during fasts, by supper. After supper there were private devotions in church, and perhaps some time in cloister or chapter house, until Compline. After Compline the monks processed to the dormitory for a few hours' sleep until the bell for Matins summoned them back to worship and another day began.

REFURNISHING THE CHOIR (1868-1873)

George Gilbert Scott laid his proposals for the restoration of the choir before the Dean and Chapter in April 1867. They were accepted almost in their entirety, and work began in the autumn.

Scott's **reredos** was erected in 1872 and dedicated on 5 June 1873 by Dr. C. S. Ellicott (bishop of Gloucester 1863-1905). It replaced the panelled work around the outer feretory wall put up in 1807 by (Sir) R. Smirke (1780-1867), the leading Greek Revival architect. The reredos is divided into three compartments each with a group of figures by J. F. Redfern, representing the Nativity, the Ascension and the Deposition of Christ.

> The figures in the surrounding niches, also by Redfern, represent Moses, the Law-giver, and King David, St. Peter and St. Paul. The statue of St Peter is of Painswick stone; the others and the groups are carved in stone from a neighbouring quarry at Cooper's Hill. The three upper turrets have figures of angels under canopies, nine in all, bearing the emblems of Christ's Passion.

The architectural structure, in which the figures and scenes are placed, reflects the 14th c. style of the choir, in particular the canopy of the shrine of King Edward II. The corner mini-buttresses, the cusping and use of ogees, the canopies and open work of the turrets are all echoes of the royal tomb. Originally in plain stone, the structure was gilded in 1896, and the scenes and figures polychromed in 1962. The **sedilia** on the south side of the sanctuary was reconstructed by G. Gilbert Scott in 1872. Writers at the time pointed out that 'little remained of the original work to guide the architect', and that the 'sedilia is so much restored as to be virtually 19th century work'. But some fragments were found, some *in situ*, otherwise Scott relied on his extensive knowledge of late-medieval architecture and considerable experience in restoration work to reconstruct it. There are traces of medieval colour on the back of the seats. The restored niches and canopies above the four seats were filled with figures of abbots and bishops.

> The figures, by Redfern, represent Abbot Edric, Bishop Wulstan and abbots Aldred, Serlo, Foliot, Thoky, Wygmore, Horton, Froucester, Morwent, Seabroke and Hanley - the great building abbots of St Peter's in chronological order.

On the cornice there are figures (late-medieval) of angel musicians, one with a drum or tambourine, the others with trumpets. Haines noted that 'the knotted rod and entwined ribbon bore the initials TO at the ends' and suggested these may be the initials of Thomas Osborne, Sheriff of Gloucester 1512-22 and Mayor 1526.

The medieval **altar** occupied the same position in the sanctuary as the present one, but Scott raised his altar on an additional step. Behind the altar the **feretory** (a narrow space containing cupboards for jewels, and beneath the altar two recesses for relics) was reinstated with its medieval features, including doors either side of the altar. It provided a way for the priest to pass round, asperge, and cense the high altar in the course of the Sunday procession. The feretory was originally roofed.

The **tile-pavement** in the sanctuary was laid down by Abbot Seabroke in *c*.1455. Samuel Lysons carried out work on it early in the 19th century adding a considerable number of alien tiles. Scott had much of the pavement carefully relaid, importing more tiles from around the cathedral. At the same time the well-preserved area around and beneath the altar was removed and relaid in the south-east chapel of the tribune. The over-all design of the pavement is best seen from the tribune.

> Thomas Seabroke, R. Brygg (Brydges), J. Applebi, W. Farlei, and Joh. Graft(on) i.e. the abbot and senior monks of St Peter's at the time are named on the tiles. W. Farlei (William Farley), who was the sacrist, became abbot (1472-98) and was responsible for completing the lady chapel. Among the alien tiles are a few from the 13th c. (including one to Richard, king of the Romans d.1271), and late-medieval tiles include those of William Malvern (*alias* Parker) and the Brydges family. There are tiles bearing the arms of Edward the Confessor and St Peter's Abbey, and many with the crowned M (*for Maria*). Among the miscellaneous tiles near the sedilia is one with the words *Croys Crist me spe de* + followed by *A ME* or *A(ve) Maria*.

In repaving the presbytery and quire (1869-70) Scott based the design of the tiles on tiles found in the Seabroke Pavement and other parts of the building, but they are larger than the medieval originals. They were made by Godwins of Lugwardine, near Hereford. In the centre of the presbytery Scott set a rectangle of brown tiles, edged with black, to mark the traditional burial place of Robert, Duke of Normandy. At the time the effigy of Duke Robert was in the north-east ambulatory chapel.

Scott also designed the eighteen Minton **sgraffito scenes** set in the floor in the centre of the presbytery [34].

(*fig 34*) *Choir; sgraffiti scene in presbytery pavement*

The subjects are delineated in black and white, set in white marble, and arranged in pairs. They represent Old Testament scenes.

Numbered from left to right, from the choir steps:

1 Adam and Eve in the Garden of Eden (Gen.2.4-24)
2 The Temptation and Fall (Gen.3.1-19)
3 Adam and Eve expelled from the Garden (Gen.3.21-24)
4 The Death of Abel (Gen.4.1-16)
5 The Flood, with the ark on the waters (Gen.6and 7)
6 The Ark on Mount Ararat: Noah and family offering sacrifice (Gen. 8)
7 Abraham and Isaac journeying to Mount Moriah (Gen.22.1-5)
8 Abraham about to offer Isaac (Gen.22.6-18)
9 Isaac blessing Jacob, Esau returning from hunting (Gen.25.19-34)
10 Joseph sold by his brothers to the Ishmaelites (Gen.37)
11 Joseph on his death bed (Gen.50.22-26)
12 The Institution of the Passover (Exodus 12.1-36)
13 The Song of Miriam, the Israelite women at the Red Sea (Exodus 15.19-21)
14 Moses with the tablets of the Law   (Exodus 19 and 20)
15 Moses showing Aaron the plan of the Tabernacle (Exodus 40)
16 David bringing the Ark from the house of Obededom (I Chron. 15)
17 The Building of the Temple of Solomon (II Chron. 3,4,5)
18 The Dedication of the Temple of Solomon (II Chron.6)

(fig 35) Choir, poppy head on 19th c. stalls

Though some of the scenes have become rather worn they remain fine examples of 19th-century sgraffito work. When first laid down, however, the scenes and the 19th-century pavement as a whole evoked considerable controversy. 'Glaring white marble in the floor of the presbytery has been inlaid with biblical scenes filled in with black cement.   It is possible from the triforium (tribune) to get a general idea of the crudity and tastelessness of the pavement which is so composed and arranged that time - the softener of all things - can never make it look appreciably better' (Masse, H. J. 1899).

Quire. G. Gilbert Scott knew of F.S. Waller's proposals (1855) for the reordering of the quire, but he urged the Dean and Chapter to keep the old monastic enclosed quire [Pl.7]. Waller's plan involved moving the organ to the north gallery, removing the choir screen and return stalls and opening up the choir to the nave. Instead Scott took out the early 18th stalls (part was later made into choir stalls for the nave) together with the mayor's stall and the bishop's throne (now also in the nave).

He extensively restored the **monastic stalls** at the back of the quire, having fourteen new misericords carved to complete the dilapidated series, and designed a new stall for the mayor and throne for the bishop. Messrs Farmer and Brindley made the **new oak stalls**, with splendid poppy-heads [35], at a cost of £ 2,775. The polychroming of the choir vault was entrusted to Clayton and Bell (at a total cost of £ 557) and, as noted above, the tiling of the floor to Godwins of Lugwardine, near Hereford. The **pulpit and lectern** were already in place. The brass lectern, the gift of J.C. Dent of Sudeley Castle in 1866, and the work of Messrs Hart & Son of London, was designed by J.F. Bentley and exhibited at the London Exhibition of 1861. The stone pulpit (1840) replaced an 18th *c.* wooden pedestal-pulpit which once stood centrally at the presbytery steps. This is now in the nave.

Chapter Seven

THE CHOIR GALLERY

A choir gallery (or, *tribune*) was an important feature of Anglo-Norman monastic churches. It was used for processions to the gallery chapels to asperge their altars, and it provided additional space around the choir on special occasions, such as the installation of an abbot or a royal visit. To add extra colour at such events and at great festivals, tapestry banners were hung from the tribune. At Gloucester no hooks survive to show how and where the hangings were suspended, as they do at Winchester where a great array of banners was hung from the gallery on the occasion of the marriage of Queen Mary and Philip of Spain.

———————————

The turret-stair in the north-west corner of the north transept leads up to the choir gallery. Though sometimes called a *triforium* this broad gallery is more accurately described as a *tribune* [36].

A *triforium* is an arcaded wall-passage facing into the interior of a church at a level above the main arcade and below the clerestory windows. It usually backs onto a sloping roof space above the aisle vault. A *tribune* is a gallery, an upper storey, above an aisle or ambulatory, overlooking the interior and usually with a series of windows in the outside wall.

The tribune extends along the east side of the north transept and continues along the north side of the choir to the north-east chapel. Then, as built in the late-11th century, it extended around the eastern apse (passing by the entrance to the axial chapel) to the south side of the choir and so around to the east side of the south transept. Here steps lead down to a wall passage, crossing to the turret stair in the south-west corner of the transept (Carter's plan 1807).

In the major reconstruction of the east end in the mid-14th century the apse, including the apsidal section of the tribune, was demolished to make space for the great east window. The north-east and the south-east chapels were left intact, and part of the axial chapel was retained. A low and narrow enclosed passage (known as the *Whispering Gallery)* was constructed outside the great east window to link the north and south sides of the tribune, and to provide access to the partially-reconstructed axial chapel. It is this passage which casts a shadow across the great east window.

Architectural Features The *massive piers* of the tribune arcade rest on those of the choir arcade which in turn rest on the strengthened piers of the crypt arcade. The piers and the arches of the arcade were cut back to accommodate the 14th *c.* wall panelling [4]. The profile and other details of the *wall panelling* which encases the choir is best studied from the tribune; and the over-all effect of the panelling best appreciated by looking across from one side of the tribune to the other. The *quadrant vault* which sweeps up from the outer wall to abut the inner wall of the choir above the arcade piers resembles a series of internal buttresses [37]. In the roof-space the quadrants are seen to be far more substantial than the ribs in the

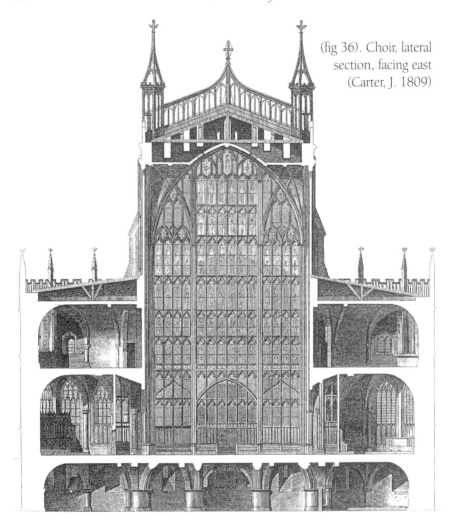

(fig 36). Choir, lateral
section, facing east
(Carter, J. 1809)

(fig 37). Choir tribune,
south side facing east
(1797)

gallery would suggest. In effect, they are flying buttresses, except that they are hidden from view beneath the tribune roof. The vault was designed to take the lateral thrust of the *high vault* which is thought to have spanned the choir from the early-12th century (Wilson,C. 1985).

At the east end, there are three *buttresses* dating from the 14th *c.* reconstruction. They spring from the outer walls at the bend of the apse and meet at a point behind the inner wall of the choir. They were built to stabilise the piers of the additional bay, and to relieve them of some of the pressure placed upon them. They also support the external buttresses above the additional bay which, unlike the buttresses to the west, have no solid foundations in the massive Romanesque piers of the tribune. The bay is splayed outwards abutting the great shafts on either side of the window. The arches of this easternmost bay are pointed, but in the other bays the wall panelling follows the line of the semi-circular arch of the Romanesque arcade. Above the pointed arches, noticeably on the south side, there is a *scar*, the remains of a relieving arch at the turn of the tribune vault, which would further strengthen the slender pier of the final bay. Set into the easternmost Anglo-Norman pier on the north side there is a small *nook shaft and capital* which seem to relate to the vaulting of the Romanesque apse. The vaulting of the apse may have been similar to the groin vault of the north transept chapel (Wilson, C. 1985).

At the west end of the tribune, over-looking the transepts, the Anglo-Norman arches back the pointed arches and panelling of the 14th-century remodelling. On the south side the internal buttress also crosses in front of the tribune opening.

Reused Stonework The demolition of the eastern apse provided the masons with material they could use in strengthening the gallery. The re-use of old stonework was a common practice, and occurs throughout the building. Re-used material can be identified in a number of places in the tribune, for example, at the angle of the outer wall opposite the north-east and south-east crossing piers, and by the entrance of the north-east chapel where a cushion capital is used as a base!

Sometimes it is also possible to identify where such material came from. For example, in the case of the tribune, it is reasonable to assume that much of the material came from those parts of the old choir which had been demolished. Thus, by comparing the material with similar work in other parts of the building, its original location can be identified. Material unlike any remaining part of the Anglo-Norman choir may have come from a demolished wall-passage or clerestory, confirming that such an upper storey existed and providing some evidence of its design [38].

*   Stones from the ovoid piers of the inner apse, demolished in *c.*1340, were re-used to raise the level of the outer wall of the tribune so that the pitch of the roof over the quadrant vault could be lowered to the sill of the new clerestory. In the roof-space on the south side there are two courses of stones with curved surfaces. Templates taken from them identify the stones as coming from the piers of the inner apse.

*   In the tribune opposite the north-east crossing pier, at the angle of the external wall, there is a pair of shafts serving as a respond for the inserted diagonal rib, each consisting of two monolithic sections, one about 0.9m. high and the other about 0.5m. Each of these composite shafts has a separate capital, one being a single scallop and the other a double scallop.

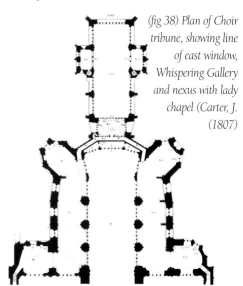

(fig 38) Plan of Choir tribune, showing line of east window, Whispering Gallery and nexus with lady chapel (Carter, J. (1807)

*   In the same position on the south side, the respond supporting the inserted diagonal rib also consists of a reused base, shaft and capital. The profile of the base is similar to that under the reused shafts on the north side. The composite shafts probably came from the same location since their dimensions indicated they belong together. The shafts and capitals were clearly free-standing, and since there is nothing remotely like them in what remains of the Romanesque choir the material probably came from a third storey in the elevation, that is from a demolished clerestory and wall passage (Wilson, C. 1985).

*   The Whispering Gallery is made up almost entirely of re-used Anglo-Norman ashlar. Outside, the small decorative arches of chevron are re-used material, and the moulding on the segmental arches which support the gallery marks the stones as coming from nook-shafts.

*   The vaulting shafts at the east end of the tribune have foundations in the crypt which were put in when the east end of the choir was reconstructed c.1340. The foundations blocks, with nook-shafts at the angles, are made up of re-used ashlar. Some of the stones have masons' marks (which do not occur on the original fabric of the crypt). The stones may well have come from the demolished apse.

Whispering Gallery   The enclosed passage is 22.6m. long and 0.9m. wide, and a little over 1.8m. high. It links the two sides of the tribune at the east end, and provides access to the axial chapel which was incorporated into the lady chapel in the late-15th century.

The passage was so named because a whisper (the lower in tone the better), or even the slightest scratch of a pin on the wall at one end of the gallery is distinctly heard at the other end. Maurice Wheeler, Headmaster of the College School (1684-1712), wrote the lines to be found on the wall of the passage:

> Doubt not but God, who sits on high
>   Thy secret prayers can hear.
>   When a dead wall thus cunningly
>   Conveys soft whispers to the ear.

At the Restoration (1660) a brick floor was laid throughout the gallery. In the 17th and 18th centuries the tribune was known as *The Whispering Place* and visited as a great curiosity and for the views it affords of the cathedral interior. In the 19th century the area was used for general storage. F.S.Waller saved a medieval wooden screen, using it to enclose the south-east chapel. In the chapel (then known as *The Museum*) he preserved medieval woodwork, tiles, glass fragments, an old clock, locks and keys, and pieces of earlier furnishings including part of the 18th *c.* classical reredos.
In 1980 the chapel was cleared and the material Waller had saved used in the Gallery Exhibition (1981). The screen was transferred to the north side. Experts from the Victoria and Albert Museum helped in sorting and identifying the material, nothing of which was removed from the gallery except for an ancient clock (preserved in the tower).

Tribune Chapels   There were five chapels in the Anglo-Norman tribune which formed part of the three-storey east-end of the abbey church. Fifteen chapels at the east-end is nearly twice as many as is usual even in churches of the same size and importance as Gloucester.

*   The north-west chapel, at the top of the stairs from the transept, contains an *aumbry* recess, and an Early English double *piscina* in an excellent state of preservation.
*   The north-east chapel contains a *piscina* in the sill of a window. The principal window was enlarged and decorated with ballflower early in the 14th century.
*   The axial chapel is entered through the Whispering Gallery. The *stone screen* in which the door is set is part of the 14th c. reconstruction. The stone screen at the back of the altar dates from the construction of the lady chapel (c.1470). A 12th-century *stone altar* with three consecration crosses on it, still *in situ*, is supported at the back by a large piece of tufa (a light porous stone sometimes used in vaults). Set into the tile-pavement are the bases of the two colonettes which supported the front of the altar. Above the altar is a weathered crucifix, originally from the gable of the lady chapel but kept for many years in the crypt. It was placed here in 1980. The *vault* is an Early English rib vault, but in the adjoining lady chapel there is a complex lierne vault with bosses. The *side windows* are set within enlarged round-headed openings. The west window, of six lights, contains glass by Hardman (1855), with flowered quarries and borders decorated with stems and oak leaves, and with medallions similar to those in the clerestory windows on the south side of the choir.
*   The south-east chapel. The windows were enlarged and tracery inserted in the 13th and 14th centuries. There is evidence of a reredos in the central bay. An interesting collection of tiles, saved from various parts of the building and relaid here in the 19th century, covers the floor of the apse. In the central area there are tiles from the Seabroke pavement, relaid here in 1872, when G. Gilbert Scott raised the high altar by an additional step. After Scott's restoration (1868-74) the chapel became known as *The Museum* (see above).

* The south-west chapel, overlooking the south transept, contains two brackets with rich canopies, and a well-preserved double *piscina* on the sill of a small window. Ballflower in two rows decorate the mouldings of the larger window, which dates the work to *c.*1320. There are also the remains of two canopies in the jambs of the windows.

Memorials These are of no great interest, most having been moved to the tribune from the nave and transepts to make space for other tablets. But one or two may be noted.

On the north side, mounted on the back of the 14th c. vaulting shaft, is a monument by John Ricketts the Elder of Gloucester, with a bust of William Lisle d. 1723.

On the south side, in a similar position, is part of the huge monument to Dr. Martin Benson, bishop of Gloucester (1734-52) which was originally in the south transept. This part, consisting of a medallion with a bust of the bishop in relief was moved here *c.*1860.

On the south side of the tribune it is possible to look down on the three medieval tombs along the north ambulatory - from left to right: Abbot Parker's Chantry, King Edward II's Shrine and Prince Osric's Tudor tomb.

THE GREAT EAST WINDOW

'The whole architectural structure built to contain the glass was itself totally unprecedented. Even today it would be a monumental undertaking for any workshop; 72 feet high and 38 feet wide, it is the second largest extant medieval window in Britain - yielding pre-eminence only to the (later) great east window of York Minster (1405). When it was deglazed for re-leading in the 1860s it was estimated that the area of glass amounted to 2000 square feet and weighed, with the lead, 35 hundredweight. The glaziers' response to the challenge of this wholly new, Perpendicular-style, stone structure demonstrated an entirely assured confidence...' (Kerr, J 1985).

The great east window was an astonishing achievement {28}. When it was erected in *c*. 1350 there was nothing in the country to compare with it in size and in the magnificence of its setting. Charles Winston, the Victorian glass historian and restorer, described it as 'the first example as well as one of the grandest of a window filled with tiers of full-length figures'. However, after six hundred and fifty years, there is truth in the succinct comment of T. Gambier Parry: 'In general effect, it is magnificent; in detail, it is a wreck'. Its magnificence is clear for all to see; it needs a pair of binoculars to see to what extent it is also a wreck. But considering the date of the window (*c*.1350) it is in an extraordinary good condition, thanks in part to the restrained and conservative restoration by Ward & Hughes under Charles Winston's direction (1814-64).

Construction of the Window The stone panelling attached to the walls of the choir rises from the floor to the sill of the clerestory windows. It then continues through the windows as mullions and transoms to the window-arches and the vault. The panels are enriched with cusping, the design of which changes at each level. The horizontal members (including the frieze at tribune level and the window sills) emphasise depth and perspective, whilst the vaulting shafts, with no horizontals crossing them, contribute to the sense of soaring height [Pl.8].

The new Perpendicular interior was created *within* the old Romanesque choir. Stone panelling was laid over the pared-down inner walls, and a tall clerestory constructed. In place of the earlier vault, a complex lierne vault was built over the entire choir from west of the crossing to a new window at the east end. The window was to be a major feature of the new interior.

The construction of the window is one of the most astonishing feats of medieval engineering and utterly unprecedented. It stands like a wall of glass across the east end. It is canted, and rests securely on the apsidal outer wall of the crypt. The bay which was added at the east end is splayed outwards to encompass the window for the window is wider than the choir itself. On the outside the two principal mullions are supported by steeped and pierced buttresses adding to the stability of the whole structure. The window hardly deserves the strictures of Bond: 'At Gloucester they pulled down the central apse, and on the (remaining) wall erected three gigantic windows, so welded together as to compose one window. So they got one of the biggest windows in the world, and one of the ugliest'.

* A significant feature of the design of the new interior is that the wall panelling extends across the east end, forming the grid-structure of the great window. Conversely, if it were possible to remove the 'backing' of the wall panelling i.e. the Anglo-Norman ambulatory and gallery, the sides of the choir would appear as a series of windows waiting to be glazed.

* The window stands like a gigantic triptych behind the high altar, the central section rising higher than the wings by two additional tiers [39]. Because the window had to be canted to follow the

(fig 39) Great East Window, upper tiers

crypt wall, and the two principal mullions buttressed for stability, the window is divided vertically into three sections, a central section of six lights and side sections of four lights (giving a grid-pattern of 4 - 6 - 4).

* The lights are basically rectangular, with cusping which, like the wall panelling, varies from tier to tier. But the cusping when viewed from outside is not always the same as on the inside. For example, the glazed panels on the tier containing saints and martyrs are rectangular and fitted *behind* the cusping. Similarly, on the lowest tier the cusping as seen from inside is simplified on the outside as a plain ogee. This peculiarity is repeated in other windows in the cathedral, but 'apart from the later east window of Exeter Cathedral the phenomenon has not been observed elsewhere' (Kerr, J. 1985).

* The grid-pattern of the window was designed for the theme of the window-glass. The main tiers contain fourteen lights, the number required for the theme *The Blessed Virgin and Christ crowned in Glory*, flanked by the twelve Apostles. In order to fit in the fourteen figures each of the lights had to be made narrower than the wall-panelling and consequently narrower than the clerestory lights. But the structural necessity of canting the window and splaying the final bay of the nave provided slightly more space.

* Horizontally, the transoms form four tiers, with a fifth extending into the tracery of the central section. This provided for the development of the hierarchical aspect of the design.

Production of the Glass No glazing accounts have survived, and the name of the master glazier is not known. But detailed contemporary accounts of the glazing of St Stephen's, Westminster makes the sequence and methods of production clear.

Once the preliminary drawings were agreed between the patron and the master-craftsman, the materials were ordered and a skilled work-force brought together.

(i) The master glass painter then prepared a full-sized drawing, or cartoon, of the agreed design. Cartoons were drawn on boards or trestle tables, prepared with chalk or whitewash and sized with water or ale. The cartoon guided the work at all subsequent stages and so was precisely set out and included all subject-matter, colour details and lead-lines.

(ii) The next task was selecting pieces of glass of the required colour, laying them on the cartoon, and cutting them to the approximate shape by splitting them with a hot iron. They were then shaped to the exact size with a grozing iron. The pieces of glass were painted with a pigment made from ground copper (or iron oxide) and powdered glass, mixed with wine, urine or vinegar, with gum arabic added to make the pigment adhere to the glass. The pigment was applied with brushes made of the hair of animals such as hog, squirrel, badger and cat.

(iii) Painting was usually done in several layers, a light overall wash, a second wash over selected areas with a heavily-charged brush, and then the outlines of facial features and draperies. Fully translucent highlights were created by picking out detail with the tip of the brush-handle (a technique known as *stick-work*). Letters of inscriptions, background ornamental patterns and other details were created in the same way.

(iv) When the pieces of glass had been painted, the pigment was fired on to them in an annealing furnace. They were then removed from the furnace and laid out again for leading. Initially the individual pieces were held together by closing or cloring nails. The lead was cast with an H cross-section and was supplied in strips known as *calmes*. All joins in the lead work were soldered and the gaps between the lead and the glass made waterproof by a filling of tallow, or later a kind of cement.

(v) The final stage was the insertion of the glass panels into the window openings. Sometimes the panels were held in place by being attached to stanchions (vertical supports), but always to saddle-bars. Instead of the elaborate iron-lattice of 13th c. windows, the great east window has a series of horizontal bars connecting the mullions. These are placed at fairly regular intervals down each light providing the framework into which the glazed panels could be fitted (Marks, R. 1993).

Contemporary Glass-painting: Charles Winston saw the stained glass of the great east window as 'a pure example of the Decorated period' and 'a striking example of the way the change in the architectural detail usually preceded by a few years that in the painted glass'. [See 40, 41, 42]

Use of yellow stain. Early in the 14th century it was discovered that if white glass is painted with a preparation of silver oxide (or chloride) and then subjected to the heat of the kiln, the parts painted are stained yellow, pale or dark according to the amount of silver used, the heat of the kiln, and the composition of the glass. When the great east window was in production (*c*.1350) the use of yellow stain was becoming widespread. The Gloucester glaziers used the technique to good effect.

Combination of figures and grisaille This is one of the most noticeable features of glass painting in the late 14th century. The extensive use of decorated quarries and geometric-patterned roundels in the window combined with tier upon tier of figures is typical of this trend.

(fig 40). Great East Window, detail, St. John the Apostle

(fig 41). Great East Window, detail, St Thomas

(fig 42). Great East Window, detail, St Cecilia
and arms of King Edward II

Development of architectural canopies. Earlier, single figures were sometimes painted in unobtrusive architectural canopies of similar design to the sculptured niches which sheltered statues outside buildings. But in the mid-14th century sculptured canopies became more elaborate, as did their painted counterparts in stained glass. In the east window the architectural detail and especially the canopies are a major feature of the design.

Style of figure-painting. A characteristic of 14th-century figure painting is its almost total lack of naturalism. There is an affectation about the poses, for example, of the angels in the top tier of the window. But this 'willowy gracefulness' (often described as an elongated S) was frequently used and much admired in contemporary art and crafts. In the great east window the lack of natural movement is compensated for in the painting of draperies in which much attention is given to the natural folds of the cloth.

Use of painted diaper-patterns on coloured backgrounds. Glass-painters of the period wanted to enrich the coloured backgrounds of their figures and often did so by using diapered-patterns. It was a way of emphasising the status and importance of those represented. The technique was simple but required care and accuracy to be really effective. There are impressive examples of the technique in the window.

> 'Like all glaziers working in the period *c.*1340-1360, the Gloucester glaziers had been influenced by the monumental painting style associated with the so-called 'Majesty Master' of the Psalter of Robert de Lisle, completed by 1339 (London BL Ms Arundel 83 pt. II). However, the Gloucester window also displays the influence of developments in English sculpture of the period, notably the Peter, Lord Grandison tomb in Hereford Cathedral (c. 1352) and the exquisite Annunciation group in wood of c. 1348 made for the Vicars' Hall at Wells' (Brown, S. 2000).

The range of colours in the window is limited. *White* glass fills more than half the total area. The glass is full of tiny bubbles which refract the light giving the window a translucent, silvery brilliance. *Blue* glass is a pure pot-metal (the metallic oxide is added to the liquid glass) so the glass is blue throughout. *Red*, or ruby, glass, however, is produced by a process known as *flashing* in which white glass is coated with a very thin layer of ruby glass. The glass has a rich, streaky character.
Yellow glass is a pot-metal made with silver oxide. In the window it is used for the yellow stars at the apex of the window and quite frequently elsewhere but, as noted, *yellow stain* is also used. Small amounts of glass of other colours, such as *purple* (murrey) and *green*, are also used. [See colour plates 29-39] 'The monochrome effect was certainly no exercise in economy. No expense had been spared in its execution, as ruby and blue, both of exceptional quality, were the most expensive colours throughout the Middle Ages' (Brown, S. 2000).

Painting Techniques The Gloucester glass-painters' techniques enabled them to achieve the impression, from a distance, of tier upon tier of *sculpted figures* in niches [40]. They did this by using bold, direct line-painting, especially for the faces and draperies, and by using a very soft brush on a wet wash surface to give a stippled effect which improved the modelling of such features (Marks, R. 1993). Kerr drew attention to the face-painting [41]. 'Once the observer has gazed into these strikingly cadaverous physiognomies with the lugubrious deep set eyes and formalized hair and beards, their powerful dignity is never forgotten' (Kerr, J. 1985).

Shading technique. Great use is made of modelling washes with highlights rubbed out. This technique is used in the niches and gives some impression of the third dimension. The third dimension is further enhanced when the draperies or attributes of some of the figures fall naturally in front of the jambs of the painted niches.

Back-painting. Back-painting was used extensively. Though some has been lost through erosion and cleaning, an enormous amount survives in extraordinarily good condition. 'Back-painting serves two purposes: most importantly it reinforces the interior painting, giving a more sculptural effect to the work. However, given that glass-painters try to avoid multi-firings, with the risks of breakage etc., it means that multiple paint layers can be applied with only one firing. In other words, there is both an aesthetic and a practical reason for its use' (Brown, S 2000).

Rinceaux, or 'stick work'. This technique is used to good effect to enrich the background of the niches in which there are figures of special significance, e.g. St Peter and St Paul. It gives the impression that the niches are lined with tapestry. It is also used, on the bottom tier, in the cusped-quatrefoils holding some of the armorials.

Yellow stain. The Gloucester glaziers used yellow stain on the figures, for crowns and for hair and beards. They also used it to pick out the folds in drapery, to give definition to the architectural detail and in heraldic work.

Repeat cartoons. A corollary of Perpendicular architecture, with its repetition of rectilinear panels on wall-surfaces and as window-tracery, is the re-use of the same cartoons in stained-glass work. This practice is very noticeable in the great east window; for example, only two cartoons are used for the angels in the top tier.

'It is abundantly clear that the glaziers were of local origin. Examination of their work reveals the exceptional quality of their design and craftsmanship, the equal of any prestige project in England. Comparison with other glazing schemes in the area, notably at Tewkesbury and Bristol, suggests that the Gloucester glaziers trained in the area, perhaps in Bristol, known as 'almost the richest city' of medieval England (Brown, S. 2000).

In its conception and execution the window is, in Gordon Rushforth's words, 'a landmark in English stained glass design'.

Painted Architecture: More than half the painted area of the window is devoted to painted architecture {28} [39]. This, as Winston pointed out, is in the Decorated style in contrast to the window's Perpendicular grid-pattern. 'It is extremely unusual to encounter a design for glazing at this time where the architecture in the glass does not conform to the framing of the stonework' (Kerr, J. 1985).

*   The painted structure is so detailed and complete that if the stonework of the window were taken down, the glass with its painted architecture would stand up on its own! Or so it is said! It is certainly true that the painted architecture is so prominent that the actual stonework of the window seems to recede, and become subsidiary. In Kerr's words: 'The depth and perspective of the architecture painting is carefully designed and articulated with the use of extensive monochrome contour washes to define the third dimension. The niches are three-quarters angled to reveal simple vaulting, heavily painted with shadow to create depth; the ribs and decorative bosses are picked out of matt wash. The side shafts are developed in segments with elaborate blind window designs in reverse, punctuated by capitals and surmounted with finials. The canopies themselves are painted with consummate skill, the high relief of the crockets boldly defined with wash and line reinforcement'.

* Though patterns for shrine-work had long been in the repertoire of glass-painters, the inspiration for the detail of the painted architecture in the great east window comes from three-dimensional models which were close at hand. There are striking similarities between the canopy of Edward II's tomb and the painted canopies above the angels. There are also similarities between the painted canopies on the lower tiers. and the canopies above the monks' stalls in the quire. The carpenters and wood-carvers were constructing the stalls at the same time as the glass-painters were at work on the window. Once noticed, details such as these emphasise the underlining integration of architectural detail and furnishings which was so characteristic of the Decorated period. Comparison may also be made with architectural works of the 1370s - for example, the tomb of Edward Despenser at Tewkesbury (d.1375) and the Neville Screen at Durham Cathedral (*c.* 1376-9).

* The canopies increase in height at each level, taking the eye ever upwards to the window arch where the canopies above the angels rise to fill the full height of the the tier above. The jambs of the niches have the same effect for they terminate not within each light, but continue up behind the transom to the tier above, terminating ultimately in the elaborate canopies of the top tiers. Furthermore, behind the crocketed pinnacles of the lower tiers shafts rise, passing as it were behind the transom, emerging to form pedestals for the figures of the tier above. 'The continuation of the canopy top to create a plinth for a figure in the tier above had already been done in Wells (east window, of *c.* 1340), but a closer comparison can be made with the contemporary carved reredos at Christchurch priory in Hampshire and the image screen on the west front of Exeter cathedral' (Brown, S. 2000).

* The strong sense of verticality is reinforced by the alternating vertical strips of blue and red glass which form the background of the painted niches. The two central niches on each tier share a ruby red background, the colours then alternating out to the sides. The shared red backgrounds in the centre of the window emphasis the status and importance of the central figures.

* The whole painted 'structure' seems to rest on a tiled pavement. The figures in the upper tiers are set on pedestals, but the abbots and bishops have their feet on the ground! Or so it appears! It should be pointed out, however, that the square pieces of coloured glass, taken to indicate a tiled pavement, may be later insertions taking the place of script. In earlier restorations fragments of script were found at the bottom of these lights.

Arrangement of the Figures The main horizontal divisions of the over-all design of the glass are distinguished no less than four times by varying the border-design. In the tracery lights, there are thin stripes of plain white glass; in the main section there are jambs and other architectural detail; in the lowest complete tier (containing the series of shields) there is a pattern of trailing vine stems, with leaves and grapes intertwining; and in the tiers either side of the entrance to the lady chapel the border changes yet again.

(i) The tracery lights contain a number of roundels with geometric patterns set within white quarries each of which is ornamented with a star-like motif and narrow black-line edging on the upper side. When such quarries are placed together they form a reticulated pattern. The two five-point flaming stars at the apex of the window are part of the original design, but between them is a 15th c. insertion of *St.Clement of Rome*.

(ii) The top tier of figures in the central section, beneath immensely tall canopies, are angels arranged in pairs looking towards each another. But in the second light from the left is a *Virgin and Child*, another 15th c. insertion.

(iii) The top complete tier of lights has a *Coronation of the Virgin* in the centre, flanked by the Apostles. But since the Virgin is wearing her crown and depicted sitting beside the Christ (who originally was also seated) the scene is more accurately described as *The Christ and the Virgin together in Majesty* (Kerr, J. 1985). Originally, the apostles all turned inwards, facing the central pair {29, 30, 31}.

(iv) The tier below contains saints and martyrs, arranged in pairs, a female saint and a male saint looking at each other across a narrow mullion; for example, on the extreme left, St Cecilia and St George {34, 35, 36}. The figures occupying the central lights are probably St Anne and St John the Baptist.

(v) The next tier has abbots and bishops, again arranged in pairs and looking at one another. The abbots, who are tonsured, probably represent abbots of Gloucester {39} and the bishops in their mitres, bishops of Worcester.

(vi) The lowest tier contains an array of shields, or armorials, including those of King Edward III and the Black Prince and a number of the king's most trusted supporters who were with him in the Scottish and French campaigns {40}.

Detailed Iconography St Clement of Rome, at the apex of the window, wears a triple-crowned tiara and holds a double cross. Winston suspected it came from the lady chapel. It probably took the place of a third star, or some representation of God, the Father, or of the Holy Trinity. The **angels**, which are painted from only two cartoons, have contrasting coloured backgrounds and nimbi. Their wings are coloured in bars, and their hair is yellow stain. One angel has a restored head - a rare surviving example of a medieval repair (Brown, S. 2000). The borders of the draperies of the *Virgin and Child* (15th *c.*) are ornamented with coloured pieces of glass stuck on (as recommended by Theophilus in *De Diversis Artibus*). The Virgin is trampling on a serpent, recalling Genesis 3.14-15. The Virgin is seated on a tasselled, tapestry cushion and half-turned towards Christ in the adjoining light. She is nimbed and wears a crown, and her hands are crossed on her breast. **Christ** has an orb and is lifting his right hand in blessing. The lower half of the figure, below the tier-bar, is from a missing apostle. The red background of the upper half is richly patterned with geometric diaper {29 & 30}.

The central pair are not given any great prominence; for example, there is no difference of scale between them and the apostles, or in the height of their canopies. They share the same red background, with rinceaux work, but the adjacent figures of St Peter and St Paul also have enriched backgrounds. Yet they are distinguished by sharing the central lights of the top complete tier, the same enriched background and they are both crowned. Originally, they were both seated whilst the apostle were all standing, and turned inwards looking at them.

In accordance with medieval convention the **apostles** are represented nimbed and with bare feet (with the exception of St Thomas). Not all the apostles are identifiable by their attributes {32, 33, 37}. St Peter (two keys and model of church) is in the position of honour; his light blue nimbus contrasts with the dark blue background. Yellow stain is used for his hair. St Paul (book in left hand, sword in right), is nimbed like St Peter, but the face is lost. St John (palm branch, and eagle perched looking into his face) has a blue nimbus. St Thomas (spear and girdle) without nimbus and wearing slippers; the figure and canopy are particularly well preserved. St Andrew (saltire cross) is a fine example of the Gloucester glaziers' work, with yellow stain on hem and border, and back-painting well preserved. St James, the Less (club of blue glass with handle of yellow stain).

The four apostles which were on the right-hand side of the window have been lost, apart from the feet and lower part of two of them.

There has been extensive damage to the right-hand side of the window, on this and the two lower tiers. This may date back to 1798 when a quantity of painted glass was stolen from the east window and a reward of fifty guineas offered for its recovery and the prosecution of those responsible. These lights have been filled with fragments of kings of larger dimension than the *in situ* figures. There are crowned heads, sceptres, swords, fragments of royal robes etc. Winston found fragments of at least ten kings in these lights and in lights of the east window of the lady chapel, and suggested they may have come from the choir clerestory windows. The lights of the clerestory are wider (by 7.6 cms) and considerably taller than those of the east window. If Winston was right, the clerestory windows contained a 'stunning array of twenty kings on either side' (Kerr). The figures, probably including King Edward III, would have formed a kind of glass 'Chronicle' of benefactors and saintly king of past centuries. The only identifiable king is St Edmund on the lower tier, with the abbots and bishops.. Sarah Brown has noted that 'a comparative sequence of lay benefactors adorns the choir clerestory of nearby Tewkesbury Abbey, in a glazing scheme of c. 1340. Something similar was probably found in the new Lady Chapel and retrochoir of St Augustine's Abbey at Bristol, also glazed in the 1340s.'

Only five of the **saints and martyrs** are identifiable by their attributes {34, 35, 38}. Like the angels above and the ecclesiastics below, they are arranged in pairs facing towards each other:

* *From the left-hand side:* St Cecilia, with a blue nimbus, wears a crown of roses and holds a book instead of one of her usual attributes, a portative organ or wheel. Her hair is yellow stain. Beside her is St George, in plate armour, with hauberk of mail, over which is a white cyclas bearing a red cross. The spurs are rowelled. He holds a spear, and the other hand rests on the handle of his sword. He has a dagger on the right side and a shield suspended by a strap from his neck. St Margaret of Antioch (face lost) is depicted treading on a dragon at her feet and spearing it. St Lawrence, tonsured and vested as a deacon, is holding a grid-iron painted black.

* *In the centre of the row,* the female saint is probably St Anne. The male saint is certainly St John the Baptist. He is nimbed and wears a short fringed tunic. He has bare feet.

* *On the right-hand side* are fragments of inserted kings, but there is the club of St Simon, and St James the Great in pilgrim hat (second from the right) who should be on the tier above. In place of the traditional shell of the pilgrim, the hat has a 15th c. insertion on which is painted a miniature head of Christ.

The **abbots and bishops**, on the next tier down, are also arranged in pairs, each turning towards the other. The abbots are tonsured and fully vested, and each holds a pastoral staff {39}. Since Gloucester Abbey did not receive the mitre until c. 1380, they probably represent some of the eighteen Abbots of Gloucester since Edric, the first abbot of the Benedictine foundation. None is nimbed, and it is not possible to identify any of the figures. The bishops are mitred and hold their crosiers.

* *In the centre of the tier* are two kings, one of similar dimension to the *in situ* figures. This is one of the original series and almost certainly represents King Edward II. The figure may have been modelled on the recumbent effigy on the tomb nearby. He is placed in a position of honour, in the centre of the tier, and shares the same rich background as the neighbouring figure. The fact that he is placed among the ecclesiastics is probably intended to emphasise the sanctity of kingship which his son, King Edward III, and the Abbey, after the events of 1327, would have been anxious to reaffirm.

To the right of Edward II is St Edmund, crowned and in royal robes, and holding three arrows. He is of larger dimensions than the *in situ* figures and is therefore an intruder, one of the array of kings and benefactors which filled the clerestory windows. Unusually, his hands, face and hair are coloured pink. Kerr conjectures that Prince Osric, the Saxon founder, was originally in this position.

The lowest tier contained fourteen **shields** [42] {40}, but only ten of them are from the original glazing [indicated by *].

The left wing, from the left:

    (i)* Arundel   (ii) * Berkeley   (iii)* Warwick   (iv) * de Bohun

The central section, from the left:

    (v) Ruydale (vi) King Edward II (vii) King Edward III (viii)* The Black Prince
    (ix) Lancaster, Henry   (x) The Instruments of the Passion

Below the central six, from the left:

    (xv) Lancaster, Thomas   (xvi) York, Duke Edmund
    (xvii) King Edward III
    (xviii)* England, Henry of Lancaster

The right wing, from the left:

    (xi)* Pembroke   (xii)* Talbot   (xiii)* Berkeley, Sir Maurice
    (xiv)* Bradeston, Lord Thomas

In the fourth light from the right is the celebrated roundel of The Golfer {41}. It depicts a small figure, wearing a short tunic trimmed with a yellow band, playing a stick and ball game. Whether the game he is playing is golf is disputed (Welander, D. 1985). There is one other pictorial roundel in the window, at the top of the window, depicting a bird sitting in an arm chair eating a stalk of corn!

Historical Context The identity of those who bore these arms provides evidence of the historical context of the window.

Local connections Those who bore the ten original shields are the king (Edward III) and his son (the Black Prince), his kinsman (Lancaster), and a group of nobles closely identified with the king as his counsellors and comrades-in-arms. Some of them had local connections; for example, Warwick and Talbot had manors in the county, and Pembroke held numerous lordships in the near-by Marches in Wales. The Berkeleys and Bradeston had estates in the county and seats within a few miles of Gloucester. The king and members of his family had given generously towards the cost of the remodelling the choir (*Historia*). Following their example some of the King's closest counsellors, particularly those with local connections, may well have done the same, though in the absence of documentary evidence this must remain a matter of conjecture. Armorial bearings, however, were often used to indicate *donation* as well as *possession*, so the arms may have been inserted in the window as the Abbey's acknowledgement of the generosity of its principal patrons. Together with the clerestory windows, the east window would have been seen as an appropriate place for the community to record its gratitude, the window being the consummation of nearly twenty years of rebuilding (1337-55).

Chivalry celebrated In view of the date of the window (*c*.1350) it is impossible to discount altogether a Crecy connection. The array of shields may be seen as a celebration of chivalry and of recent success in arms. A wave of euphoria swept across the country with the success of the French campaign, with the king instituting the *Order of the Garter* at Windsor in 1349. Those who bore the ten original shields fought with Edward III in his French campaigns, being commanders in the Battle of Crecy (1346) or present at the Siege of Calais (1347). The Black Prince commanded the first division, assisted by Warwick; the Earls of Arundel and Northampton commanded the second division; the King personally commanded the third; Lord Berkeley and his brother, Sir Maurice, together with Richard, Lord Talbot, and Thomas, Lord Bradeston were probably among the bannerets. Lancaster was not at Crecy as he and Pembroke were fighting elsewhere in France, but they joined the king the following year at the Siege of Calais. Sir Maurice Berkeley was killed at Calais, and two years later Pembroke died from wounds received in battle. These were all renowned for their military prowess and bravery. 'The original heraldry in the window confirms that the glass had been commissioned before 1360 and perhaps as early as 1348. While the traditional interpretation of the window as a war memorial of the Crecy campaign is now questioned, the heraldic display confirms the close link between the choir of Gloucester and the court of Edward III' (Brown, S. 2000).

Donors of the Window Drayton in his *Notes on the Heraldry of the East Window of Gloucester Cathedral* (1916) argued that Thomas, Lord Bradeston was the sole donor. He gave the window in memory of his friend and comrade-in-arms, Sir Maurice Berkeley. For this reason Bradeston's arms are in the so-called donor-position at the bottom right-hand corner, and his arms distinguished by being the only ones with a coloured background. It is doubtful, however, whether Bradeston could have afforded such a costly commission - Thomas, Lord Berkeley, Maurice's half-brother, was Bradeston's feudal overlord. It is true that Bradeston's social status had been steadily rising since he was knighted and given custody of Gloucester Castle 'for the better maintenance of the knightly rank lately conferred on him' (1330). He was later ennobled, and in 1351 built a family burial chapel at Winterbourne in Gloucestershire. Presumably it was for his war record and as Constable of Gloucester Castle that he was included here among the great men of the kingdom. However, it is most unlikely that the window was the gift of one man. The *Historia* makes it clear that the Abbots initiated and motivated the whole building project, funding it, in the main, from the Abbey coffers with substantial help from the Royal purse.

Liturgical Significance Though it was a window of national significance, its context is the choir of a Benedictine abbey. Its design would have been suggested and approved by the community in the person of the abbot, Adam de Staunton (1337-51).

*   The monastic community would have seen in the window a 'formalized hierarchy' (Kerr), expressing the derivation of authority from heaven to earth. At the apex, the symbols of the Godhead, the flaming stars, and below the angels representing the heavenly host. In the vault (from which the window cannot be disassociated) is an angel orchestra playing and singing a *Gloria in excelsis Deo*. Angels abound around the choir, on tombs and doorways, above sedilia as well as in the stained glass. The window expresses the community's conviction that in their daily round of worship they were joining 'with angels and archangels and all the company of heaven'.

*   Below the angels are the figures of *Christ and the Virgin enthroned in Glory*. The central pair were seated and crowned whilst the apostles stood, turned towards them. Christ and the Virgin were the principal focus of medieval devotion and particularly in the liturgy of the Benedictine Order. The Virgin was frequently celebrated, and devotion to her expressed in works of art, in stained glass, in paintings and illuminations, in statues and reliefs.

*   On the next tier, is an array of saints and martyrs of the church. As with the apostles on the tier above, the community was able to identify each of the figures. But more importantly they were able *to identify with them*, for they were not merely figures of the past but a part of their daily lives. They were intercessors, to whom and through whom they prayed. They studied the *Lives of the Saints and Martyrs*, which challenged them to greater devotion and sacrifice.

* On the tier below the members of the community were reminded of their *lords spiritual*, the bishops of the church and abbots of their Order and community. They were reminded of the long history of their own religious house from its foundation in early Saxon times, and through the centuries since the Conquest; of their great founder-builder, Abbot Serlo, and of some of his distinguished successors. Among them, in a central position, they recognised their royal patron whose shrine nearby was their daily care.

* On the lowest tier, they were reminded of their *lords temporal*, of their power and achievements, and in particular of those who were their benefactors, for whom they prayed constantly.

The community gathered in the choir at night, the occasional lamp casting a dim light and shadow on carved figures of saints and angels. Then as dawn broke and the sun rose the great window was brilliantly illuminated as with heavenly light. They saw the Christ, only half turned towards the Virgin, holding up his hand in blessing, and all around the apostles, saints, and martyrs 'came alive' against the silvery light. This great array of saintly figures seemed as one with the *Christ and the Angel choir* in the vault above them. The myriad of bosses were like stars in the firmament. The choir was 'a closed world, fenced in, in a very literal sense, by the net of tracery which surrounds it' (Coldstream, N. 1987). The community had created a 'heaven on earth' so that when they gathered in worship they found themselves in the presence of the Christ and the Virgin, the apostles and martyrs, the angels and the whole company of heaven, and were caught up in heaven's unceasing worship, praise and thanksgiving.

Chapter Nine
THE NORTH TRANSEPT

The remodelling of the north transept took less than six years. 'The aisle of St Paul (the north transept) was begun the day after the Epiphany of the Lord in the forty-first year of King Edward, the third of that name after the Conquest, and was fully completed at the Vigil of the Nativity of the Lord in the forty-seventh year of the above mentioned king. The cost of this work...was as much as £ 718 1s. 2d., out of which the said abbot (Thomas Horton) paid £ 444 1s. 2d., as is made clear in the records of the above mentioned work' (*Historia*).

The remodelling of the north transept (1368-73) completed the transformation of the eastern arm of the abbey church. Building work had been going on almost continuously in and around the choir since 1331, beginning in the south transept (1331-36), and then in the choir itself (1337-1355).

Transept Transformed As in the south transept, the shell of the Romanesque transept survives. Behind the stone panelling on the east side a wide arch spans the entrance to the chapel and a smaller arch the entrance to the north ambulatory. Above these arches and behind the panelling, the great piers and arches of the tribune are also intact. In the north-west corner of the transept the Anglo-Norman turret-stair survives, its ashlar walls unadorned apart from string courses. But whilst much of the original fabric remains much had to be taken down, mainly to make space for the construction of windows [2].

Perpendicular Windows: As in the south transept, much of the terminal wall had to be demolished, together with its windows and wall-passages, to allow for the construction of the large window which now fills the space between the corner turrets. A new wall-passage was built beneath the window and behind the gables of the reliquary (see below), to provide access, via the turret-stair to the gallery on the east side of the transept. Much of the west wall was also demolished to make way for the construction of a large window, and a smaller window over the north-aisle arch. Above the tribune, two more windows were built.

Raised Clerestory: In their determination to get additional light into the dark Romanesque choir and transepts, the 14th c. builders raised the height of the presbytery and transepts; the south transept and presbytery to a height of 26.2m., and the north transept 2.4m. higher. At the time, similar tall clerestorys were being built (but with an earlier type of tracery) in the choirs of Lichfield and Wells. 'But for what was to be the glory of the closing years of English Gothic architecture - the 'Lantern' church - credit must be given to the architects and masons of Gloucester in the 14th century' (Bond, F. 1912).

Rectilinear Panelling: At the same time stone panelling was grafted onto the walls. The panelling is far more developed than that in the south transept. Angular mouldings are used in the place of round mouldings, and the mullions of the side windows rise directly to the main arch instead of branching off into ogee tracery. The open panelling in front of the wall passage also rises as tracery through the great window to the main arch. Similarly, on the east side of the transept, the panelling extends over the gallery openings and through the windows to the vault. The tracery of these east windows is similar to the tracery of the great east window. As in the south transept, to ensure that the panelling was truly vertical it was rebated into the north-east crossing pier. But no internal buttress was considered necessary, partly because the pier was not leaning outwards to any degree, and also because it had been strengthened only recently at tribune level.

Lierne Vault: In the south transept the net-like vault was constructed on a geometric pattern and without bosses. In the north transept a more complex vault was constructed more akin to the choir vault, with parallel ridge ribs and bosses. The springing of the vault resembles fan-vaulting in that the junction of the main and transverse ribs are rounded rather than angular, with smaller ribs springing from *between* the larger ones a little above their union with the top of the supporting shafts. But just as the springing of the choir vault is still angular, the north transept vault is not yet truly conical. In the adjoining cloister walk, however, fan-vaulting had already arrived (*c.*1355-68), though spanning only a comparatively small area.

St Paul's Chapel The chapel is entered up steps which, like the flight into the choir ambulatory, were necessary to accommodate the height of the crypt [43]. The original **arch** over the entrance springs from twin attached-shafts, with single scallop capitals and shared abaci, similar to that at the entrance to the ambulatory. The chapel arch is wider than that at the ambulatory entrance 'perhaps to emphasise the relative importance of the chapel' (Willis, R. 1860). On the north side of the chapel, above the doorway, there is a round-headed arch set into the wall. This is not a blocked up window but reticulation, or decoration, of the wall surface (the horizontal masonry line shows that this is how the wall was built). Such inset **wall-arches** are a feature of the Anglo-Norman building also occurring, for example, at the west end of the north ambulatory and in the south-east ambulatory chapel. The doorway itself has Perpendicular cresting, with angels bearing scrolls (with messages) lying in the hollow moulding. The radiating **groin vault** is most unusual. There is a circle at the apex, and the lines marking the sections of the vault are carried down to the piers. Willis considered this 'quite unique'. It is possible that the design may reflect a rib-pattern in the semi-dome over the demolished apse at the east end of the choir (Wilson,C. 1985). The **reredos** is one of the most perfect in the building. Though much restored, it is not 'late 19th century' (New, A. 1980). It was restored in 1870 at the expense of Edward Law, Earl of Ellenborough and one-time Governor-General of India *in mem.* members of his family. The niches are filled with figures, by J. F. Redfern, representing St Peter, St Paul and St Luke. The **window** is obscured by the reredos, even so Burlison and Grylls produced a striking design (1870).

> Christ is depicted seated in majesty, clothed in a crimson robe and white mantle, surrounded by an aureola with cherubim and fourteen angels kneeling in adoration and holding palm branches and crowns. In the upper lights six angels hold scrolls inscribed with *Te Deum Laudamus*. The side lights extend the theme, with ten angels arranged in four tiers playing various stringed instruments, pipes and a small organ. Their dresses are white, relieved with yellow; the background throughout is blue, spangled with yellow stars.

Early English Reliquary
The reliquary screen is a tripartite structure, with a doorway in the central bay and window-like openings on either side [43]. The scars in the stonework above each of the openings suggest that originally crocketed gables surmounted the screen. The doorway has a trefoil head set under a pointed gable, and above

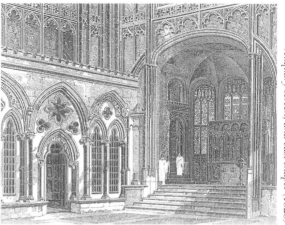

reliquary screen, and east chapel (1828)   *(fig 43) North Transept,*

two small trefoils and a large eight-cornered star whose diagonal corners are pointed trefoils. Purbeck shafts with well-preserved stiff-leaf capitals are set at the angles, and corbel-heads at the springing of the arches. There are uncut blocks of stone where carvings once were. On the extreme left, at the top of the vertical moulding, there is a tiny head of a mitred abbot or bishop. Inside the screen there is a rib-vault with bosses, the boss in the central division is particularly delicate and finely cut.

The original position and purpose of the screen has excited much discussion. Bonnor (1796) thought it served as a punishment cell; others as a lavatorium or a confessional, or even as an Easter sepulchre. Bazeley (1904) suggested that it did not stand here originally but formed the entrance to the early-13th *c.* lady chapel which, he believed, was a remodelling of the Anglo-Norman axial chapel. He thought the entry-screen was moved to the north transept when the present lady chapel was built in the late-15th century. There are difficulties, however, with this: (i) would the screen have fitted across the entrance of the chapel without restricting movement around the ambulatory? (ii) would the crocketed pinnacles have fitted under the groin vault of the Anglo-Norman ambulatory?

The screen was almost certainly designed to stand in its present position and to serve as a reliquary (Tudor Craig, P. 1981). It was therefore *in situ* when the north transept was remodelled (1368-73). With the construction of the wall-passage the crocketed pinnacles of the reliquary were removed and replaced by castellation.

On the extreme right of the screen where it abuts the panelling of the east wall the stone-work has been disturbed. This must have occurred either when the panelling was put up, or later when a niche for a figure was set into the angle. For some reason the damage was never made good. In the corner on top of the niche, Bartlett shows a stone with the arms of Abbot Parker (abbot 1514-39) carved on it. It was probably lodged here much later for safe keeping, but if there was a connection with the Abbot he may have been installing a figure at the time of the Dissolution, and the project was never completed.

Cathedral Treasury The reliquary screen now forms the entrance to the Cathedral Treasury, which was the gift of the Goldsmiths' Company of London and set up in

1977 in the eastern slype. Access from the cloister at one end, and to the precinct gardens at the other has been cut off by steel security grills. Two bays of the Anglo-Norman wall-arcading were demolished to make a way through to the transept.

The Treasury contains an interesting and valuable collection of church silver from the medieval period to the present day, much of it on loan from the parishes of the diocese. The display is changed periodically, but at present (1999) there are several pieces of the cathedral's Restoration plate displayed, including two chalices and two patens, a credence paten and two flagons (1660), an alms dish (1661) and two altar candlesticks (1661). Also displayed are a credence paten (1705) by Humphrey Payne, given to the cathedral in 1905, and chalices of 1817 and 1862; and a bishop's mace (1737) given by Dr. Martin Benson, bishop of Gloucester (1734-52). There is also a chalice (c.1900) designed by Henry Wilson, in silver, parcel gilt, enamel, niello and semi-precious stones, and a flagon (1891) designed by J. D. Sedding. Among other cathedral treasures are: Two verges dating from the reign of King Charles II which are still in regular use. Also in use is a silver cross and matching candlesticks by Stephen Dykes Bower, and an *Art Nouveau* processional cross by Omar Ramsden (1922). A silver processional staff depicting St George and the Dragon, by Leslie Durbin (1959) is used on occasions by the dean's verger.

Memorials Under the larger west window are two curiosities: A **painted monument**, on wooden panels against the wall, to John Bower, an apothecary, and his wife (1615). They had 'nyne sones and seaven daughters' who are represented in perspective. At the top of the monument is an inscription: *Momento more, Vayne, vanytie, witnesse Solomon, all is but vayne*. The figures are full of interest, especially in depicting period costume. The paint-work has suffered considerably from the heat and fumes of a Gurney stove which stood nearby for many years. Above the memorial is a sumptuous **Art Nouveau clock** (1903) designed by Henry Wilson (1864-1934), and given *in mem*. of the Revd. Bartholomew Price (1818-98), a notable astronomer, Master of Pembroke College, Oxford, and Canon of Gloucester. Below the clock the small tablet to Canon Price is also by Wilson [44].

(fig 44) North Transept, wall clock by Henry Wilson (1864-1934)

The hours, indicated by Roman numerals, are represented by bronze medallions depicting the signs of the zodiac. In the centre is a large bronze relief containing two figures, a woman standing in front of a gateway, crowned and with a nimbus, and a helmeted man wearing a short tunic and sandals holding a spear or lance in his left hand. The woman seems to be restraining him from using it. The hands are in the form of flying birds. The clock face and the tablet below were restored by Donald Smith in 1997.

Almost all the **burial slabs** are without their brasses and inscriptions. But a large mutilated slab has an inscription of which some of the lettering in the border is legible. Browne Willis in his *Survey* (1727) records that this was to a certain Robert Stanford, but that a small brass to Wm. Lisle (1723) had been let into it. Abbots Horton, Boyfield and Froucester are all thought to have been buried in the transept, but beyond associating the stone that shows the trace of a mitre to Froucester, there is no indication of who is buried where.

Stained Glass The two east windows contain some medieval glass, fragments of the original glazing, restored by Clayton & Bell. The borders are broad and decorated with crowns and *fleur-de-lys*.

The border of crowns is matched with quarries with a leaf motif; and the border of *fleur-de-lys* with a rose motif. The roundels are of different designs - some have decorated borders and contain stars, others are of geometric designs, and others have leaf motifs. In the four small *oculi* in the tracery there is glass from the original glazing (c.1370). The smaller of the two west windows also contains fragments of glass of the same date in the cusping and tracery.

The large **north window** is by Hardman (1874). At the foot of the window are the arms of the Hicks-Beach family who donated the window. Sir Michael E. Hicks-Beach Bart. MP. PC. (1837-1916) devoted much of his life to politics and was twice Chancellor of the Exchequer. He later became the first Earl St Aldwyn (Johnson, J. 1989).

Appropriately in a transept known in medieval times as *St Paul's Aisle*, the window depicts scenes from the life of St Paul. Four scenes from the martyrdom of St Stephen occupy the eight lights above the transom; they are the stoning of St Stephen, the conversion of St Paul, the vision that sustained the martyr as he was being stoned, and his death. Below the transom are two tiers of eight lights depicting scenes from the life of the Apostle as described in the *Acts of the Apostles*. Each scene is vividly portrayed and repays careful study with binoculars.

The large **west window** is by C. E. Kempe (1894) on the theme *Artistic Gifts and Learning*, and is *in mem.* William Philip Price MP. The richly vested figures, so typical of Kempe's work, are Bazalel, Solomon, St Gregory and St John Chrysostom. Below is a scene from their lives, illustrating their work.

In the tracery on the left, the window is signed with the heraldic device assumed by Kempe and which served as his trademark viz. three golden wheat sheafs on a ruby field. In a similar position on the right are the initials of **A E T**ombleson, a skilled craftsman and fine artist who for many years was the master glass-painter of the Kempe studio. Though Tombleson frequently 'signed' his windows in this way Kempe rarely, if ever, allowed his other artists to do so (Stavridi, M. 1988).

Choir and Clergy Vestries (*not open to the public*) Access to the choir vestry is from St Paul's Chapel. The room is long and narrow, built over the eastern slype (*the Cathedral Treasury*). Here the choristers practice, in preparation for the daily services, and robe with the lay-clerks.

26

27

26. Choir, looking west into the quire
27 & 27b. Choir vault and key to
rib construction

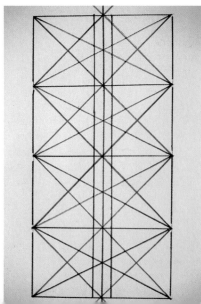

27b

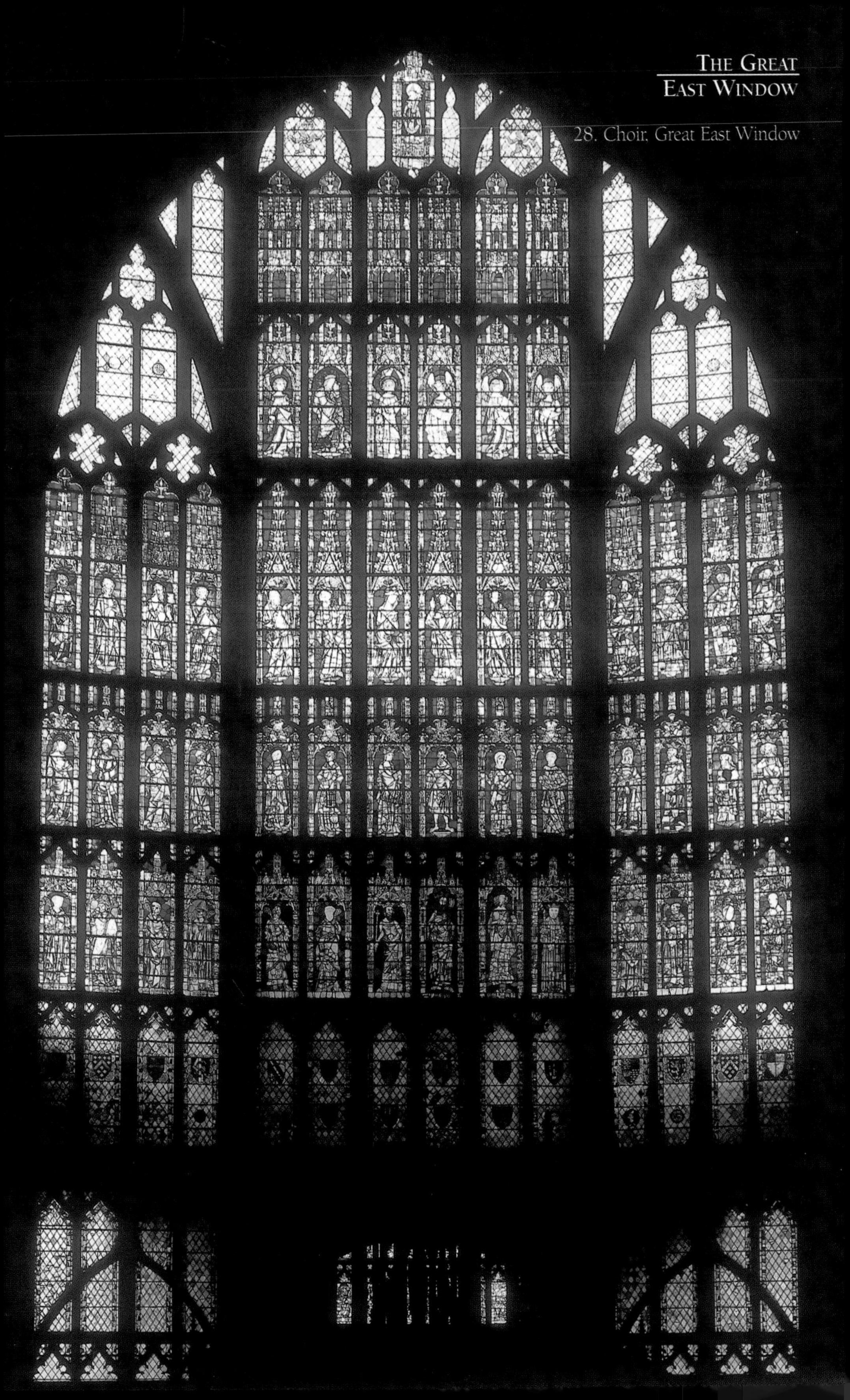

28. Choir, Great East Window

29

30

29. Choir, GEW detail, The Virgin Mary

30. Choir, GEW detail, Christ in Majesty

31. Choir, GEW detail, panel of Christ and the Virgin

32. Choir, GEW detail, St. Thomas and St. Peter

33. Choir, GEW detail, St. Paul and St. John

31

32

33

34

35

36

37

38

34. Choir, GEW detail, St Cecilia
35. Choir, GEW detail, St. George
36. Choir, GEW detail, St Cecilia and St. George
37. Choir, GEW detail, An Apostle and St. Andrew
38. Choir, GEW detail, St. Margaret and St. Lawrence

39. Choir, GEW detail, an abbot (? of St. Peter's Abbey)

40. Choir, GEW detail, arms of the Earls of Lancaster   41. Choir, GEW detail, The Golfer' roundel

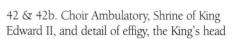

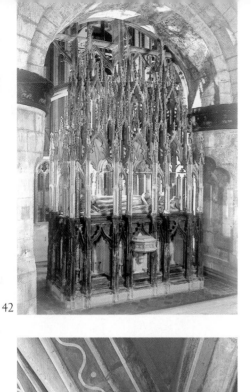

42

42 & 42b. Choir Ambulatory, Shrine of King
Edward II, and detail of effigy, the King's head

43. Choir Ambulatory, an Angel musician in vault

44. Choir Ambulatory, Robert, Duke of Normandy

45. Choir Ambulatory, Prince Osric, founder, detail

46. Choir Ambulatory, detail of effigy of Abbot Parker

42b

43

45

44

46

CHOIR AND AMBULATORY

47a. Three shepherds with crooks, and dog following (15)

47b. Giant with a club being attacked by a knight (3)

47c. Two youths playing with a ball (32)

47e. Elephant with cart-horse feet and tail (35)

48. Choir, the great organ, facing into the choir

47d. Bear baiting (5)

47f. Hawking, with beater in background (27)

In monastic times the room was probably used as a store for account books and valuables. In the 18th century the small room at the east end of the vestry (now the choristers' practice room) was known as the *Chapter Room* (at the time, the *Chapter House* was the library). From the mid-18th century the 'singing men' (lay-clerks) used the chapel off the south transept which had been blocked up to provide wall space for a memorial to Dr. Martin Benson (bishop of Gloucester 1734-52). The medieval *Reliquary* was used for choir robes. A drawing by Bonnor (1796) shows wooden grills fitted into the openings and central doorway.

The **clergy vestry** is on the south side of the transept, beneath the north crossing arch [45]. It is bounded on the choir side by the high wooden screen at the back of the stalls, and on the transept side by a Perpendicular stone screen.

In medieval times it was the *Chapel of St Anthony*. On the back of the choir stalls there are almost life-size paintings of saints, revealed by Clive Rouse in 1972. The paintings are of St Margaret of Antioch, emerging from a dragon, and St Antony of Egypt carrying his tau-headed cross or staff, and with his attributes of pig, bell and rosary.

(fig 45) North Transept, clergy vestry and crossing (1829)

Below the panels there is a series of **eight miniature paintings** (*c*.1375) of the *Fox and Geese* legend. In contrast to the work of contemporary glass-painters which was formal and stylised, the animals in the miniatures are extraordinarily life-like and animated. Glass-painters had their own conventions and, as expected by their ecclesiastical patrons, a reverential attitude towards their subjects. No such constraints were felt or imposed on the painter, or painters, of the miniatures.

The top row, from left to right, depicts:
(i) Reynard the fox running off holding a goose in its mouth and flung over its back; (ii) The fox is arrested and brought before Ysengrin the wolf; (iii) Reynard is dragged by three yoked geese to execution; (iv) Reynard is hauled up by goat, hare and goose, and is hanging from a gibbet.

The lower row depicts:
(v) The stag and hind begin to sing the burial service; (vi) The animals celebrate the death of Reynard (this painting is not very clear); (vii) Reynard is lifted off the bier as the service is read by Baucent the boar and Courtois the hound, with 'bell, book and candle'; (viii) Noble, the lion, holds a celebration feast, with Fiere, Brun, the goat and the monkey.

Chapter Ten

THE GREAT CLOISTER

The idea of a cloister originated in Classical times in the warmer and more settled climate of Mediterranean countries where an open cloister provided welcome coolness and shade. But in the vagaries of English weather open cloisters were bitterly cold and cheerless in winter, especially if the cloister was on the north side of the church, as at Gloucester. Nevertheless, from the 10th century English monasteries arranged their domestic quarters around a garden (*garth*) which was roughly rectangular and surrounded by covered ways. From the late-13th century there was increasing pressure to rebuild cloisters replacing the open walks with walks partially or entirely enclosed, using window tracery and stained glass. 'Cloister walks became more than covered ways, they formed the innermost enclosure of the monastery where the monks lived and worked. Naturally, the community wanted their living-space to be as pleasant and as beautiful as possible; the cloister at Norwich and especially at Gloucester are notable examples of just how beautiful a medieval cloisters could be' (Coppack, G. 1990).

Arguably, Gloucester's cloister is the most beautiful in the country. 'No Perpendicular interior in England can vie with the long vistas of Gloucester's cloister, at least from the point of view of uniformity. Here, if anywhere, the aesthetic ideal of the style finds its fulfilment' (Kidson, P. 1978). The fan vaulting turns each walk into an avenue of trees with overhanging branches. When built, the deep hues of the early 15th-century glass which filled the windows, and the painted decoration on the vault and walls added richness and warmth. As Leland (1541) noted, it is 'a right goodly and sumptuous piece of work' [46].

(fig 46) Great Cloister, west walk, from the south

Construction of the Cloister

The Great Cloister was built in the second half of the 14th century on the foundations of the Anglo-Norman cloister. The first six bays of the east walk were built (*c.*1360) by Thomas Horton (abbot 1351-77). There was then a break of 'many years' (*Historia*) before work resumed. The cloister was completed by Walter Froucester (abbot 1381-1412). The cloister may be seen as part of the rebuilding programme which began in 1331 and which gave the community a magnificent choir and then an equally magnificent cloister. The new choir provided the monks with a 'heavenly' setting for their daily round of worship, and the cloister with a singularly beautiful setting for other activities.

Fan Vaulting is a uniquely English form of vaulting. When it appeared in the mid-14th century it was a new concept in vault design and construction. Gothic vaulting was conceived as a series of supports or ribs between which were placed the warped surfaces of the webs. Transverse arches and ribs were placed in position, and the webs were built up.

In contrast, fan vaulting was made up of interlocking masonry, part of the tracery pattern being cut into each piece. Thus the ribs of the cones are not functional but purely aesthetic. 'The Gloucester cloister vaults are constructed entirely of jointed ashlar blocks each of which includes part of the tracery and part of the plain surfaces between' (Wilson, C. 1985). Because the jointed blocks in each course of the fan is identical, a large number of them could be cut from the same template ready for assembly - an early example of mass-production. The vault is held in place by the heavy, square key-stone in the central spandrel of each bay (Fitchen, J. 1961).

Fan vaulting was probably inspired by and derived from 13th-century rose windows.

> This possibility can be demonstrated by taking a photocopy of a picture of a rose window, such as that in the south transept of Notre-Dame in Paris, cutting around it and then cutting from any point on the circumference to the centre to form a cone. Held up above eye level the cone will look remarkably like the half-cones of Gloucester's fan-vaulting.

The earliest fans appear to have been small-scale, decorative forms, in tombs and chantries. The development of fan vaulting for larger architectural projects, such as a cloister, was probably centred in the Gloucester, Tewkesbury and Hereford area. The vaulting at Gloucester is the earliest, large-scale, fan vaulting to have survived, with the first bays of the east walk constructed before 1365. The two fan-vaulted monuments at Tewkesbury, though probably earlier, are on a far smaller scale. But Dr. Kidson has drawn attention to the 'complete assurance with which the fans are handled' at Gloucester which suggests that some earlier experiments had been carried out elsewhere.

The small holes in some of the cones were drilled soon after the outbreak of the Second World War (1939-45) so that, in the event of an incendiary attack, the fire-fighters' water would drain away before it caused serious damage.

Windows and Wall Panelling The east walk of the cloister is divided into ten bays, nine of which contain a Perpendicular window of eight lights crossed by a broad transom projecting externally like a shelf. The shelf was designed as a gutter to collect rain water, and to prevent rain from driving in through the unglazed lower part of the windows. Outside, buttresses with sculptured spouts (gargoyles) were designed to channel the water from the lean-to cloister roofs and throw it clear of the walls. In the north-east corner of the garth there is, for example, a gargoyle in the form of a man-servant pouring from a ewer.

The design of the window tracery in the east walk differs from that in the other walks. The east walk has nine windows of eight lights, and one of four; the other walks each have ten windows of six lights. In the east walk the window tracery is divided, with two main arches and a horizontal element at springing level made up of interlacing ogee archlets. This produces two pairs of elongated hexagons cusped equally top and bottom with a third pair centrally at the top, all with supermullions and Y tracery. The tracery of the windows in the other walks is less elaborate, the ogees do not interlace and there is one large elongated hexagon at the top. The design of the tracery, in all the walks, is repeated as blind tracery on the wall opposite.

There are simplifications in the design of the fans in the later walks, for example the use of trefoils and quatrefoils in the vault of the south walk, but these are comparatively minor and do not effect the harmony and beauty of the cloister as a whole.

Stained Glass   The medieval glass was extensively damaged during the Commonwealth. But when the windows were repaired in 1662-3 (using white, or clear, glass) some medieval glass was preserved. Possibly at the same time, the unglazed lower part of the windows was bricked up and plastered over. Since, at the time, the garth was the dean's private garden, this provided more privacy. When the reglazing of the cloister began in the mid-19th century the lights below the transoms were reopened, over a period of years, and glazed. In 1854 Dr. Jeune proposed that 'all the windows should be filled with painted glass depicting the *Story of Man's Redemption*'. The plan was to begin in the south-east corner with the Annunciation and the Nativity, and continue round to the north walk with the parables and miracles of Christ, and with incidents from his life and ministry. The west walk would tell the story of Christ's Passion, and the south walk his Resurrection and his Appearances to his disciples, concluding with the Ascension. Donors of glass were asked to restore the stonework of the windows as well as supply the stained glass. Brass plates below the windows in the east walk record their *in memoriam* donations. The first window to be inserted (E 5) was given by Mrs. Evans, widow of Dr. Thomas Evans, headmaster of the College School. Shortly afterwards another was given (E7), by Mrs. Claxton, widow of one of the canons. Dr. Jeune left Gloucester to become Bishop of Peterborough in 1864, and though the scheme continued to be supported for a while, in 1868 (the year Dr. Jeune died) interest turned to G. Gilbert Scott's major restoration of the choir (1868-73). As a result the iconographical scheme was never completed, even though reglazing resumed in the 1890s.

East walk

E 1	The Garden of Eden	Hardman 1865
E 2	Prophecy of Christ's Birth	Hardman 1865
E 3	The Nativity	Hardman 1866
E 4	The Visit of the Magi	Hardman 1865
E 5	The boy Jesus in the Temple	Hardman 1855
E 6	Jesus and John Baptist	Hardman 1866
E 7	The Baptism of Jesus	Hardman 1856
E 8	Christ and the Children	Ballantine of Edinburgh 1864

E 9 The Temptations of Christ   Hardman 1865
E 10 Christ's Healing Miracles   Clayton & Bell 1868

North walk

N 1-5 were bricked up until 1895 when the Freemasons of Gloucester glazed the windows, largely through the generosity of Baron de Ferrieres of Cheltenham.

N 6 The Lavatorium glass: depicts Biblical scenes with the theme of water. Hardman 1868   (designed by John H. Powell).

N 6-9 Over the Lavatorium, continuing the Biblical theme of water. Lavers and Westlake 1896

N 10 Christ, the Good Shepherd   Hardman 1898

N 11 The Virgin Mary with St Agnes and St Dorothy
Morris & Co. 1924 (designed by J.H. Dearle)

West walk

The stonework of the windows was restored (1856-7) and the windows filled with clear glass, preserving medieval fragments in the tracery.

South walk

S 1 The Resurrection of Christ   Hardman 1868
S 10 The Conversion and Martyrdom of St Paul   Hardman 1874

The carrels were glazed by Hardman over a number of years (1857-69) at the expense of Thomas Holt (hence the initials in the lower corners of the windows). On the central heraldic window, see below.

Ledgers and Memorials It was commonplace during cathedral and parish church restorations in the 19th century to re-lay ledgers and relocate memorials. Many of those in the nave, the lady chapel and the apsidal chapels were moved as well as those in the cloister. Most of the grave-slabs along the cloister walks date from the 18th and 19th centuries. But at the east end of the south walk the stone-bench incorporates a medieval grave marker with a plain floriate cross. A number of the wall-memorials are of interest, including those in the south walk to the Waller dynasty of Cathedral architects.

Cloister Garth The present lay-out of the cloister garden is the result of extensive work carried out under the supervision of the Cathedral architect, Basil Comely, in the 1990s {13}. Necessary excavation work revealed a cobbled working surface, possibly of the late 13th to 14th centuries; pottery fragments, some of Roman date, a Roman melon bead, and a carved stone head of a 14th c. knight. Several 18th c. monuments, buried in the 19th century, were also found. In the north west corner of the garth, outside the *lavatorium*, a 13th *c.* stone reservoir, excavated in the 19th *c.*, was backfilled and paved over. A nearby buttress was repaired, and a sculptured head of Kenneth Jennings (dean, 1988-96) set into it. 'The sculptor surprised us all with a delightful mini sculpture of a left-handed mason on the blind side of the buttress' (Basil Comely). On a buttress on the other side of the cloister door there is a sculptured head of Sieriol Evans (dean, 1953-73).

The garden was constructed with gravel paths and grey-sandstone steps, and new gravel and turfed areas. An innovation was the water feature in the centre of the garden, with water gently cascading down. The beds were restocked with plants suitable for the surroundings.

Monastic Cloister

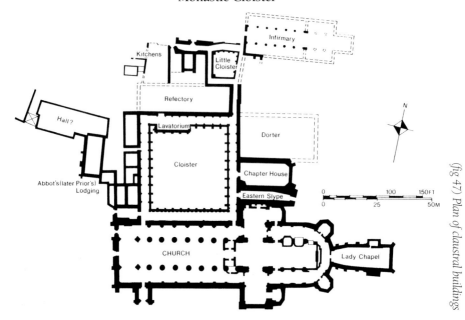

(fig 47) Plan of claustral buildings

The way in which the claustral buildings were arranged around the cloister of Westminster Abbey (built 1042-66, by Edward the Confessor) became the standard layout of Benedictine houses throughout the country [47]. This *Benedictine plan* was followed almost exactly at Gloucester, except that the cloister was built on the north side of the church and not on the sheltered south side. Nevertheless, *mutates mutandis* the arrangement of the buildings at Gloucester corresponds closely to the arrangement at Westminster, and at Durham as described in some detail in *The Rites of Durham*.

East Walk

There is no stone-bench along the east walk because the walk was used mainly as a passage connecting the main domestic buildings to each other and to the church. The first bays adjoin the wall of the north transept but then there are several doors which lead, or led, into claustral buildings.

Buildings which no longer exist are noted, but marked (+).

The first door led into the **eastern slype** (*locutorium*). The semi-circular arch of the original entry can be seen behind the wall tracery above the small door. The entry was apparently blocked up when the cloister was rebuilt in the 14th century. The small doorway was opened in 1874 and the slype used to store building materials and equipment. The slype now houses the Cathedral Treasury (1978), the entrance to which is in the north transept.

The locutorium was built against the end-wall of the transept and originally was only as long as the transept is wide. When the muniments room (now the choir vestry) was built over the slype, and then the library over the muniments room, the locutorium was extended eastward to almost twice its original length. There is wall-arcading on each side of the passage, with fifteen arches on the north but, originally, only eleven on the south (the space between the transept turrets). Along both sides of the slype there are the remains of stone benches, now covered over; medieval pigment survives on some of the arcade arches on the north side.

> Just inside the old entrance from the cloister there is a cresset which provided light at the west end of the long barrel-vaulted chamber. The rule of silence, strictly observed in the cloister, was relaxed in the locutorium so that members of the community could briefly discuss matters of immediate concern. The locutorium was also used as a passage from the cloister to the monks cemetery. Near the east end of the passage there is a door with steps leading down to the north-west crypt chapel, and another leading up to the east end of the library.

The next door leads up to the **library** (*librarium*). Built in *c*.1350, it is a large room, 26.2 m. long and 5.5 m. wide [48]. It retains much of its original open roof and some well-carved wooden corbels but none of its original fittings. There are eleven windows along the north side, each with two square-headed lights which provided light in each of the study bays. The wooden partitions have not survived. The large windows at either end are late Perpendicular. At Durham the library is described as 'standinge

(fig 48) Cathedral library (1990)

betwixt the chapter house and the Te Deum wyndowe, being well replenished with ould written Doctors and other histories and ecclesiasticall writers' (*Rites of Durham*).

> The library provided additional space in which the monks could pursue their literary and artistic interests, and for the abbey's growing collection of manuscripts and books. When Abbot Froucester completed the great cloister (*c*.1400) the monks also had a series of twenty study-recesses in the south walk. The south walk may have served as a *scriptorium* from time to time, but there were several rooms in the monastery which could have been used, including the library. The *Acta* show the importance of the Gloucester scriptorium and indicate the extent of its work. Though all-too-little of its output has survived, Professor Patterson in his edition of the *Original Acta of St Peter's Abbey c.1122-1263* identified the work of a number of scribal monks (albeit mostly anonymous) who were engaged on administrative work (Patterson, R. 1998). Apart from recording transactions and appointments, the scriptorium would have been used

for producing copies of texts required by the novices, and liturgical and devotional works for the monks themselves.

After the Dissolution the room was used by the boys of the College School, founded by King Henry VIII in 1541. An etching by Thomas Bonnor (1796) shows the schoolroom as it was in the late-18th century. The room was damaged by fire in 1849, and a new schoolroom was built on the north side of the chapter house. The old monastic library was then repaired and returned to its original use (1856). The library set up in the Chapter House during the Commonwealth was taken over by the Dean and Chapter in 1660. The collection was small but grew steadily over the following two hundred years.

> The library now contains abbey records, the Chapter Act Books, together with more than 6000 volumes on a wide variety of subjects. There is a published catalogue (1972) which includes a brief history of the collection and of the library-room.

Next, is the doorway of the **chapter house** (*capitulum*). The impressive 12th *c.* doorway, with its zig-zag ornament, was over-restored in the 19th century. Originally, there were round-headed openings on both sides of the entrance, but that on the right is blocked

(fig 49) Chapter House, as library (1798)

by the library stair. The large rectangular room (23m. long, and 10.4m wide) is divided into four bays, three of which are Anglo-Norman [49]. On each side there is a wall arcade of four arches to each bay. The shafts carrying the vaulting ribs are set back on the wall. The high barrel-vault is slightly pointed. The eastern bay, which is 15th-century Perpendicular, replaced the original apse, and was probably the work of Richard Handley (abbot 1458-1472).

The chapter house contains earlier work than the main structure. The way the north wall abuts the west wall suggests the blind arcading on this side was added *in front of* an earlier wall. The lower part of the west wall is reddened by fire, caused by the conflagration of 1102 'when the church together with the city was burnt with fire... (*Historia*) and 'flames destroyed the wooden cloisters' (Verey, D. 1978). It seems there was an earlier chapter house on the site, a timber-framed building erected even before work on the church began (1089).

> The *Historia* indicates that the foundations of the entire eastern arm were marked out before the foundation-stone was formally laid in 1089. Once the alignment of the great church was fixed, the position of the north transept could be determined, and a cloister and chapter house built on the site. The adjoining barrel-vaulted *locutorium* (eastern slype) must be one of the oldest parts of the monastic complex.

Abbot Serlo's rapidly growing community would have required an adequate chapter house. The first Baron Lacy is recorded as having been buried 'in the chapter house' in 1085; this prompted Masse to state the obvious: 'If he was buried in the chapter house, there must have been a chapter house for him to be buried in'.

The community gathered in the chapter house every morning after the Morning Mass :

* The original apse would have had a stone-bench around it providing seats for the abbot and prior and other senior obedientiaries, as at Durham. There were seats for the monks along the side walls beneath the arcading. The line where the seating abutted the wall can still be seen, particularly on the south side.

* Proceedings usually began with a commemoration of the saints and martyrs of the day, followed by prayers for the dead. Then the reading of a chapter of the *Rule of St Benedict* (hence the name of the building). This was followed by discussion of matters of common concern and the allocation of various administrative tasks. Time was also given to ventilating grievances, announcing and even inflicting punishment.

* Punishments varied from being separated from their brethren in the frater, being put on a diet of bread and water or allocated a junior place in the choir. More public humiliations could include lying down at the door of the church so that the rest of the community had to step over the penitent on their way in. The most serious punishments included imprisonment, exile or even expulsion from the Order.

* William the Conqueror held his Christmas court at Gloucester in 1085. This was the occasion when, in the words of the *Anglo-Saxon Chronicles*, he had 'deep speech with his witan' and ordered the great statistical survey of the country recorded in *Doomsday Book* (1086). Unless the Court met a mile to the north at the old Saxon royal palace at Kingsholm (Heighway, C. 1978), the King and his nobles would have been entertained by Abbot Serlo at St Peter's Abbey and held their witan in the timber-framed chapter house.

In the 13th century the community decided to commemorate some of its early benefactors. The names of only eight are recorded in the wall arcading though there was plenty of space for others. They included, on the south side, Robert, Duke of Normandy, the eldest son of the Conqueror: *Hic jacet... Robertus Curtus.* Below each name is an outlined heater-shield suggesting an intention to display the real or attributed arms of those commemorated, but there is no trace of colour within the shields. John Leland noticed the names when he visited Gloucester in 1541, and recorded them. But the chapter house was later whitewashed, and the names remained hidden until they were uncovered and restored in 1853.

On the north wall:

Left   Hic jacet Roger Lacey, Comes Hereford
        Hic jacet Ricus Strongbowe, filius Gilberti Comitis Pembroke

Right   Hic jacet Gaulterus de Laceio
        Hic jacet Phillippus de Foye miles

On the south wall:

Left   Hic jacet Berunardus de Novo Mercatii
        His jacet Paganus de Cadurcis

Right   His jacet Adam de Cadurcis
        His jacet Robertus Curtus

The first Baron Lacy fought with the Conqueror at Hastings and died in 1085. Another member of the family, Walter Lacy, was sent as a boy to St Peter's Abbey and became abbot (1131-39). He arranged the burial of Duke Robert (1134).

The east window, by Christopher Whall, is a memorial to those who fell in the South African War (1899-1902); below the window are panels giving the names of the officers and men of the Gloucestershire regiments who died. Beneath the carpet there is a 19th c. tile pavement. The designs of the tiles were copied from the tiles of the medieval floor which was revealed when, after two hundred years (1655-1855), the wooden floor of the Commonwealth library was removed.

The next doorway led up to the 14th c. **monks' dormitory** (*dorter*)+. The first dorter was aligned with the east wall of the cloister, north of the chapter house door, and may have extended over the east walk. But it was demolished in 1303, following a fire, and a new dormitory was built along the north side of the chapter house. The dorter was completed by 1313 - long before the apse of the Romanesque chapter house was demolished. Its position and date is confirmed by a window jamb (with a small ballflower attached to the capital of a slender shaft) adjoining the north-east corner of the chapter house.

At Gloucester little of the dorter undercroft survives because of the demolition of both the earlier and later dormitories, and rebuilding on the site. But the dorter undercroft usually consisted of three separate rooms, generally vaulted and entered from the cloister walk. In the area to the north of the chapter house there would have been a parlour, a warming house and other vaulted chambers, as well as the infirmary slype which has survived. Off the eastern end of the dorter was the reredorter (latrine block, or *necessarium*). In small monasteries the reredorter was sometimes only the width of the dorter, but in large houses, such as Gloucester, it often extended at right angles for a considerable length. Within the reredorter gallery there was a row of seats, which were divided by partitions, and in larger houses each cubicle had its own window. The great drain below the reredorter was flushed by a running stream; otherwise water was stored and the drain flushed at regular intervals.

Many chapter houses were low enough to allow access over the west end to a night-stair. This meant the monks could leave the dormitory and go to the choir for the night-time offices by way of a passage which led directly down a flight of steps into the transept. But in larger Benedictine houses, such as Canterbury, Worcester and Gloucester, owing to the height of the chapter house this arrangement was not possible. The monks had to go down the day-stairs and along the cloister walk into the church.

> There are examples of monastic dormitories at Durham and Westminster, at Cleeve in Somerset and at Ford in Dorset. At Durham the dorter still has its medieval roof, but nowhere do the internal partitions survive which, in the later Middle Ages, divided dormitories into individuals cubicles.
>
> The *Rites of Durham* has a description of 'the faire large house where all the monnks and the novices did lye, every monncke having a little chamber of wainscott...'. The obedientiary with responsibility for discipline, a sub-prior, slept with the monks in their dormitory and accompanied them to supper, eating with them in the frater. He locked the dormitory at night, opening it again when the monks were roused for the night

offices. Every night at about mid-night there was a 'privy serche by the supprior who did caule at every monnkes chambre, so se good order keapt, that none should be wanting' (*Rites of Durham*).

At the north end of the east walk is the **infirmary door**, leading into a vaulted passage (*infirmary slype*) and on through a small cloister which was also part of the infirmary range. Behind the Perpendicular panelling surrounding the doorway are the remains of an Early English doorway. There was a doorway of the same date and design (of two orders of colonettes and a richly moulded arch) at the other end of the north walk, but this is now filled with tracery and stained glass. The doorways date from the mid-13th century at the time when the frater and infirmary hall were rebuilt. Later, when the abbot's lodging was built on the north side of the precincts (*c.*1330), a passage from the lodging led past the west end of the infirmary hall, through the little cloister and slype to the great cloister and so to the church.

North Walk

The eastern bays of the north walk were probably used by the novices. Evidence of their presence may be found half-way down the walk in the stone bench on which

(fig 50) Monks' washing place

there is incised the 'board' used for such games as *Nine Men's Morris* and *Fox and Geese*. The novices would meet here with the novice-master for their lessons or, at other times, in one of the nearby chambers of the dorter undercroft.

At the west end of the walk is the monks' **washing place** (*lavatorium*, or *lever*) which extends out into the cloister garth [50]. It is exceptionally fine and well-preserved. It has a miniature fan vault similar in design to the vault in the cloister walks, and a series of eight two-light windows, and windows at each end. Half the width is taken up by a stone ledge on which there stood a lead tank containing water, with spigots extending over the lead-lined trough. Waste water ran out through holes in the trough to stone gutters outside and so into a drain.

* The laver was always sited near the entrance to the refectory for it was here that the monks washed before meals. It was 'architecturally distinguished to emphasise its spiritual and social importance, and was the most elaborate feature of the cloister' (Coppack, G. 1990).

* The curious opening in the cloister wall on the west side of the laver may be associated with a summoning bell. At Durham there was such a bell near the laver which was rung to summon the brethren to meals. Otherwise it may have been opened when the

lavatorium was used as a laundry, perhaps for passing baskets through to washing lines in the garth, or receiving buckets of water from the well.

* The drain outside the laver may be part of Helias' improvements to the abbey's water system when he ' made a channel for running water' (*Historia*). If so, it was built as a reservoir to serve the lavatorium in the Anglo-Norman cloister and, with the building of the present cloister in the 14th.c., it was converted into a drain.

* After the Dissolution the lavatorium continued to be used until early in the 18th century, mainly as a laundry. The drain was then filled in. It was excavated in 1887 but back-filled in 1996 to preserve it.

Opposite the lavatorium, in the thickness of the wall, is a groined recess, a **towel cupboard** (*manutergia*). At meal times, after washing their hands and faces and hanging up their towels, the monks proceeded in order of seniority to the frater. To the left of the towel cupboard where there is now a

(fig 50) Monks' drain outside lavatorium

window, there was the doorway. The door opened into a corridor, off which there was a broad flight of stairs leading up to the vestibule at the west end of the refectory.

When the frater was demolished early in the 17th century the doorway was bricked up. But at the end of the 18th century it was partially opened, fitted with tracery and glazed with fragments of medieval glass. In the words of a contemporary, this created a 'very pleasing aspect at the end of the west walk'. The window was enlarged in 1865 and filled with glass by Ballantine of Edinburgh, who had recently glazed a window in the east walk (E.8. 1864). It now contains glass donated by the Revd. C. H. J. Wilton, designed and installed in 1924 by H. Dearle of Morris & Co. of Merton Abbey.

The monks' **refectory** + (*frater*) was usually built along the side of the cloister walk opposite the church and usually on the ground floor. But because the cloister at Gloucester is on the north side of the church the refectory was raised on an undercroft. In 1246 a new refectory was built on the site of the Anglo-Norman refectory but extending a little further east. The sills of the windows were at the level of the top of the cloister walk's sloping roof. Remains of some of the sills can still be identified. The refectory was the largest room in the monastery being nearly 40m. long and more than 12m. wide, extending the full length of the north walk.

The vestibule of the refectory would have been screened off from the rest of the hall, and there may have been a loft or gallery above it. The service doors from the kitchen and the buttery usually opened onto the vestibule, and near the central door leading into the refectory there were often cupboards for napkins.

The internal arrangements of the frater included a raised dais at the far end where the abbot or prior sat flanked by the more senior obedientiaries. There were often mural decorations, frescoes or sculptures in relief, set into the wall above the high table; there is a notable example at Worcester. Along the side walls there were the benches and tables for the rest of the community. As at Durham, the hall was probably 'finely wainscotted on the north and south sides as also on the west' (*The Rites of Durham*). Set into the walls at the upper end of the hall was usually a *pulpitum*, or reading platform, from which a member of the community read from some suitable work as the monk ate in silence. A sign language enabled them to look after each others needs during meals (Harvey, B. 1993).

Part of the frater was badly damaged by fire shortly after the Dissolution, but it continued to be used until the early years of the 17th century when it was finally demolished. However, parts of the east end and a fragment of the north wall have survived together with the lower part of the south wall which is common to the cloister walk. What appears to be one of the responds of the Anglo-Norman undercroft (cellar) survives in the south-east corner of the infirmary cloister.

West Walk

The west walk has a stone bench along its entire length. In some monasteries this walk was used by the novices, and by the monks for exercise and meditation [46]. There are three doorways off the walk:

The prior's door The ogee-arched doorway (c.1400) led to a small courtyard behind the prior's lodging (now part of *Church House*). In the late 1970s this area and the adjoining undercroft were developed for the benefit of visitors; lavatories were built and a restaurant opened.

The *parlour door* The door at the south end of the walk leads down steps to the outer parlour. This vaulted chamber, with a stone bench along its walls, has been shortened. Here members of the community were allowed to meet visitors, family or friends, or do business with merchants and others.

The *processional door* The doorway in the thickness of the nave wall is vaulted and retains its original wooden doors. On the cloister side the doorway is unimpressive, but in the nave it is enriched with stone panelling for painted figures of saints, and jambs with niches for figures {14}.

This was the principal doorway leading into the quiet walks where the monks' lived and worked, and through which, on Sundays and at great festivals, the monks walked in procession, with their censers, lights and banners, returning to the church and to their places in the choir. The doorway would have added to the impressiveness of their entry, which would have been watched by those standing around in the aisles, or if aged and infirm, sitting on the stone benches (the sick and frail 'went to the wall').

South Walk

In the south walk there are twenty study recesses (*carrels*) each with its own small, two-light window {15}. The **carrels** are surmounted by a rich embattled cornice. As at Durham, a wainscot, or projecting wooden screen, probably divided them. The walk was closed off at the east end by a curtain and possibly at the west end.

There is a stone bench along the walk where those who were not working in the carrels could sit and read. The *Rites of Durham* describe how 'everyone of the old Monks had his carrell, severall by himselfs, that when they had dyned, they dyd resorte to that place in the cloister and there studyed upon there books, every one in his carrell, all the afternonne

(fig 51) South walk, Prinknash heraldic glass

unto evensong tyme. This was there exercise every daie'. The monks had access to a variety of works including 'the old auncyent written Doctors of the Church as other prophane authors, with dyverse other holie mens wourks, so that every one dyd studye what doctor pleased them best, havinge the librarie at all tymes to goe studie in besydes there carrells'. In view of the rule of silence, the south walk would rarely have been used as a *scriptorium*. There were other rooms in the monastery which could have been used, such as the library.

In the central window of the south walk there are twelve **heraldic panels and roundels** of Tudor date [51]. A panel in the window states: 'This glass came from Prinknash Park. Six panels were placed there by Abbot Parker, late abbot of St Peter's; the remainder by Dorothy Braye, wife of Sir Edmund Bridges of Coberley, later Lady Chandon of Sudeley and foundress of Winchcombe Almshouses'. At the Dissolution, Prinknash Park passed into the possession of the Brydges' family, Sir Edmund Brydges and his wife Dorothy owning the house from 1544 until 1573. These examples of Tudor heraldic-glass remained in the drawing-room windows at Prinknash until 1928 when, on the initiative of W. St Clair Baddeley of Painswick, they were bought for the nation and placed here (1930-31).

The glass is arranged in the following order:

Abbot Parker

Dorothy Braye	Edward VI (as Prince of Wales)	Sir Edmund Brydges (as Berkeley, Bray and Chandos)	Sir Edmund Brydges
Badge of Katherine of Aragon	Attrib. arms of Prince Osric	Henry VIII	Henry VIII and Jane Seymour

Badge of Abbot Parker   Attrib arms of
                                                          Prince Osric

After the Reformation there was little demand for stained glass of traditional design; instead heraldic glass (which often was of little religious significance and so caused no offence) was much in demand. The Royal Arms and badges, for example the badge of Katherine of Aragon (pomegranate), are particularly fine.

Chapter Eleven
THE LADY CHAPEL

A chapel dedicated to the Blessed Virgin (called 'Our Lady') was usually built eastward of the high altar, often forming a projection from the main building. From the 13th century onwards the practice of constructing such chapels as part of larger churches became common in England. At Gloucester in the 15th century it was decided to construct a large (semi) detached building to the east of the great east window. The chapel was built without aisles, but with little transepts; with the side elevation almost one continuous sheet of glass, and with a superb vault. The galleries of the 'transept' chapels have book-rests, and were probably meant for the singers of harmonised music, which at the time was just coming into fashion, but not as yet allowed in monastic choirs. The lady chapel had to be joined up to the presbytery, but the great east window was in the way. However, the difficulty was surmounted by 'a series of ingenious shifts and dodges, which must be seen to be believed' (Thorold, H. 1986).

The lady chapel was built between 1468 and 1482, during the abbacies of Richard Hanley (1457-72) and William Farley (1472-98). A chapel 'dedicated to the blessed Mary' (*Historia*) was built early in the 13th century but this was not an entirely new building. It was probably an extension of the axial chapel. Below the chapel, in the crypt, there is clear evidence that the crypt axial chapel was extended in the 13th century, presumably to provide foundations [24].

In the 14th century when the east end of the choir was reconstructed the Early English lady chapel was retained, and the axial chapel at tribune level also survived, at least in part. With the building of the present lady chapel [Pl. 11] in the late-15th century further modifications had to be made to both chapels to incorporate them as vestibule and gallery {4}. The tribune chapel retained its connection with the choir gallery; no staircase was built to provide direct access from the ambulatory, or the lady chapel itself.

Vestibule A Perpendicular screen backs onto the arched entrance of the Anglo-Norman chapel. It was glazed in the 1980s and wooden doors were made for the entrance. The walls of the vestibule are splayed outwards, resting on the extended foundations in the crypt. In both style and construction the vestibule is distinct from the main body of the building. Whereas the lady chapel was an entirely new four-bay rectangular building, the vestibule and gallery-chapel incorporate remains of earlier buildings. But a new elements is the low **pendant vault**. The earliest examples of such vaulting are at Oxford, at the Divinity School (*c*.1450) and at Christ Church. In Henry VII's Chapel at Westminster, where the pendants form the centres of fan-cones, the series of fans appear to be suspended in space from transverse ribs. The pendant vault here is a modest but still pleasing enrichment to the chapel. The **lead font** (*c*.1140) on the podium in the centre of the vestibule

(fig 52). Lady Chapel, section showing north elevation

*(fig 53) Lady Chapel,
12th c. lead font (Lancaut font)*

[53] came from the ruined Norman church of St James at Lancaut on the banks of the River Wye in Gloucestershire. It was removed from the church in 1890, and later restored by the Marling family of Stroud - as recorded on the inscription inside the rim of the font. The Marling family were patrons of the parish and owners of Sedbury Park estate in Tidenham. The family gave the font to the cathedral in 1940, and it was set on the podium in 1987.

* The font was probably made in the Bristol area. England was a principal producer of lead in the Middle Ages, and Bristol one of the more important centres for the production of lead-ware. The font was made from the same moulds as five others in Gloucestershire. The most complete of these cast-decorated lead fonts is at Frampton-on Severn (Glos) *c*.1130-40 They were cast in flat strips, which were then welded together to form a cylinder, the bottom being cast last. The other fonts have a strip of delicate palmettes at the top and bottom, but the bottom strip is missing on the Lancaut font.

* The decoration around the font comprises an arcade in low relief containing alternately scrolls and seated figures, probably intended to represent Apostles. Four of the fonts are decorated with twelve arcades, one with eleven and the Lancaut font, the smallest, with only ten.

   'The scrolls within the arcades resemble designs in manuscripts, for example, in the *Winchcombe Psalter c*.1130. The linear and decorative treatment of the figures resemble the Anglo-Saxon figure-style in, for example, the *Troper*, though the chip-carved band across the robe of one figure is a typically Romanesque device. The font is an impressive example of the continuing popularity of pre-Conquest designs in the 12th century' (Zarnecki, G. 1985).

The stained glass in the vestibule is by Christopher Whall (see below).

Gallery Chapel The chapel is supported on the east side by a substantial arch which is deeply moulded and contains a band of thirteen cinquefoils with shields, which originally contained armorial bearings. Resting on this arch is an open screen, rising to the full height of the building {4}. The structural importance of this arch and screen become clearer when the vault is examined in the roof-space. The vault over the gallery chapel is an Early English rib-vault and quite distinct from the lady chapel lierne vault, but they come together and rest on the arch of the open screen. The vault and the three windows which light the chapel can be seen through the stone screen. The west gallery window faces the great east window but the gap between them is wide enough to ensure that some light can pass through both. The only access to the gallery is from the choir tribune and through the Whispering Gallery.

LADY CHAPEL (1468-1482)

The lady chapel proper is divided into four bays. Only the vaulting shafts, which contain brackets and canopies for figures, separate the windows. There are traces of original colour on some of the niches. A stone bench runs along the side walls which are panelled to the window sills [54].

Design of the Chapel In its basic design and in its detail the chapel owes much to the adjoining choir, indeed it is a free-standing version of the choir on a smaller scale [Pl.11]. It has the same rectangular plan. The wall panelling continues as

tracery through the windows. The east end, above the reredos, is a wall of glass. The vault is a copy of the choir vault, on a smaller scale. It is as though the choir has been lifted out of its supporting framework, reduced in size and attached to the east end.

But the lady chapel is not the only late-15th *c.* building in the country to be influenced by the 14th-century remodelled choir. After more than a hundred and twenty years, such major buildings as St George's Chapel, Windsor (begun 1474), King's College Chapel, Cambridge, and the magnificent Edward VII's Chapel (1485-1500) at Westminster Abbey owe their basic design to Gloucester's Perpendicular choir. Referring to King's College, Cambridge Dr. Kidson comments:

(fig 54) Lady Chapel, view to the east end

'The nearest prototype is Gloucester's choir, and of all the Perpendicular buildings in England which were influenced by *that precocious design* it is the only one which deliberately takes up the problem of the homogeneous Perpendicular interior at the point where it was left at Gloucester, and finds for it a wholly satisfying solution. The chapel was conceived as Gloucester choir, with all the extraneous masonry removed - that is, with all the panels free to be filled with glass' (Kidson, P. 1978).

Lierne Vault At this period (1468-82) one might have expected a fan-vault to complement such a fine Perpendicular interior. Instead the master mason went for a replica of the choir vault, with its net-work of ribs and bosses, and a ridge-rib with a parallel rib on either side. 'Here and at Great Malvern the independent school of vaulting that had begun with the nave at Tewkesbury retained its individuality to the end, preserving as its hallmark a pair of subsidiary longitudinal ribs on each side of the main ridge' (Pevsner, N. & Metcalf, P. 1985). Yet Kidson is surely right: 'The choir and lady chapel vaults at Gloucester strike the only discordant note. The vaults have what is undoubtedly the most involved lierne pattern ever devised in England. Yet few people would acclaim the result as something visually satisfying.

It is evident that the intense congestion was an attempt to match and complete the all-over patterns on the walls and windows below. But whereas lierne vaults accord well with Decorated window tracery, their irregular compartments merely look untidy when they surmount tier upon tier of rectangular panels' (Kidson, P. 1979). One can only imagine how magnificent the lady chapel would be with fan-vaulting. The **bosses** are all of foliage designs, with six exceptions; a grotesque centaur, three fishes arranged in a triangle, a fish curved round so that the tail and head come close together, a dragon coiled up between spreading three-lobed leaves, two dragons fighting head to head, a dragon biting the tail of another dragon and two dragons each biting the tail of the other!

Chantry Chapels In the second bay from the east end there are small chantry chapels (*oratoria*), with singing galleries (*cantoria*) above them. It has been suggested that they were the chantries of the two abbots who built the lady chapel, but there is no record of their being buried in them. At ground level the chantries have fan vaults, ingeniously adapted to a fairly narrow rectangular plan. The galleries have rib vaults with bosses which have been polychromed. Access to these galleries is by way of small staircases set into the angle of the wall. Each gallery is supported by a strong ogee arch, set into the screen in front of the lower chapel. The stone screen extends up in front of the gallery on the south side but there is no such screen in front of the gallery on the north side. The intention may have been to put an organ in the open gallery. At the front of the upper chapels there are sloping, stone shelves for books and music.

> Cut into the stone of the book-rest of the north gallery is a country scene showing a gentleman of the Commonwealth period with his dog, and in the distance a church with a tall spire. This graffiti may have been the work of a pupil of the College School. The school used the lady chapel for morning prayers and for lessons over many years.

The **north chantry** contains a full-length effigy of Bishop Goldsborough (d.1604) lying on a tomb-chest. The bishop is robed in his white rochet, black chimere, with lawn sleeves, scarf, ruff and black skull cap {6}. There are fragments of medieval glass in the windows, but the three-light window at the east end, designed by John W. Lisle, was made in the Kempe studio (1895). It was given *in mem*. A. J. Lawford of Oswestry (1859-85) and depicts St Martin:

(i) on horseback being approached by a beggar
(ii) as a bishop and
(iii) being visited by Christ on his deathbed.

The **south chantry** contained the tomb of Dr. William Nicholson (bishop of Gloucester 1660-72) but in 1896 it was dismantled and the memorial tablet which blocked up the east window was removed to the nave. The altar-tomb is to Thomas Fitzwilliam (d.1579). The reredos has embroidery designed by W. H. R. Blacking. The stained glass in the chapel is in memory of church musicians, including Samuel Sebastian Wesley (d.1876), a notable composer of English church music and one time organist of the cathedral (by James Fisher of London 1896); Sir Alfred Herbert

Brewer, organist of the cathedral 1897-1928 (by Veronica Whall 1929); Dr. Charles Harford Lloyd, organist of the cathedral 1876-82 (by Christopher Whall jnr. 1921), and panels by Caroline Swash (1992) in memory of the composer, Herbert Howells; and by Fiona Brown (1997) in memory of Dr Herbert Sumsion. The design of the Sumsion glass is 'very fluid and attempts to echo the flow of his music in the horizontal lead-lines' (Brown). The panel reflect the seasons, and includes Sumsion's signature above the inscription: 'Composer and Cathedral Organist 1928-1967'.

Reredos The reredos was almost totally destroyed soon after the Dissolution or possibly during the Commonwealth (1651-60). In 1980 the Dean and Chapter commissioned Professor Evetts of Newcastle University to design, and Mrs. M. Pallister of Cheltenham to work, panels for the three main niches. These depict, left to right, the *Annunciation, the Nativity* and *the Visit of the Shepherds*.

In the past attempts have been made to cover up the damage, or to improve the appearance of the reredos in some way. Dr. Martin Benson, bishop of Gloucester (1734-52), put up a huge *Radiance*, a golden sun of stucco in front of the central section (T. Bonnor's engraving 1796). In the early years of the 20th c. three Gothicised painted panels were erected in front of it. In the 1960s a large curtain was hung over it. Though a ruin it is best left as it is and not covered up, or 'restored' in any way. It is part of the history of the building and a salutary reminder of the damage done to the country's architectural and artistic heritage by those whose religious zeal led to death and destruction.

When first erected (c.1480) the reredos would have looked magnificent, richly coloured and with polychromed figures in its three main niches, surrounded by thirty-six smaller figures. Part of the original paint-work survives, the colours including yellow, blue and red. The reredos is unusual in possessing contemporary graffiti giving the names of the saints whose statues once adorned it. Names are incised in the stone at the back of a number of the niches. All were written after the reredos had been assembled for certain letters are scratched across the cement between the stones. Clearly, the purpose was to ensure that each figure was placed in the right niche. Among those named are: Arilda, King Lucius, Keneburga, Dorothy, St John the Evangelist, Botolph, Bridget, Margaret of Antioch and St Thomas the Apostle. There is a certain symmetry in the arrangement of the saints, and appropriately in a lady chapel, virgin saints and martyrs predominate. Among those named is a high proportion of Celtic saints - evidence of the abbey's links with the Welsh church, but others like Keneburga relate specifically to the history of the abbey.

East Window The east window, of nine lights, is divided by two transoms into three tiers. It contains medieval glass which is in such a confused and disordered state that it is difficult to make any sense of it {9}. Kerr called it 'a salad of richly-toned fragments'. The glass is mainly of the 14th and 15th centuries and from other windows in the cathedral, though there are fragments of the original glazing, some still *in situ*. These fragments are quite distinctive in their tonal quality and style of painting, and are mainly to be found in the tracery and in certain lights, in the cusped heads of the lights, and in the small *oculi* of the lowest tier. The window was probably leaded up in its present form at the end of the 18th century when interest in antiquities, ancient and medieval, was becoming widespread. This was seen as a way of preserving fragments and larger areas of medieval glass. Fragments from other windows were arranged to form limbs and draperies, and remains of heads were placed two-thirds up each light to give the impression, from a distance, of standing figures.

A *rebus* conceals the identity of the **donor** of the original window. In some of the small quatrefoil openings of the lights on the bottom tier (for example, the second light in from the left) there is a medieval comb and a tun (or, barrel). The comb, on the left, is preceded by an initial E, and followed by the letters TO, and the barrel or tun, on the right, has CO written beside it. This is the rebus for the surname COMPTON (comb-tun). The reference is probably to Edmund Compton, father of Sir William Compton (1482-1528) who was a friend of Henry VIII and who became Constable of Gloucester Castle in 1512, and of Sudeley in 1513, and Chief Steward of the abbeys of Gloucester and Cirencester. The glass could have been given by Edmond Compton, or by his son, Sir William, in memory of his father.

Though the glass is so fragmented, it repays close study with binoculars {10}.

* The three central lights at the top of the window are filled, for the most part, with inserted glass, possibly from windows in the north aisle of the nave.

* The smaller tracery lights on either side contain fragments of the original glazing, some fragments being *in situ*. The principal figure on the left is a crowned Madonna, and as there are remains of a similar figure in the small lights at both ends of the top tier, these four lights may have contained miraculous stories about the Blessed Virgin.

* On the tier below, the second light in on both sides appears to be scenes in the open air, the blue sky or landscape being continued into the cusped heads. At the top of the light on the left there is a group of tonsured heads, with the fragments below suggesting a group of monks in procession, one carrying a processional cross. Similarly, at the top of the light on the right-hand side, there is a group of mitred heads, presumably bishops (or mitred abbots) also in procession and preceded by a more ornate processional cross {10b & c}.

* In the cusping of other lights on this tier, there are fragments of architectural canopies, suggesting figures-in-niches alternated with pictorial scenes. This was a feature of stained-glass design from the end of the 15th century into the 16th (e.g. the east window of St Margaret's, Westminster, completed 1519).

* In the extreme right-hand light of the middle tier there are substantial remains of a *Madonna* in a deep red robe with jewelled border, standing on the crescent moon in the midst of a glory of gold rays. The head of the Infant Christ has been replaced by imported fragments. But at the bottom of the light is an inscribed band of text: *S(an)c(t)a Ma(ria) cel(es)t(i) luminei.* This figure probably occupied a central light.

* The three central lights of the bottom tier contain glass from a Jesse Tree window.

The glass may have been made at Great Malvern. A comparison of fragments in the window with the late-medieval glass at Malvern Priory seems to confirm the possibility. Dr. Richard Marks argues that the window was made at the Twygge-

Wodshawe workshop. 'Patronage links explain some of the more important commissions undertaken by the workshop. Its first major patron was Bishop Alcock of Worcester who between July 1480 and October 1482 entrusted it with the glazing of the east window of Little Malvern Priory. Alcock moved in the same royal administrative circles as Bishop William Waynflete of Winchester. Alcock would have been acquainted with Abbot Farley of Gloucester under whom the lady chapel was completed. The workshop could, therefore, have been responsible (at least in part) for the glazing of the lady chapel in the period c.1472-93 (Marks, R. 1993).

Tile Pavement Originally, the entire chapel was tiled. In the vestibule the tiles (now covered by carpet) have lost most of their glaze and pattern through the treading of feet and years of neglect. In the floor near the Clint memorial (half way up on the right) there is a miscellany of medieval tiles from different parts of the building relaid here in the 19th c. to preserve them. In the sanctuary there is considerable patching, but the pattern of the original tile-pavement is still discernible, particularly on the north side. Between rows of dark tiles set diagonally to the axis of the building decorated tiles are laid in groups of four and sixteen. In the 17th and 18th centuries the lady chapel became a favoured place for burials, with the result that the medieval pavement was all but destroyed. In the late-19th century restoration of the chapel there was some rearrangement of the ledgers.

Monuments The most prominent monument is the impressive figure of *Sir John Powell* (d.1713), one-time town clerk of Gloucester city, and a judge of the Queen's Bench who is represented in his gown, hood, mantle and coif. It is a noble figure by one of the outstanding statuaries of the early 18th century, Thomas Green of Camberwell. The putti on the base are beautifully sculpted, but sadly damaged {7}. To the east of the Powell monument is a memorial to *Elizabeth Williams* (d.1622), wife of W. J. Williams {8} and daughter of Dr. Miles Smith, bishop of Gloucester (1612-24). The bishop is buried near-by beneath a simple ledger. Elizabeth is shown laying on her side, raised on one elbow, with an infant on a pillow. The inscription records that she died in childbirth. On the wall opposite there is a smaller memorial with a frontal-kneeling figure and another moving inscription. This is to Elizabeth's sister, *Margaret Clent* (d.1623) who also died in childbirth {5}. Both memorials are by Samuel Baldwin of Stroud (Verey, D. 1978). Near the Clint memorial is a bronze tablet by Drury to *Dorethea Beale*, founder and first Principal of Cheltenham Ladies College. The inscription is by Eric Gill c.1907.

Stained Glass In November 1897 Christopher Whall (d.1924), who was one of the acknowledged leaders of the Arts and Crafts Movement of the late 19th century, was asked to submit sketches for the two windows in the vestibule. These were accepted and the following year he was commissioned 'to reglaze the windows of the lady chapel excluding the windows in the sanctuary' [55], {11 & 12}.

Reacting against the production-line approach of many of the Victorian stained glass firms, he worked with his staff supervising each stage of the craft process. He sketched out the designs in all their Ruskinian detail, with tangled stems and foliage in place of the conventional medieval architecture. The slab glass he used, known as Prior's Early English, had been recently invented and was renowned for its subtlety of hue and texture combined with a brilliance and range of colour. The contrast between his glass and that of Heaton, Butler & Bayne's sanctuary window could hardly be more stark. Aware of the architectural context of the windows, Whall insisted on large areas of pure white glass, both in quarry glazing and

(fig 55) Lady Chapel, detail of Christopher Whall glass

figures, giving them a medieval 'silvery' quality and a brilliance which accords well with the varied hues of the lady chapel east window. In the cusping of some of the lights there is glass from the original glazing. Whall preserved further fragments in the tracery lights. He emphasised to his students and apprentices that 'ancient glass must be isolated out of respect and as a lesson'. (Note, however, that the fragments in the cusping of S IV were leaded up by C. H. Dancy in 1892). Whall was a master in the use of the lead-line. For him the lead was not simply a functional expedient, a necessary evil, but an integral part of the design of the window (Whall, C. 1905, reissued 1999 by Peter Cormack). In this connection the windows should also be studied from outside the building (as should the Denny windows in the south east ambulatory chapel).

The **iconographical scheme** for the glazing is masterly. In Whall's words: 'The general idea illustrated is the Dignity to which Human Nature has been raised by the Incarnation of Christ through the Virgin Mary' (Whall, C. 1905).

In the vestibule is *The Fall and Deprivation of Paradise* on the north side, and on the south side The *Restoration in the sacrament of the Eucharist*. In the main body of the chapel at the top of each window is an archangel, and below one or more of the nine Angel Choirs. In the main tier below the angels, and occupying one or more lights in the centre, is an incident in the story of the *Incarnation*, between figures of saints. On the next tier down, are British saints, with saints of the church in the north on the north side, and saints of the church in the south on the south side. In the chancel, on the north side, the window contains Scriptural saints, and at the bottom of the window incidents connected with the Incarnation {12}.

The subjects of the individual windows and their dates are as follows (numbered from the east end, the east window being designated as EI).

N II   1909   The Reconciliation of Man to God through the Incarnation
N III   1913   St Cecilia
N IV   1901   The Annunciation
N V   1901   The Childhood of the Blessed Virgin Mary
N VI   1899   Man's Fallen State
S II   (A window by Heaton, Butler and Bayne - see below)
S III   1926   St Christopher (by Veronica Whall in mem. of her father)
S IV   1901   The Nativity
S V   1902   The Salutation
S VI   1900   The Eucharist

Whall later produced a design for the south window in the sanctuary which had been specifically excluded from his contract; it was never made, but the cartoon survives in the archives of the William Morris Museum, Walthemstow, London.

Peter Cormack points out that the glazing of the lady chapel was 'Whall's first opportunity to work in a major medieval building. It offered him a 'daunting challenge, to combine, on the one hand, his frankly modern style and personal approach to workmanship and materials with, on the other, an acute sensitivity to the architectural context. That the Gloucester windows remain, a century later, the finest post-medieval ensemble of stained glass in any English cathedral testifies to Whall's profound understanding of the distinctive national tradition of glazing. Challenging as the Gloucester commission was in terms of design, the limited funds available also meant that little or no profit could be made, so Whall had to undertake the work in a true spirit of sacrifice. His own dedication and enthusiasm, however, were infectious and his staff readily agreed to a reduction in wages for the duration of the commission' (Cormack, P. 1999).

Sanctuary Window S II Just months before Whall was given his commission to reglaze the chapel, the Dean (Dr. H. D. M. Spence-Jones) had given permission to the family of Sir Joseph Lee of Ross, Herefordshire, to glaze the south window in the sanctuary in memory of Sir Joseph and three of his children. The window was made by Heaton, Butler and Bayne. Beside the brilliance of the medieval fragments of the east window and surrounded by Whall's fine series of windows, the Lee window is shown up as a hideous example of late-Victorian trade-glass. The window prevented Whall from completing his iconographical scheme.

The window, however, has some interest as an example of 19th-century 'family album' design. Note the photographic likeness of various members of Sir Joseph's family used as heads of angels, prophets and apostles. The beards of members of the Edwardian family contrast with the more conventional representation of other figures, and the women of the family, with their 'buns', somewhat date the angels! Five of the grandchildren appear as cherubs at the bottom of the window.

There are few medieval monastic foundations in the country with a greater range of claustral and precinct buildings than Gloucester. Among the buildings which have survived, entire or in ruins, are the main gateway and the gatekeeper's accommodation, the abbot's (later the prior's) lodging including his private chapel, the great cloister with the monks' washing-place and a row of twenty carrels, the chapter house, the library, the outer parlour and eastern locutorium, the cellarer's office, cellars and undercrofts, the infirmary hall (in ruins), the infirmary cloister and dining hall, and remains of the infirmarer's lodging. There are fragments of other medieval buildings embedded in houses around the precinct, but little remains of the monks' dormitory and refectory [Pl. 4].

West Side

When the Anglo-Norman abbey was being laid out in the late-11th century the way

(fig 56) Cathedral west front (Bartlett, W.H. 1828)

in which buildings were arranged within the precincts of Benedictine monasteries was well established and widely adopted. At Gloucester this *Benedictine plan* appears to have been followed closely, with the great court on the west side of the church, between the main entrance and the cloister. In some larger monasteries, such as Gloucester, a range of buildings divided the great court into an outer and inner court, with a gateway in the dividing range {23}.

West Front This is not one of England's most impressive but it is not without interest [56]. Built by John Morwent (abbot 1420-37) it replaced the original Anglo-Norman west front, as altered in the 13th century.

> Many details of Morwent's work such as panelling and niches have been lost together with statuary. A graceful balustrade over the west door has been replaced by a castellated parapet, a dull and inappropriate piece of early Victorian work. Behind this parapet there is a passage linking the turret stairs on the south side with stairs on the north side which lead to the north aisle roof space.

The **great west window** is set well back on its foundation wall. According to Leland's informant (1541) the window was intended to match the great east window. The principal mullions are buttressed, and the buttresses are pierced (to allow as much light as possible into the church). Again, as in the great east window, plain transoms cross the lights on the outside, but inside the cusping is elaborate. The **balustrade** above the window is set forward of the roof-line, which is somewhat unusual.   At the top of the window graceful counter-curves sweep upwards to enriched crockets and finial. There is a small sculpted figure enclosed within them. The ornate cross at the apex is a copy (1987) of a mid-19th century cross which replaced a far-simpler cross (Carter, J. 1809 & Britton, J. 1829). At either end of the balustrade there are turrets of open work supported by miniature flying buttresses [Pl.10].   The **west door** is rather plain, with shields in the spandrels for the royal arms and the arms of the abbey. To the left of the side-door (the *Dean's Door*) and at a lower level there is a door leading into a vaulted chamber (the monks' *parlour*) with steps up to the great cloister {17}.

Church House, which adjoins the west front on the north side was originally the abbot's lodging [Pl. 2, 3 & 9]. In the 14th century the abbot moved into a new and larger house on the north side of the precincts and his old lodging was assigned to the prior. The oldest part of the building is a Norman tower, about 10.4 m. square, consisting of three large chambers, one upon another, which were the abbot's **private apartments**.   These still have windows enriched with zig-zag mouldings. In the north-east corner there was a **garderobe**, now demolished but shown on Carter's plan (1809). The arched doorways are blocked up, but they retain their original decoration. There is another blocked doorway with 12th c. decoration in the north east corner of the basement.

Between the original tower and the church there is a two storey building. At ground level is the **parlour** {17} leading to the cloister, and above it there is a vaulted room which may once have been used as a **chapel**. A late-medieval tile pavement at the east end was probably the sanctuary area. In the 13th century a vaulted **antechamber** was added in front of the original tower.

On the ground floor of the original tower there would have been a reception room and probably accommodation for one or two servants. The enlarged first floor consisted of the abbot's dining room, bedroom, solar and chapel. Above the abbot's apartments there were probably **guest rooms**, for special guests such as high ecclesiastics, royal visitors and nobles. At the back there was a **courtyard**, probably enclosed by covered ways on the north and west sides so that the abbot, and later the prior, could cross to the cloister under cover, entering through a small doorway in the west walk. Part of the courtyard remains (on the left at the foot of the steps off the cloister west walk).

In the 13th century a large hall, with an undercroft for domestic purposes, was added on the north side. It was connected to the abbot's lodging by a turret stair and landings. This was the hall where he entertained guests. The **hall** has been substantially altered over the centuries, especially its fenestration. It is now divided into two rooms, one of which (*the Laud Room*, after William Laud, dean of Gloucester 1616-21)) is lined with Jacobean panelling and its 15th c. roof underdrawn by a plaster ceiling. In the other part of the hall, which is known as the *Henry Room*, the timbers of the open roof have curious painted decoration.

To the north of the abbot's hall there is a larger hall, also with an undercroft, which was part of the almoner's range and which, from the 13th century, divided the great court into two. Originally this **great hall** {18} extended westward as far as the inner gate, but at sometime before the end of the 15th *c.* it was shortened (see below). At the dissolution of the monastery (1540) the prior's lodging became the Deanery. A range of buildings adjoining the cloister wall had been removed by the mid-1730s and a brick coach house and stable built on part of the site.

The old **Deanery** was restored and remodelled in 1863, and the west front including the tower was virtually rebuilt. At the same time additional domestic accommodation was built at the back of the north block (hence the blocked up windows in the east wall of the Henry Room). In 1940 the dean moved to a house on the west side of Miller's Green, and the south block of the old Deanery became diocesan offices (1948) and was renamed *Church House*. In the 1950s the north block, including the great hall, was extensively restored, and thereafter used for meetings and social functions.

St Mary's Gate, the 'great gate' of the abbey, is first recorded in 1190 {16}. Though the west facade is not over-impressive it is typical of monastic gateways of the 12th century. The entrance arch is low and pointed in keeping with the Transitional character of the whole building. The gateway consists of a *gateporch*, with an inner arch where the gates were hung, and a gatehall, an inner vaulted area which had another pair of gates at the far end opening into the great court. There are two arched recesses in the south wall, and a door on the north side with stairs leading up to a large room (now entered from St Mary's Square). The vault of the gatehall has pierced chevron ribs. There is similar deeply undercut and pierced chevron at Ozleworth, Gloucestershire.

> Gatehouses had a least one upper storey, providing accommodation for the gatekeeper. He would close the gates at night and open them in the morning, check the wagons entering and leaving the monastery and ask all visitors to state their business.   There were other gates set into the abbey walls, notably *King Edward's Gate* on the south side, but only its west tower has survived.

When Bishop Hooper was burnt at the stake outside St Mary's Gate in 1553 notables were said to have viewed proceeding from the room over the archway. A Victorian memorial now marks the spot where the Bishop died.

The house adjoining St Mary's Gate on the north side (*Community House*) was rebuilt *c.*1774 and designed to face into the Green. It contains medieval work and is probably on the site of the **almonry** (though the timber-frame house on the south side of the gate is often said to be on the 13th *c.* undercroft of the old almonry). At the almonry the abbey's charity was distributed to the poor and sick, and to all who came to the 'dole-house' door seeking help. A group of pensioners, and others who needed and deserved more long-term care, were housed and fed there, and in some monasteries boys who were being educated at the abbey, lodged with the almoner. There was a variety of other buildings around the **great court** having to do with general maintenance and the practical needs of the community. There were barns for storage and stabling for horses. In the south-west corner of the precincts (College Yard) was the miskin, or dung heap. In large monasteries there were permanent masons' lodges, carpenters' workshops and drawing offices, and workshops for plumbers and glaziers. In describing the fire which swept through the city on 11 May 1190 the *Historia* states that 'almost all the workshops attached to the abbey were set on fire, as were 'two churches, the church of St Mary in front of the abbey gate and St Oswald adjoining the wall'. Workshops, either free-standing or lean-to, being made of wood easily caught fire. Somewhere in the outer court was the **guesthouse** for the poorer classes. Its exact position is not known, but it was probably against the south precinct wall or on the west side near the stabling. Guests and travellers of higher rank were entertained in the great hall at the east end of the almonry range (*magna aula*, also described as *aula hospitum*). Hospitality at monasteries was organised according to rank or status, with distinguished guests being entertained by the abbot or prior. The king himself, with his entourage, often stayed at large abbeys since they provided the most suitable and sometimes the only adequate accommodation.

Precinct houses Adapted from monastic to domestic use soon after the Dissolution, many of the houses around the Lower Green were rebuilt in the 18th century.
The row of four houses on the **west side** (nos.10-13) was built in 1735-36 on the site of the bishop and dean's stables and coach houses. The tall sash windows of no. 12 were designed for a ground floor assembly room, used in the 18th century for concerts and social gatherings.
One of the most imposing houses in the Green (no.9) stands at the south end of this row. Built in c.1707, it is of three storeys and five bays, with a central pediment and angle-pilasters. A new doorcase was added in the mid-18th century (Herbert, N. 1988).
The houses along the **south side** were substantially altered in the 18th and 19th centuries. No.7 was given bow windows and much altered internally, and the house on the corner (no.6), the former sexton's house, was extensively remodelled in 1813 and given a late Georgian front.
On the **north side** beside St Mary's Gate is *Community House* (see above). For many years a prebendal house, it is now used as offices. On the other side of the inner gate is another house built in the 17th century but later remodelled. For many years it has been the residence of the cathedral organist. The east end of the house adjoins entrances to the *Parliament Room* and the *Undercroft Restaurant*.
Standing in the centre of the Lower Green is a war memorial to the Royal Gloucestershire Hussars Yeomanry (1923). The bronze panels with bas reliefs are by Adrian Jones, an army veterinary surgeon who in his retirement modelled horses. He had work exhibited at the Royal Academy from 1883. The panels depict incidents from the regiment's campaign in the Middle East.

Miller's Green

The **inner gate**, leading into Miller's Green, dates from the 14th century and consists of a single passage covered by a simple lierne vault. There is a blocked door on the west side which probably led into the almoner's lodging.

> The *Deanery* (no.1) is the large house on the **west side** of the Green. The tall house adjoining it on the north side (no.2) is thought to be on the site of the abbey mill. Further to the north, beyond the high wall, is the 19th c. Bishop's Palace, now part of the King's School (see below).
>
> On the **east side** the Queen Anne house (no.6) was built in the late 17th century. Beside it is a small dwelling, built in the lane which once allowed access to the cellars and kitchen area. At one time it was a washhouse and stable associated with a house around the corner (No.3). The house on the corner (no.4) was once two separate houses, 'the schoolmaster's and the usher's house' (Eward, S. 1985). On the **south side** the organist's house (no.7) was built c.1670 on the site of the demolished west end of the great hall.

Great Hall (*Parliament Room*) On the south side of the Green is what remains of a one-time large and important building, the abbey's great hall {18}. This timber-framed building stands on a 13th *c.* undercroft and originally extended westward as far as the inner gate. It was a building of considerable architectural interest as may be seen from the jamb of an elaborate window at the north-west corner. The oriel windows were added in the 1960s (rather inappropriately considering the date of the building). According to St John Hope the banquet, during which King Edward II made his famous remark, took place in the great hall, or *aula magna*, rather than in the abbot's own hall (Hope, St J. 1898). The *Historia* records that 'the abbot received the king with honour. Sitting at table in the abbot's hall and seeing there paintings of the kings his predecessors, he jokingly asked the abbot (John Thoky) whether he had his portrait among them or not; to which the abbot replied, prophesying rather than merely talking, that he hoped he would have him in a more honourable place'.

When King Richard II held his parliament (1378) at Gloucester, the king and his nobles used every available hall in the abbey. The *Historia* notes that 'discussion of laws about arms took place in the refectory; the guest hall was decided upon for general parliamentary matters; secret debates among the nobles were held in the guest chamber, and general debates in the chapter house'.

Around the inner court in medieval times were the kitchens, storerooms and cellars, the pantry, buttery and larder, the mill and probably the brewery and bakery. Little is known about these buildings from historical records. The **bakehouse** may have stood in the corner near the great gate, and the mill was on the north side of the court. There is a **mill** stone in the basement of no.2. The abbey mill was leased out and continued to be used until the early years of the 18th century. In the north-west corner of the precincts (now the garden of the King's School) there was an orchard and **vineyard**. The *Historia* refers to 'the Vineyard which was earlier cultivated for the fruit of various trees, as well as vines'.

North Side

King's School, founded by King Henry VIII, occupied the old monastic library until 1850 when a new schoolroom was built on the north side of the chapter house. With the growth of the school in the years after the Second World War (1939-45) it took over the *Bishop's Palace*. This huge building was erected on the site of the abbot's lodging in 1860-2. The architect was Ewan Christian (1814-96).

The medieval **Abbot's Lodging**, which the bishops of Gloucester occupied until 1856, was begun by John Wygmore (abbot 1329-37) when he was prior [Pl.5].

It was a baronial-style residence, more in keeping with the times and with the dignity and demands of the abbot's office than the old residence beside the west end of the church. Its resemblance to a secular manor house is the result of it being free-standing, its plan not influenced by the necessity of being attached to the claustral ranges. In the later Middle Ages it was enlarged and enriched, culminating in the work carried out by the last abbot, William Parker (abbot 1514-39) which included the construction of oriel windows in the long gallery. The remains of the windows can still be seen in the gallery wall which forms part of the north precinct wall in Pitt Street.

At the Dissolution the lodging comprised of two halls, two dining chambers, two kitchens, four butteries, four pantries, a court room, thirteen other chambers, two galleries, a chapel and various cellars and storerooms. This was the Bishop's Palace for more than three hundred years, during which time other improvements were carried out. Plans of the old building (made in 1856) were reproduced in *Records of Gloucester Cathedral* (1897) with notes by St John Hope. In 1849 the old medieval building was almost totally destroyed by fire and the charred remains had to be demolished. The present building was then erected on the same site. Part of the building was left standing, for example the north fascade on the south side of Pitt Street, which now serves to screen the 19th c. house from the road. After the Second World War (1939-45) a more suitable house was built for the bishop at the other end of Pitt Street (1954), and the *Old Palace* or *Palace House*, as it came to be called, was then taken over by the King's School.

On the east side of Miller's Green and around to the infirmary arches were the buildings of the cellarer's range, and the infirmarer's range [Pl.4].

Cellarer's Range The cellarer was responsible for the bulk provisioning of the monastery and had charge of the cellars which were usually beneath the buildings on the west side of the great cloister. Beyond no.3 Millers Green there is a small 13th c. doorway, beneath the overhang of a timber hall, which could be the door of the **cellarer's checker** (office), where wagons bringing in provisions would be checked, off-loaded, and the stores taken to the adjoining cellars. The undercroft of the hall consists of three bays each with low rib-vaults springing from just above floor level. Nearby, beneath the frater, there were more-extensive **cellars** which would have been used for the storage of grain, ale and wine. The refectory cellars were a little over 3m. high, and divided down the middle into two alleys by a row of square Norman piers which, with a series of responds along the side and end walls, supported a plain rubble vault {20, 21}.

* In the wall on the south side of the *Infirmary Cloister* there are two blocked openings. The larger is an archway 3.65m. wide and nearly as high through which large barrels and other bulky stores could be brought in. The smaller opening was a narrow doorway which opened into a passage in the thickness of the wall with three steps down at the end. At the bottom an archway, on the east side, opened into a passage about 5.2m. long and over 1.8m. wide which led under the *Infirmary Slype* to a building on the other side now long since demolished (St John Hope 1897 & Carter, J. 1807).

* An infirmary cloister was built or rebuilt with the frater in the 13th century, probably at the same time as the *Infirmary Hall*. In the south walk of the cloister against the frater wall, there is part of a moulded half-arch that crossed it at its east end to carry the thrust of the frater gable, and also some of the corbels which supported the lean-to roof. But this earlier cloister differed considerably from the present cloister since there must have been some way of bringing carts through to the archway into the frater cellars .

* The frater was situated between the cellarer's range and the north walk of the great cloister. The south wall of the cellarer's checker and undercroft stop short of the line of the refectory by about 3.65m. leaving sufficient room for a cartway from the inner court. A lane may have run from where the small cottage (no.5) now stands, providing access to the kitchen and to the cellars beyond.

The **kitchen** + was to the north-west of the refectory but its exact location and dimensions are not known [Pl. 4]. There are few remains of the buttery and pantry, and other offices that served the frater. Monastic kitchens were usually large and lofty buildings surmounted by pyramidal roofs; there are fine examples at Ely and Durham, and at Glastonbury (the *Abbot's Kitchen*).

Infirmarer's Range More of the infirmary range survives than first meets the eye. The survivals include the infirmary slype and cloister, the dining hall (the *misericord*, or flesh-frater), and the remains of the infirmary hall and infirmarer's lodging {20 & 21}. In most monasteries the infirmarer's range was a detached group of buildings, as at Gloucester, sited near the great cloister but well away from the noise and bustle of the outer court. The **infirmary dining hall**. During restoration work in 1967, it was discovered that the rooms resting on the 13th c. undercroft beside the timber-framed building above the cellar's checker, had been formed by dividing a medieval hall. The hall retained much of its original roof timbers, and apparently included a solar and garderobe. At first it was thought the hall was part of the cellarer's lodging, but the discovery of a *Majestas* (a painting of the Holy Trinity, now in the Parliament Room) in the roof space at the north end of the hall indicated that it was more probably the infirmary dining hall. The position of the hall in the infirmary range, near the monastic kitchens, also makes this highly likely. The original ceiling was elaborately painted to represent stone vaulting, with painted ribs, bosses and angels.

From the late 12th *c.* the relaxation of strict dietary discipline meant that meat off the bone as well as meat dishes were regularly available in the monks' refectory as well as in the infirmary dining hall. By the end of the 14th century there was often little distinction between the food available in the frater and that served in the misericord . Nevertheless, obedientaries and other senior monks sometimes had rooms near, or adjoining, the infirmary so that they could be away from the pressures of daily life in the monastery and enjoy the richer and more varied fare of the misericord (Harvey, B. 1993). At Canterbury

and Westminster the infirmarer came under considerable pressure to reserve rooms for abbey officials, and to allocate rooms as part of a monk's corrody (provision, or pension). The **infirmary cloister** served as a covered-way linking the various buildings of the range [57]. It also served as a sheltered area where aged and infirm

(fig 57) Infirmary Cloister (Little Cloister)

monks could rest or take gentle exercise. In warmer weather they could sit or walk in the infirmary garden. The cloister is not an exact square or rectangle, but each side is divided into five traceried openings of good Perpendicular work. The central area may have been cultivated as a herb-garden (*herbarium*) but there were more open and extensive gardens nearby.

> The **north and east** walks have been unroofed, partially during the Commonwealth and finally with the demolition of *Babylon* (see below).
> The **west** walk forms part of a medieval house, built over it and to the west of it. The house includes what is thought to have been the infirmary dining hall. For many years a prebendal house, more recently it has been used by the King's School.
> The **south** walk is still covered with a lean-to roof built against the north wall of the frater cellars.

The **infirmary hall** was the central building of the range [58]. On the site there are now only six arches, of Early English date, and the bases of piers of the north arcade.

(fig 58) Infirmary Hall, west entrance and ruins of south arcade

The main doorway is set within the west wall. The hall was a large nave-like building with a central day-area and aisles where beds were arranged at right angles to the walls. Here infirm and aged monks were allowed to live out their days no longer subject to the daily pressures of choir and cloister. Until the end of the 13th century the aisles of infirmary halls were usually entirely open, but with the trend towards greater privacy in the later Middle Ages partitions were erected. The monks were then allocated a cubicle in which they had a bed, a chest and a few personal belongings. Later still, in some monasteries, cubicles became rooms with fireplaces and other amenities.

When other members of the community fell ill they were also cared for in the infirmary, as were those recovering from blood-letting (*seyney*). The latter were allowed to rest for a day or two enjoying the richer fare provided by the infirmary kitchen.   Sometimes in larger monasteries there was a resident physician, otherwise a local physician was called in to advise on treatment for the sick and injured. The infirmarer himself, or one of the monks who had studied herbal remedies, was often sufficiently skilled in medical matters to carry out routine treatment and minor operations.

The **infirmary chapel** +(dedicated to St Bridget) adjoined the east end of the hall, but it was demolished soon after the Dissolution. What remains of the infirmary hall probably escaped destruction because, as at Canterbury, the south aisle had already been divided up into sets of rooms. If so, this was the beginning of the tenements in and around the old infirmary which were later known as *Babylon*. {20/21}

> Part of the tenements was demolished in 1831 and the remainder in 1854. The ruins of the infirmary hall were exposed and the area around landscaped. Though all that remains of the hall are ruined walls and arches they are strangely evocative of the time when the aged monks lived here, walking in their cloister and in the gardens, eating together in the *misericord*, saying their offices in chapel, and sleeping together in the hall.

Within *Dulverton House*, at the east end of the infirmary ruins, there is a medieval building at least 15.3 m. long, running north-south. This must have been part of the infirmary range, and was probably the **infirmarer's lodging**.

The **infirmary slype** links the infirmary and the great cloister. It has a stone vault divided into four bays, supported by heavy moulded ribs springing from corbels.

The passage, which is wider in its northern bays than in its southern bays, is lit by a narrow window, a single light with trefoiled head and wide internal splay. At its wider end there were two other openings, now blocked; one had a transom two-thirds up, above which the rear-arch is moulded; the sill of the other has been cut down and the opening made into a doorway, which led into a house outside, as shown on Carter's plan (1807). The house was demolished in the mid-19th century.   The **infirmary garden** was to the north of the infirmary hall adjoining the abbot's lodging (*Historia*). At Christchurch Priory at Canterbury the layout of the late-12th c. infirmary garden is clear from a contemporary drawing of the monastic waterworks. Labelled *herbarium* the enclosure is shown with rows of plants and wooden trellises, and probably a cistern for watering the plants (Coppack, G. 1990).

Many of the herbs found in the gardens of medieval monasteries can be identified from contemporary herbals. In the cathedral library, bound up with the Gloucester copy of the *Historia* (MS.34) is a late medieval herbal with an alphabetical list of herbs, Alleluya-Zipperis. Many of the herbs listed are given English names. Also included in the manuscript is an alphabetical list of herbs which could be used as substitutes, as well as a large miscellaneous collection of recipes, a few in English.

There were several other cultivated areas in the precincts, for example, on the west side of the abbot's lodging where there was vineyard and orchard; the great cloister garth would also have been cultivated, at least in part. Between the cemetery wall and the east wall of the abbey there was another cultivated area. In addition to herbs for cooking and medicinal purposes, a variety of vegetables and fruit would have been grown.

East Side

The ground on the east side of the cathedral, known for many years as *The Grove*, is shown in 18th and 19th *c*. drawings full of over-grown shrubs and trees, with paths running through them. It was a favourite area for members of the College, and their wives and children. A grassed area near the schoolroom (the monastic library) was used by the boys as a playground. But in *c*.1850 the whole area was laid out as a garden, with lawns and beds for shrubbery, and with paths and a carriage way.

On the west side of the garden, extending north from the transept are:

(i)   a three-storey building, with the eastern slype (11th c.) at ground level; above it the choir vestry (13th c.); and above the vestry the library (14th c.);

(ii) the chapter house, with its late 15th c. east end, and in its north-east corner a jamb of a window of the 14th c. monks' dormitory (with a ballflower attached);

(iii) a 19th-century schoolroom and playground.

Abbey Water Supply The Abbey's main supply came from the Fulbrook, a stream which originated in the Cotswold Hills and which entered the town near the North Gate [Pl.4]. A culverted water supply was diverted from it into the precincts on the east side. An abbey community required enormous quantities of water for cooking and brewing, for washing and sluicing, and for general domestic purposes. It also required water in the gardens and for turning the mill.

*   The supply from the Fulbrook was divided into two channels, one passing under the dormitory to flush the reredorter, and then flowing on through the cloister garth passing by the lavatorium. The other split into two south of the infirmary hall, one channel passing under the infirmary and on to supply the 14th c. abbot's lodging, before going on to fed the abbey mill; and the other passing under the infirmary cloister. During excavations in 1962, Fullbrook-Leggatt discovered that 'water still flows here at a depth of about 14ft. (4.26m.)'.

*   From the infirmary cloister this channel passed the cellarer's checker before dividing, one arm passing the kitchens and going on to the mill, and the other passing by the kitchens and turning into the prior's lodging.

*   The stream from the mill and the outflow from the lodging came together in the great drain near the inner gate and flowed westward out of the precincts beneath the precinct wall north of St. Mary's Gate (Heighway, C. 1991).

*   The supply of water from the Fulbrook was augmented by well-water drawn from a number of wells in various parts of the precincts, including the well in the cloister. These provided fresh or, as the Historia calls it, 'living water'.

*   In order to improve the water supply, Helias, the sacrist (*c.* 1230) is thought to have constructed the reservoir in the north-west corner of the cloister garth. During the reign of Edward II (1307-27) the abbey was granted permission to draw further supplies from Mattesdune (Robinswood Hill). The reservoir in the garth then became a drain, and served as such when the lavatorium was built at the end of the 14th century. From the early 18th c. the reservoir remained hidden and forgotten until it was re-discovered and excavated in 1888. It was filled in again in 1997.

Cathedral Exterior

There are fine views of the cathedral from the gardens around the east end, with the roofs of the lady chapel, the choir and the central tower forming, as it were, great steps skyward.

Features of interest   At the foot of the tower, in the north east corner just above the tribune roof, there is the base of a 12th c. rounded **turret tower** (a feature of the Anglo-Norman tower) and a bay and a half of blind arcading. This is a fragment of a decorative frieze which probably ran around the whole of the eastern arm of the building beneath the eaves (as at Tewkesbury) indicating the height of the exterior walls of the Romanesque choir. The round-headed **windows** of the Anglo-Norman building have been enlarged and filled with tracery, which involved reducing the splay, and lowering the sills, thus breaking the string course. The tribune **chapels**, on both sides of the choir, have been raised in height and given an embattled parapet. The north-east tribune chapel has a Decorated window with ballflower ornament. Below, in the crypt chapel, there is a blocked up doorway where there was once a window. This was opened in the 18th century to provide access to and from the crypt (and so to the choir) from *The Grove*.

The **great east window** is canted resting, as it does, on the eastern apse of the crypt. The two main mullions are buttressed to strengthen the structure and protect it against wind pressure. The buttresses are pierced to allow as much light as possible through the window. On two tiers of the window the transoms are plain, but they are cusped on the inside. This simplified the glaziers' task in that the panels could be rectangular. Above the window the outer hood-mould turns into an ogee shape and rises to the perforated parapet of the gable, which is flanked by pierced pinnacles. The window is 'perhaps the *tour de force* of the whole edifice' (Verey, D. 1978).

The **lady chapel** is almost detached from the main building {19}. The Anglo-Norman axial chapel in the crypt forms the foundation of its western end. Early in the 13th c. the axial chapels at ground and tribune level were extended eastward and squared off to form a chapel dedicated to St Mary the Virgin. When the great east window was erected in c. 1350 the chapels were not entirely demolished since parts of them were later incorporated into the lady chapel (1468-82) as vestibule and west gallery chapel.

The **enclosed passage** (*Whispering Gallery*), constructed outside the Great East

Window, links the two sides of the tribune and passes by the west gallery chapel. It is carried on segmental arches, or *bridges*, built, in the main, with masonry recovered, presumably, from the demolished east end. The passage is an extraordinarily ingenious solution to the problem of how to link the two sides of the tribune once the eastern apse had been demolished.

The **vaulted passage** under the lady chapel sanctuary. According to the *Historia* the 13th *c.* lady chapel was built 'in the cemetery'. The present lady chapel was built out to a wall which in the 15th century bounded the cemetery on the east side. Thus a passage had to be constructed under the east end of the chapel to provide access from one part of the burial ground to the other.

South Side

On the south side of the lady chapel, in the angle of the projecting chantry, there is a turret stair with a **small window**. The string course and masonry lines show that there was once a doorway here.

> In 1721 the Dean and Chapter gave John Cocks (who lived opposite at what is now the Headmaster's House) permission 'to make a way or passage from the bottom stairs leading up to a little chapel on the south side of the Ladies Chapel belonging to this Church into a walk leading to the house of the said John Cocks for the use and convenience of him and his family to come to Divine Service in this Cathedral' (*Chapter Act Book 1720*). At the time, the ground level outside the lady chapel was considerably higher than at present. When John Cocks died in 1737 the next tenant, Sir Robert Cocks of Dumbleton, was told that the *Act of Chapter* granting permission for the doorway 'was illegal', and that the Chapter had ordered 'the said passage be forthwith stopped up'.

On the south side of the choir ambulatory, it is very noticeable how the splay of the windows has been reduced and the original string course broken through the enlargement of the windows.

The *Upper Green* is bounded on the east and south sides by houses, roughly marking the line of the abbey wall. House-building had begun by 1616, and by 1649 there were houses ranged along the east wall, and along the south wall between St Michael's Gate, in the south east corner, and King Edward's Gate, at the end of College Street. From the south precinct wall near St Michael's Gate a wall extended to the east corner of the south transept [59]. The wall separated the inner (monks) cemetery from the outer (lay) cemetery. It was still standing in 1827; and part of it is still standing behind the houses on the east side of the Green. The south side of the church was known as the *Upper Churchyard* and used for burials until the 1770s when Dean Tucker closed it as part of his precinct improvements.

St Michael's Gate is a small pedestrian gate dating in its present form from the 15th century. It has a flattened archway and canopied niches on either side. The upper part has been replaced by a small room built of brick. The gateway, appropriately called after St Michael, the archangel, led into the cemetery from a narrow street off

Westgate. An earlier gate on the same site was mistakenly thought to have been used by pilgrims visiting the tomb of King Edward II, and entering the church through a door in the south wall of the transept. **King Edward's Gate**, which was built at the expense of King Edward I (1272-1307), was by far the most imposing of the abbey gates. A wall was built from the west side of the new gateway to the south west corner of the nave, the purpose of which was to enclose the great court, separating it from the now more-public south side of the abbey church. The gate was largely rebuilt by William Parker (abbot 1514-39), but all that now remains is part of the west gate-tower which stands beside the modern wrought-iron gates.

> In a niche on the south face of the tower is a stone bearing the attributed arms of Prince Osric, as King of Northumbria. It was dug up on the north side of the cathedral in c.1828 and placed here. The tower contains a newel stair which led up to the rooms over the gateway, which were leased as a dwelling until 1805; the rooms were then demolished leaving only the two gate-towers. The east tower was taken down in 1893 when the narrow medieval street (College Street) was widened.

South aisle of the nave was reconstructed by Abbot Thoky in c.1320 in the Decorated style (ballflower featuring prominently). He first strengthened the aisle wall by adding free-standing buttresses which rise well above the parapet forming a series of crocketed pinnacles. In the upper part of the buttresses there are niches which originally contained an array of saintly figures [Pl. 10].

> In 1854 seven figures were still *in situ* but now there are only three, and the head of one of these is a 19th *c*. replacement. After World War II it was proposed to restore all the buttresses, renewing the ballflower and filling the niches with figures, but after one buttress had been restored the project was abandoned.

In contrast with the north aisle, the arches of the Anglo-Norman windows were removed, and the enlarged openings filled with three-light **windows** with unusual 'butterfly' tracery. The windows are festooned with ballflower inside and out. Even the easternmost window, enlarged and reglazed early in the 15th century, is decorated with ballflower. When the work was completed anyone entering the precincts through King Edward's Gate could not have failed to be impressed by its architectural detail and rich display of statuary. It could be said that this was as near as Gloucester ever got to an imposing 'west front'. The clerestory was reconstructed in the 15th century, retaining the shallow Anglo-Norman buttresses with chevron at the angles.

South Transept (*St Andrew's Aisle*) was substantially altered (1331-36) in the reconstruction of the east end following the burial of Edward II.

The **walls** up to the sills of the windows are Anglo-Norman, together with the transept-turrets at the corners. The **turrets** have ornamented arcading in two tiers, one with intersecting arches and the other with zig-zag. They are both capped with conical roofs (not the originals). The **gable** of the south front has stepped, round-headed, blind arches ornamented with zig-zag. In the centre at the base of the gable a small door provides access from the south transept roof-space to a narrow passage, behind the pierced parapet.

(fig 59). South transept and central tower (Bartlett, 1828)

Whether it was possible to construct the great window without taking down and later rebuilding the gable is uncertain. If it was dismantled (1331-36) it was re-assembled with great skill retaining the pitch of the roof and the typically 12th c. stepped blind arches. The **window frame** is reset Anglo-Norman chevron supplemented with additional chevron made for the 14th *c.* reconstruction. Some of the earlier chevron was replaced in the 19th century. Unlike the Anglo-Norman work, which has only one chevron (>) to each stone, the stones inserted later have two, and sometimes more. On either side of the great window are tall vertical lines of chevron which appear to be *in situ*. The **south window** itself is the earliest surviving Perpendicular window in the country (1335-36). Panel tracery, super-mullions and vertical hexagons fill the window, but most significantly the mullions rise to strike the arch perpendicularly for the first time. The **doorway** and the small recess in the wall are thought to be evidence of a *sacristy* which once extended from the south wall of the transept. In 1867 remains of a Roman tessellated pavement were discovered near the south front of the transept. The area would have been just inside the old Roman town walls. The **windows** on the east and west sides of the transept were constructed using graceful flowing tracery, with liberal use of ogee curves. On the west side a buttress, designed to strengthen the south-west corner of the tower, crosses the window; a transom crosses the larger of the two windows at the level of the sill of the smaller window.

Central Tower The great Perpendicular tower dominates the exterior of the building, rising to a height of 68.6m (225ft.). Begun by Thomas Seabroke (abbot 1450-57), the tower is divided into two main tiers, surmounted by a coronet of open-work parapets and tall delicate corner turrets [59] {22}.

> Like the rest of the building it was built of local oolitic limestone which in bright sunlight takes on a silvery brilliance and in the evening as the sun sets in the west a rich honey colour. Light and shade make the decorative detail on the wall surfaces, the deep recesses of the louvred openings and the bold projection of the diagonal buttresses, stand out in sharp relief.

In the choir, the crossing piers (dating to 1089-1100) of the **Anglo-Norman tower** are still in place, though the broad arches which once spanned them have gone. But around and above the mid-14th c. arches there is Anglo-Norman masonry which suggests that when the present tower was built more of the Anglo-Norman masonry than meets the eye was left in place.

* Around the base of the tower, below the decorative work, there is comparatively plain, ashlar walling. Behind this precise ashlar, the base of the Anglo-Norman tower survives, partially rebuilt and refaced when the present tower was built. As Professor J. Heyman (1990) has confirmed 'most of the original Norman build survives behind the 15th century facing'.
* At the north-east corner of the tower there are substantial remains of a circular turret and fragments of external wall arcading.
* The Anglo-Norman tower probably rose to the height of the floor of the present ringing chamber. It might have been a little higher, but it could not have been lower since it had to support the high-pitched roofs of the four arms of the

Romanesque building. The 14th c. buttresses at the south-west and south east corners were designed to strengthen the base of the Perpendicular tower. Considering the weight of the tower (estimated at over 5000 tons), raising the tower on foundations which were more than 300 years old involved considerable risk. But it paid off!

It is not known for certain who designed the tower. There is a tradition that the builder was a certain John Gower, whom Dr. J. Harvey identifies as one of two masons named John Gore who worked as setters at Eton College for four weeks in the summer of 1445. Robert Tully, one of the monks of St Peter's Abbey, was in financial control of the project, and after Abbot Seabroke's death in 1457 he completed the tower before leaving to become Bishop of St David (1460-81). Beneath the window high up on the west side of the crossing, there is an inscription in Latin which translated runs: 'This work (the tower) which you see built and adorned was done by the labour of Tully, at the command of Abbot Seabroke'.

'And a very imposing tower it is; fully able, from its massiveness as well as from its height, to gather together the masses of the building - all the more so because the transepts are so short. It succeeds where the central towers of Worcester and Hereford fail; in fact, it is as effective in its way as Salisbury spire. The pinnacles bear witness to the architect's love of harmony and unity - each pinnacle with its two ranges of 'windows', is a repeat of the two stages of the tower below' (Bond, F. 1912).

--------------X--------------

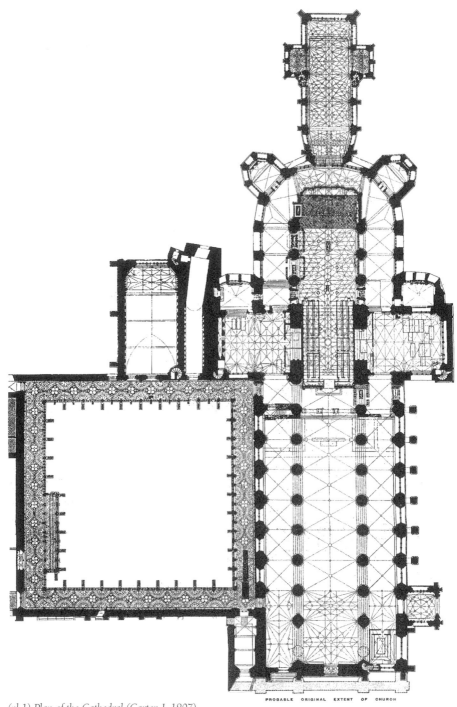

(pl 1) Plan of the Cathedral (Carter, J. 1807)
Varied vaulting: Barrel (east slype), groined (chapels, ambulatory, orig. crypt), quadrant (tribune), Anglo-Norman quatrepartite rib (north aisle), Early English (nave), Decorated (south aisle), lierne, simple (south transept), lierne complex (choir, lady chapel, nave west end), fan (great cloister).

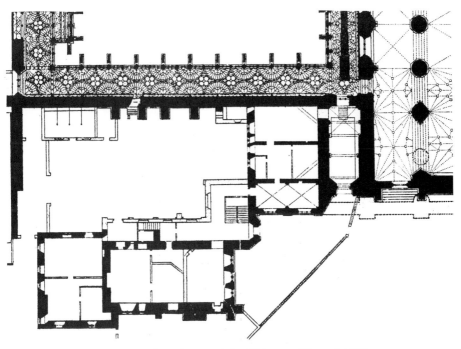

(pl 2) Plan of the Cloister and the old Deanery (Carter, J. 1807)

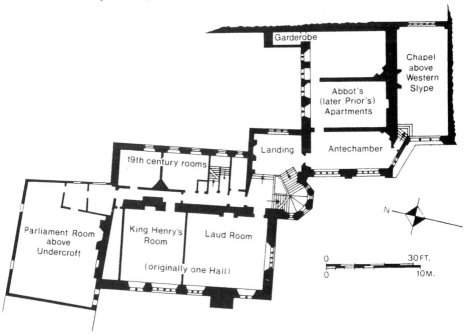

(pl 3) Plan of the old deanery after mid-19th reconstruction, and as it is, as Church House, today

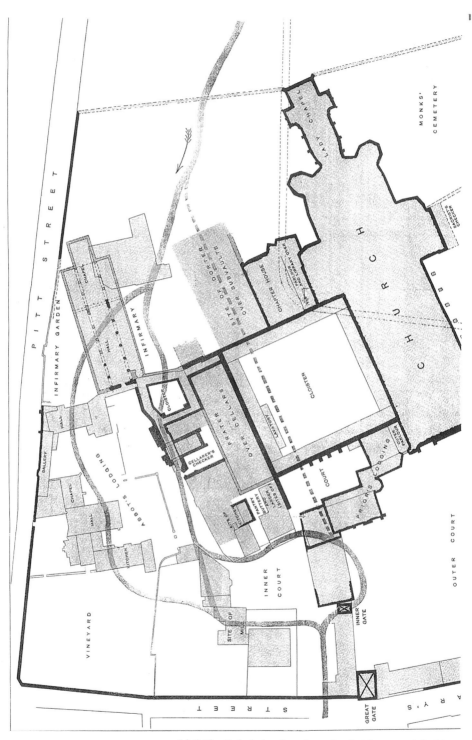

*(pl 4) The Cathedral and precincts, showing the monastic buildings,
the line of the Roman walls and the abbey water supply*

(pl 5) Plan of the windows of the nave, transepts and choir

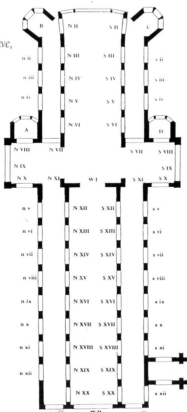

The black and white photographs of the Great East Window (E1) taken by Sydney Pitcher, the Gloucester photographer, in the late 1930s document the state of the window at the time. They detail with remarkable clarity (in a way that colour photographs often do not) the main features of each figure e.g. St. George (left) is armed to the teeth, with lance, dagger and sword, and St. Thomas (right) wears patterned slippers and holds a spear in one hand and a girdle in the other. Tradition has it that the Virgin's girdle was dropped to St. Thomas at her Assumption.

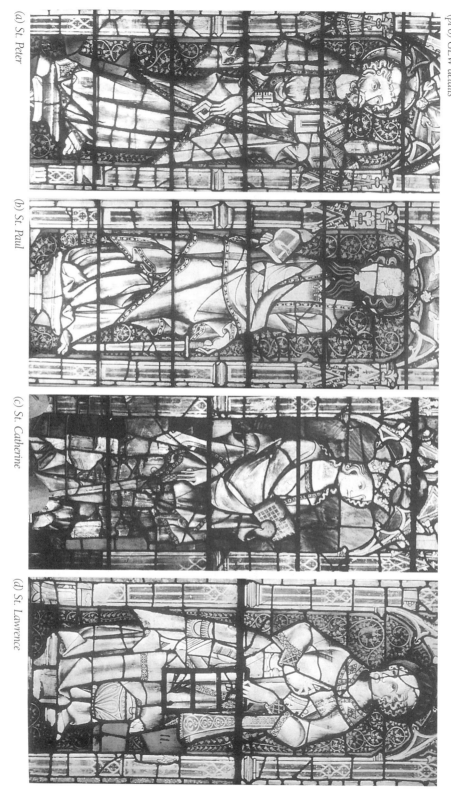

(pl 6) GEW details

(a) St. Peter

(b) St. Paul

(c) St. Catherine

(d) St. Lawrence

(pl 8) Detail of the north elevation of the choir (Carter, J. 1807)

(pl 8) Detail of the north elevation of the choir (Carter, J. 1807)

(pl 9) *Cathedral exterior, west end, with the old Deanery before the mid-19th c. reconstruction (Carter, J. 1807)*

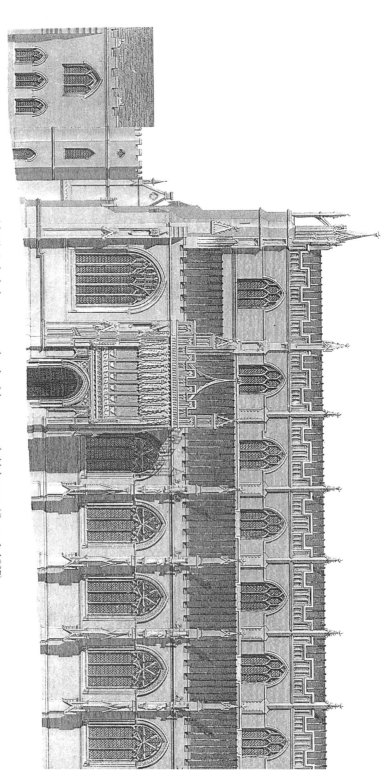

(pl 10) Cathedral exterior, south side of the nave, and old deanery (Carter, J. 1807)

APPENDICES

PRINCIPLE SOURCES

The principal source for the history of Gloucester's abbey church, from the 12th century to the end of the 14th century, is *Historia Monasterii Sancti Petri Gloucestriae*, compiled by Abbot Froucester (1381-1412). Froucester compiled his account from the abbey's official documents, charters and annals, memoranda, historical notes, biographical notes and chronicles written by monks from time to time. The Latin text is in the *Rolls Series No 33, edited by W.H.Hart (1863-1867)* in three volumes. There is a 15th c. copy of the *Historia* in Gloucester Cathedral Library (MS 34 ff 1v-43v), and a translation by the Revd. W. Barber in Welander, D. 1991).

The *Historia* begins with an account of the foundation of the first monastic house on the site by Prince Osric of Mercia in c.681, and of the period leading up to the introduction of Benedictine monks in c.1022. It then details the work of the twenty abbots "after the Conquest" , beginning with Serlo (abbot 1072-1104) and ending with Abbot Froucester. Professor Christopher Brooke in his study of the chronicle and its attached index concludes: "We are in contact here with a large amount of authentic information, much of it written down - as monastic annals often were -year by year as events happened. A glance at Froucester's chronicle will confirm this impression"

Among surviving records of the abbey are ten volumes of deeds etc. dating from Norman times. The first volume of these *Acta*, covering the years c.1122 to 1263, edited by Prof. Robert Patterson was published in 1998. Like the five Registers containing information about the abbey's *officia* and estates, these are a valuable source for the history of the abbey. The fabric rolls (building accounts) of the abbey have not survived.

There are references to the abbey, and in particular to its abbots and their achievements, in the writings of William of Malmesbury, Gerald of Wales and Gregory of Caerwent. Gerald, for example, in his *Life of St Remigius* tells how Roger, bishop of Worcester (1163-1179) visiting the abbey in September or December 1164/5 witnessed the collapse of one of the western towers.

There is only scant documentary evidence for any construction work after 1400. Sir William Dugdale in his *Monasticon Anglicanum* (1655 vol.1) prints a tract known as *Memoriale Ecclesiae Cathedralis Gloucestriae Compendiarum* which traces the history of the abbey/cathedral down to 1607, but from an anti-monastic point of view. It was published anonymously, but is thought to be the work of William Loe, a Puritan prebendary of Gloucester. It is of doubtful historical value. At the end of the medieval period there are *inter alia* the notes of Leland, based in part on the precollections of "an auld monk" of St Peter's Abbey whom he met in 1541 on a visit to Gloucester.

The legal documents relating to the foundation of the diocese, and records of the bishops' Visitations etc. provide information about the church and its endowments from 1540. From 1621 the *Chapter Act Books*, are an invaluable source of information about all aspects of the cathedral, its buildings and endowments, its clergy and collegiate life. The Dean and Chapter's legal documents and accounts, and records of the cathedral architects (from c.1840) provide detailed information for the cathedral fabric in the 19th and 20th centuries..

Drawings and etchings of ancient buildings, particularly of cathedrals and old abbeys were much in vogue in the early years of the 19th century. These provide information about the internal furnishings and external features of the cathedral at the time. Of particular importance is *An Account of the Cathedral Church of Gloucester with Plans, Elevations, and Sections of that Building*, published by the Society of Antiquaries of London in 1809. The drawings of Thomas Bonnor (1796), John Britton (1829), James Storer (1814-1819), H.Ansted (1827) and W. H. Bartlett (1818) are also of interest. Associated with some of these collections of etchings are descriptions of the cathedral's history and architecture. A number of Histories of the City and County of Gloucester were published in this period including those by: Rudge, T. (1807), Fosbroke, T.D.(1807) , Rudge.T. (1811). Also of interest are Furney, R. *Extracts* (1807) in the Bodleian Library, Oxford. Of particular importance, on the

Victorian restoration of the cathedral, is the report by F. S. Waller entitled *General Architectural Description of the Cathedral Church....with plans and sketches of its pecularities and beauties*, published in August 1856.

There is no shortage of information from the mid-19th century, with publications covering every aspect of the cathedral's life and history, fabric and furnishings. Of particular note are the published lectures of Willis, R. (1860) and Hope, St J. (1897); *The Records* of the Gloucester Cathedral Society, volumes 1 & 2; Haines, H. *A Guide to the Cathedral Church of Gloucester* (1867); *The Bell Guide* by Masse,H.J. (1899) and more recently Pevsner's *Buildings of England: Gloucestershire* by Verey, D. (1978), revised (in part) by Pevsner, N. and Metcalf, P. (1985), Herbert, N.M. *A History of the County of Gloucester* vol. IV (1988); Eward, S. *No Fine but a Glass of Wine* (1985); British Archaeological Association *Transactions* of the Gloucester conference (1981), published in 1985, and the present author's *The Stained Glass of Gloucester Cathedral* (1985) and *The History, Art and Architecture of Gloucester Cathedral* (1991). Patterson, R. *The Original Acta of St Peter's Abbey, Gloucester 1122-1263* (1998).

BIBLIOGRAPHY

Ashwell, B.,   *Report on the Restoration of Gloucester Cathedral 1960-1982 (1982)*

Bayle, M.,   *English Romanesque Art 1066-1200 (Exhibition Catalogue 1984)*

Barrett, P.,   *Barchester: English Cathedral Life in the Nineteenth Century (1993).*

Billett, J. H. A.,   *Gloucester Cathedral - a Guide (1880).*

Blair,J. & Ramsay,N. (ed),   *English Medieval Industries (1991).*

Bonnor, T.,   *Itinerary, with Notes (1796).*

Bartlett, W. H.,   *Drawings, engraved by Woolnoth W. (1892).*

Bond, F.,   *The Cathedrals of England and Wales (1912).*

Bony, J.,   *Gloucester et l'origine des voutes d'hemicycle gothique (1939);*
                      La Chapelle episcopale de Hereford... (1959);
                      French Gothic Architecture of the 12th and 13th c. (1983).

Browne Willis,   *A Survey of the Cathedrals... (Gloucester) (1727).*

Carter, J.,   *Some Account of the Cathedral Church of Gloucester (1807).*

Clapham, Sir A.,   *English Romanesque Architecture after the Conquest (1934).*

Coldstream, N.,   *The Art of Chivalry (Exhibition Catalogue 1988);*
                      The Decorated Style 1240-1360 (1994).

Coppack, G.,   *Abbeys and Priories (1990).*

Cormack, P.,   *Introduction to Whall, C. Stained Glass Work (1905, re-issued 1999)*

Eward, S.,   *No Fine but a Glass of Wine (1985).*

Fernie, E.,   *The Architecture of the Anglo-Saxons (1983).*

Fitchen, J.,   *The Construction of Gothic Cathedrals (1961).*

Gillingham, M.,   *Gloucester Cathedral Organ (Friends of Gloucester Cath 1971).*

Geddes, J.,   *Medieval Decorative Ironwork in England (Soc. of Antiquaries of London 1999).*

Haines, H.,   *A Guide to the Cathedral Church of Gloucester (1867).*

Harvey,B.,   *Living and Dying in England 1100-1540 The Monastic Experience (1993).*

Harvey, J.,   *The Perpendicular Style (1984).*

Heighway, C.,   *Gloucester: A History and a Guide (1985).*
                      Heighway, C. and Bryant, R. et al. The Golden Minster (St Oswald's Priory,
                      Gloucester) (1999).

Herbert, N.,   *The Victoria County History of Gloucestershire 1988).*

Hewett, C.,   *English Cathedral and Monastic Carpentry (1985).*

Heyman, J.,   *Report to the Dean and Chapter on The Central Tower (1990).*

Hurtig, J.,   *Armored Gisant before 1400 (Ph.D. thesis 1979).*

Johnson, Joan,   *The Gloucestershire Gentry (1989).*

Kerr, J.,   *The East Window at Gloucester Cathedral (BAA Report 1985)*

Kidson, P.,   *A History of English Architecture (1979).*

King, R. J.,   *Gloucester Cathedral (1874).*

Leedy, W. C.,   *Fan Vaulting: A Study of Form (1980).*

Leland's   *Itinery (1541), ed. Toulnin Smith.*

McAleer, J. P.,   *Some Reused Romanesque material in the Choir Tribune (TBGAS 1986).*

MacCulloch, D.,   *Thomas Cranmer (1996); and Tudor Church Militant (1999).*

Marks, R.,   *English Medieval Industries (contrib. Ed. Blair J & Ramsay N. 1993).*

Masse, H. J.,   *The Cathedral Church of Gloucester (1899).*

Metcalf, P.,   *The Cathedrals of England Vol. 2. (1985).*

Morganstern, A.M. *Gothic Tombs of Kingship (Pennsylvania State U.P. 2000).*

New, A.,   *A Guide to the Cathedrals of Britain (1980).*

Patterson, R.,   *The Original Acta of St. Peter's Abbey, Gloucester 1122-1263 (1989)*

Pevsner, N. & Metcalf, P.   *The Cathedrals of England (1985).*

Poyntz-Wright, P.,   *Article in Daily Telegraph (May 1991).*
Rowley, T.,   *Norman England (1997).*
St John Hope, W.H., *Notes on the Benedictine Abbey of St Peter, Gloucester (1898).*
Stravridi, M.,   *Master of Glass: Charles Eamer Kempe 1837-1907 (1988).*
Thorold, H.,   *Cathedrals, Abbeys and Priories of England and Wales (1986)*
Thurlby, M.   *The Elevations of the Romanesque Churches of Tewkesbury*
                     and Gloucester (BAA Conference (1981), et al.
Tracey, C.,   *English Gothic Choir Stalls 1400-1540 (1990).*
Tudor Craig, P.,   *Unpublished paper to the BAA Conference, Gloucester (1981)*
Waller, F. S.,   *The Present State of the Cathedral Church (Report 1856);*
                     General Architectural Description of the Cathedral Church
Watkin, D.,   *The Architecture of Britain (1979).*
Welander, D.,   *The Stained Glass of Gloucester Cathedral (1985);*
                     The History, Art and Architecture of Gloucester Cathedral (1991).
Whall, C.,   *Stained Glass Work (1905, re-issued 1999)*
Willis, R.,   *Lecture (in The Archaeological Journal 1860).*
Wilson, C.,   *Abbot Serlo's Church at Gloucester (BAA Conference Report 1985);*
                     The Gothic Cathedral (1990).
Verey, D.,   *Gloucestershire (The Buildings of England: Pevsner, N.) Vol 2. 1980).*
Zarnecki, G.,   *Romanesque (in Herbert History of Art and Architecture 1989).*

ILLUSTRATIONS

COLOUR PLATES

PLANS AND DRAWINGS

GLOSSARY

Abacus	A flat slab on the top of a capital.
Ambulatory	A walk-way, or aisle, around the sanctuary.
Apse	Semi-circular or polygonal termination of a church or chapel.
Arcade	A series of arches supported on piers or columns. When attached to a wall surface, known as blind arcading.
Arch	A structure of wedge-shaped blocks of stone over an opening which support one another by mutual pressure. Arches take a variety of forms.
Ashlar	Hewn and squared stones prepared for buildings.
Aumbry	A cupboard or recess for the sacred vessels for the Mass.
Ballflower	A globular flower of three petals enclosing a small ball. A form of decoration used in the early 14th. century.
Barrel vault	A continuous vault of semi-circular section like a tunnel.
Battlement	A parapet, with a series of indentations (embrasures) with raised portions (merlons) in between, from which archers could shoot. Such a parapet is said to be castellated. Often used decoratively.
Bay	Compartment or division in a building, as defined by regular vertical features such as columns, windows or arches.
Billet	Norman ornament of small half-cylindrical or rectangular blocks.
Boss	An ornamental knob or projection at the intersection of ribs in a vault or ceiling, often carved with foliage.
Bowtell	A form of roll moulding, usually three-quarters of a circle in section, an edge roll or for small shafts in clustered piers, in window and door jambs, mullions etc.
Buttress	A mass of masonry projecting from or built against a wall to give additional strength, usually to counteract the lateral thrust of an arch, roof, or vault.
Cable,	or *rope* moulding, like twisted strands of a rope.
Capital	The head or crowning feature of a column, free-standing or attached. Occurring in a variety of forms, with distinctive decoration according to successive architectural styles.
Carrel	A compartment in a cloister where a monk might sit and work
Cartouche	An ornamental panel in the form of a scroll, usually bearing an inscription and sometimes ornately framed.
Centring	Wooden support for the building of an arch or vault, removed after completion.
Chamfer	(lit. corner-break) a surface formed by cutting off a square edge or corner.
Chevet	A French term for a chancel or choir with an ambulatory and radiating chapels.
Chevron	A Romanesque form of decoration, a V-shape used in series or double series, and sometimes called zigzag.
Clerestory,	or *clearstory*. The upper stage of the main walls of a church, above the aisle roofs, pierced by windows.
Corbel	A projecting block, usually of stone, supporting a beam or other horizontal member.
Crockets	A decorative feature of Gothic architecture, resembling leafy hooks. projecting at regular intervals from the angles of spires, pinnacles, canopies, gables etc.
Crossing	The central space at the intersection of the nave, chancel and transepts; often surmounted by a crossing tower or dome.
Crypt	A vaulted chamber, usually underground, beneath the east end of a church.
Cusp	Projecting points formed at the meeting of the foils (q.v.) in tracery.

Dagger	A tracery motif of the Decorated style, elongated ogee-ended lozenges.
Diaper	All-over surface decoration formed by the repetitive use of lozenges or squares, flat or in relief.
Encaustic tiles	Earthenware tiles fired with a pattern and glaze.
Engaged	or *attached column* A column which partly merges into a wall or pier.
Fenestration	The arrangement of windows in a building.
Feretory	The area behind the high altar where the chief shrine was placed or the treasures of a church were kept.
Finial	The ornament finishing off the apex of a canopy, gable, pinnacle etc
Foil	A lobe or leaf-shaped curve formed by the cusping of a circle or an arch. The number of foils involved is indicated by a prefix e.g. trefoil. Used of window tracery, wall panelling, and details of furnishings such as the canopies of choir stalls.
Gable	The triangular upper portion of a wall at the end of a pitched roof. Normally it has straight sides, but there are variations e.g. crow-stepped, which has stepped sides.
Garderobe	A medieval lavatory.
Gargoyle	A water spout projecting from the parapet of a wall or tower, and often carved into a grotesque figure, human or animal.
Groin	The sharp edge formed by the intersection of vaulting surfaces; hence groin vault.
Grisaille	Monochrome painting on walls or glass.
Hoodmould	A projecting moulding to throw off rain water, on the face of a wall, above an arch, doorway or window. When horizontal often called a *label*; hence a *label stop*, a plain or decorated terminal to mouldings, or at the end of hoodmouldings.
Impost	Horizontal moulding at the springing of an arch. An *impost block* is the block between abacus and capital.
Keystone	The central stone in an arch or vault.
Lady Chapel	A chapel dedicated to the Virgin Mary (Our Lady)
Lancet	A slender single-light pointed-arched window.
Lavatorium	In religious houses, a washing place adjacent to the refectory.
Lierne	A tertiary rib, that is, one which does not spring either from one of the main springers or from the central boss. A *lierne vault* is a ribbed vault with liernes
Linenfold	Tudor panelling carved with simulations of folded linen.
Lintel	Horizontal beam or stone bridging an opening e.g. a doorway or cupboard.
Lynchgate	(*lit. corpse-gate*); a roofed gateway to a churchyard for the reception of a coffin.
Misercord	(*or, miserere, meaning mercy*) A bracket on the underside of the seat of a hinged choir stall which, when turned up, served as a support for the occupant whilst standing during long services.
Narthex	In general medieval sense, an enclosed covered vestibule at the main entrance to a church or chapel.
Nave	The body of a church west of the crossing or chancel often flanked by aisles
Newel	The central or corner post of a staircase, so *newel stair,* ascending round a central supporting newel; called a *spiral stair* or *vice* when in a circular shaft.
Night stair	Stair by which religious entered the transept of their church from their dormitory for the night services.
Nook-shaft	A shaft set in the angle of a pier, a respond, a wall or the jamb of a window or doorway.

Oculus	A circular opening.
Ogee	A double curve, bending first one way and then the other. So an *ogee*, or *ogival arch*.
Oratory	A private chapel in a church (or house).
Oriel	A window of one or more storeys projecting from the face of a building, starting above ground.
Parclose	A parclose screen separates a chapel from the rest of the church. A Rood (screen) stands at the entrance of the chancel.
Parlour	In a religious house, a room where the religious could talk to visitors; in a medieval house, the semi-private living room below the *solar* (the private upper chamber)
Perpendicular	English Gothic architecture *c*. 1335-1530, the name being derive from the upright tracery panels used on the walls and as tracery in the windows.
Pier	Large masonry support, often for an arch.
Piscina	A shallow stone basin (provided with a drain) set in, or against, the wall on the south side of the altar for washing the Communion or MAss vessels. *Pillar piscina*, a free-standing piscina set on a pillar.
Plinth	projecting courses at the foot of a wall or column, generally chamfered (q.v.) or moulded at the top.
Poppyhead	Carved ornament, usually of leaves and flowers but also of animals and figures, serving as a finial for a bench end or stall.
Presbytery	The part of a church laying to the east of the choir where the main altar is placed.
Pulpitum	A stone screen, in major churches, erected to shut off the choir from the nave dividing choir from nave.
Putto	(plural *putti*) Small naked boy.
Quarries	Square (or diamond) panes of glass supported by leading strips (*cames*). Also used of square floor slabs or tiles.
Quatrefoil	Four lobes or foils (*lit.* leaf) formed by the cusping (q.v.) of a circular or other shape in tracery. Also *trefoil* (three), *cinquefoil* (five).
Quions	Dressed stones at the corners, or angles of a building.
Rebate	A rectangle recess or groove cut along the edge of stone or wood to receive a shutter, window or door etc.
Rebus	An heraldic pun e.g. Belton represented by a bell and a barrel (tun).
Reredorter	(lit. behind the dormitory); latrines in a medieval monastery.
Reredos	A wall or screen at the back of an altar. Usually ornamented with panelling and sometimes enriched with a profusion of niches, buttresses, pinnacles, statues etc. painted with brilliant colours
Respond	A half-pier of half-column bonded into a wall and carrying one end of an arch.
Ridge rib	A rib extending along the internal ridge of a vault on which the upper ends of the other ribs rest.
Roll moulding	Medieval moulding of part-circular section.
Romanesque	Architectural style current in the 11th and 12th centuries, In England often called *Norman* or *Anglo-Norman*.
Rood	A crucifix flanked by the Virgin and St. John, standing on a wooden beam (*rood beam*) and set across the east end of a nave, usually over the entry into the chancel or choir.
Rose window	A circular window with tracery radiating from the centre.

Sacristy	A room in a church for the sacred vessels and vestments
Sanctuary	The area around the main altar of a church, the *sacrarium*.
Sedilia	Seats for the priests (usually three) on the south side of the sanctuary.
Sgraffito	Decoration scratched, often in plaster, to reveal a pattern in another colour beneath.
Shaft	The trunk of a column between the base and the capital. In medieval architecture, one of several slender columns attached (in a cluster) to a pillar or pier, door jamb or window surround.
Slype	Covered way or passage leading east from the cloisters, between transept and chapter house.
Soffit	The underside of an arch (also called *intrados*). *Soffit roll*: medieval roll moulding on a soffit.
Solar	A private upper chamber in a medieval house, accessible from the high end of the great hall.
Spandrel	The roughly triangular space between the side of an arch and its containing rectangle; or the surface between the arches of an arcade.
Splay	A sloping, chamfered surface cut into the walls,. Usually applied to the widening of doorways, windows or other wall-openings by slanting the sides
Spring	or *springing* The level at which an arch or vault rises (springs) from its supports. The bottom stone of the arch resting on the impost each side can thus be called a *springer*.
Stiff-leaf	Type of Early English foliage decoration, often found on capitals of the period.
Stop	A plain or decorated end to mouldings or chamfers, or at the end of hoodmoulds and labels (*label stop*) or stringcourses.
Tas-de-charge	The lower courses of a vault or arch which are laid horizontally.
Terracotta	Moulded and fired clay ornament or cladding.
Tessellated pavement	Mosaic flooring made of *tesserae*, i.e. cubes of glass, stone or brick.
Tracery	Openwork pattern of masonry (or timber) in the upper part of an opening, especially a window opening. When applied to a wall, it is known as *blind tracery*.
Transom	Horizontal bar of stone or wood across the opening of a window or across a panel
Triforium	An arcaded wall-passage facing on to the nave, at a level above the arcade and below the clerestory windows (if any). The term is often wrongly applied to a tribune or gallery (see chapter seven).
Undercroft	A vaulted room or rooms beneath a medieval house or church (Cf. *crypt*).
Vault	Arched stone roof, of various types e.g. *barrel, groin, rib, fan etc*.
Vault shaft	The wall-shaft leading up to the springing of a vault.
Voussoirs	Wedge-shaped stones forming an arch.
Weepers	Small figures in niches along the sides of some medieval tombs.

-------------X-------------

Notes